BICYCLE RIDES
Santa Barbara & Ventura Counties
** 68 Trips Including 15 Best Mountain Bike Rides **

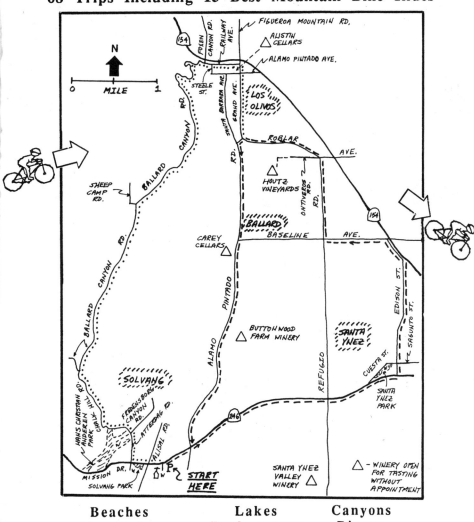

Beaches   **Lakes**   **Canyons**
Mountains   **Backcountry**   **Rivers**

BY DON AND SHARRON BRUNDIGE

Other Books by Don and Sharron Brundige:
Bicycle Rides: Los Angeles and Orange Counties (Out of Print)
Bicycle Rides: San Fernando Valley and Ventura County (Out of Print)
Bicycle Rides: Orange County
Bicycle Rides: Los Angeles County
Bicycle Rides: Inland Empire
Bicycle Rides: San Diego and Imperial Counties

Printed by Griffin Printing & Lithograph Co., Inc.
Glendale, California

Published by B-D Enterprises
122 Mirabeau Ave.
San Pedro, California 90732-3117

Photo Development by A-1 Photo, San Pedro CA.

Photography by Don and Sharron Brundige
Cover Photos: Atop The "Wall"-Susan Cohen; Gibralter Reservoir-Sam Nunez

All rights reserved
Library of Congress Catalogue Number 94-094025
ISBN 0-9619151-6-1
Copyright © 1994 by Don and Sharron Brundige
Published in the United States of America

We want to hear from you!

Corrections and updates will make this a better book and are gratefully appreciated. Publisher will reply to all such letters. Where information is used, submitter will be acknowledged in subsequent printing.

TABLE OF CONTENTS

DEDICATION

To Margaret Thelma Davis
...Who is not here to share in the joy of our book
and
To Mama & Papa "B"
and "Auntie" Holly
...who are

ACKNOWLEDGEMENTS

We offer our thanks to family, friends and bicycling acquaintances who gave us ideas, advice and plenty of encouragement while developing this biking book. This includes a "thank you" to the state, county and city agencies and individuals who offered their services and publications. We show particular gratitude to the folks that were kind enough to review and comment on our manuscript: Walt and Sally Bond, Susan Cohen, Al Hook, and Jill Morales. Additional kudos to Walt and Sal, and Sam Nunez, for sharing the "off-roaders" and to Susan for supporting us with her photographic skills.

Finally, we acknowledge getting some nifty ride ideas from the following sources: *The Official Bicycle Map of Santa Barbara* by the Santa Barbara County Bicycle Safety Project, *Bicycling Country Roads* published by Western Tanager Press, *Bicycling Santa Barbara* published by McNally and Loftin, several articles written for *California Bicyclist* by Bob Winning, Walt and Sally Bond and the many cycling comrades that we have met along the way.

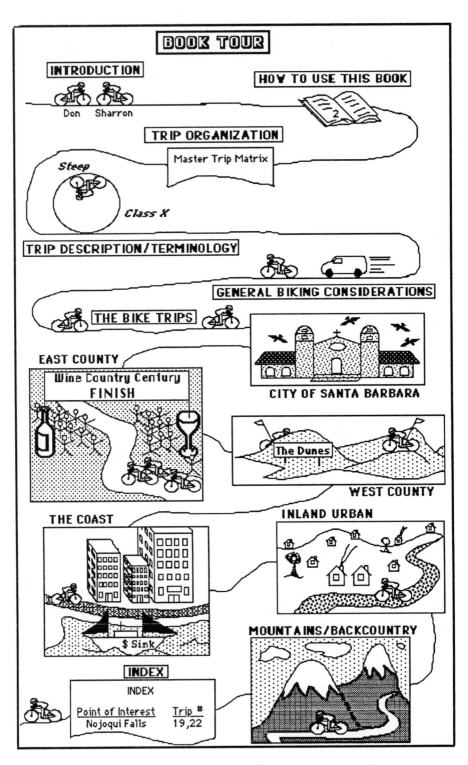

INTRODUCTION

As with all our books, we wanted to provide a trip guide that concentrates on trip navigation, contains a large number of well-documented trips, provides the necessary trip maps, and is reasonably priced. Hopefully we have succeeded!

This guide has been developed based on biking trips taken in 1993-1994. There are over 1700 one-way bike miles described! The document identifies 68 biking trips in Santa Barbara and Ventura Counties. Each trip is written to be as complete and self-standing as possible. The authors used eighteen-speed bicycles (a touring bike and mountain bikes fitted with road tires), although a vast majority of the trips can easily be ridden with ten-speeds. Included are **54 on-road trips** and **15 mountain bike (off-road) trips,** which require fat-tire bikes.

A cross section of trips is provided. There are some short-length family trips on separated bike paths, many longer exploratory and workout trips for more experienced bikers on various quality bike routes, and a few "gut-buster" trips on both on- and off-roadway for the most physically fit and motivated bikers. The trip domains include valleys, canyons, parks, rivers, lakes, mountains and basins. The trips vary from extremely scenic to austere (e.g., the eastern stretches of the Cuyama River). There's a little something for everybody! **The mountain bike trips are among the best in the two counties and most do not require exceptional technical skills or training.** However, some are remote and on poor surfaces--take them at your own risk.

The strong emphasis in this book is "getting from here to there." This navigation is provided using detailed route descriptions in terms of landmarks, mileage and a quality set of trip maps. Scenery, vistas, scenic or historic landmarks, and sightseeing attractions are regularly noted for each trip, although detailed information about these features must be sought out in other publications. Public restrooms and sources of water are identified on trips where these facilities are scarce. Pleasant rest spots are also pointed out. Finally, "wine and dine" spots are noted for two specific circumstances: 1) where places to eat along the trip are scarce; and 2) where the establishment is too unique or exceptional not to mention.

Mountain Biking--a word to the wise. As fervent hikers, we have been agitated with mountain bikers more than once as they swooped by on narrow trails, forcing us to scatter with little warning. We have seen numerous damaged switchbacks and water bars beat to a pulp, sporting an array of bike treads. Like some hikers, there are cyclists who do not carry out their trash. We have talked to disappointed outback property owners who have graciously allowed cyclists to pass through, expecting that they will not stray off the throughway, will not disturb residents or cattle, and will not damage surrounding terrain. There have been problems!

Have no doubt, there are many hikers, property owners, naturalists and other interested parties that are beginning to say "enough!" They seek an outright ban on off-roaders in both backcountry and frontcountry areas or, as a minimum, want to severly limit the areas in which bikers can transit. You must understand that many of their concerns are legitimate. Learn to share the trails with your fellow outdoorsmen or stand the risk of losing an immeasurable freedom. A little courtesy and common sense will keep us all on the back roads and trails together!

1

HOW TO USE THIS BOOK

There are two ways to use this book, one way for the person who wants to enjoy the research along with enjoying the bike ride, and another way for the biker who is just anxious to get out there "amongst em" on a bike ride.

For the "anxious biker," follow Steps 1 through 5 below and split!

1. Use the "Master Trip Map" in the "TRIP ORGANIZATION" section to select areas of interest for the bike ride. Note the candidate trip numbers. (Another option is to select a trip based on landmarks and sightseeing attractions referenced in the "INDEX.")

2. Go to the "Master Trip Matrices" in the "TRIP ORGANIZATION" section and narrow down the number of candidate trips by reviewing their general features.

3. Read about the individual trips and select one.

4. Read and understand the safety rules described in the "GENERAL BIKING CONSIDERATIONS" section.

5. See you later. Enjoy the ride!

For the more methodical folks, continue reading the next chapter. By the time you're through, you'll understand the trip description and maps much better than the "anxious biker."

TRIP ORGANIZATION

This bike book is organized by trip number. Trip numbers are in a general sequence governed by whether the tours are in Santa Barbara or Ventura County. Refer back to the "TABLE OF CONTENTS" for the entire trip list.

The "Master Trip Maps" show the general location of trips by a circled reference number (i.e., ⑦ refers to Trip #7). Extended length trips are identified by circled numbers at both beginning and terminal points.

The "Master Trip Matrices" provide a quick reference for selecting candidate trips for more detailed reading evaluation. The matrices are organized by trip number. The key trip descriptors provided in those matrices are briefly explained in the footnotes at the bottom of the last matrix (page 11). A more detailed explanation of those descriptors is provided in the "TRIP DESCRIPTION/TERMINOLOGY" section which follows.

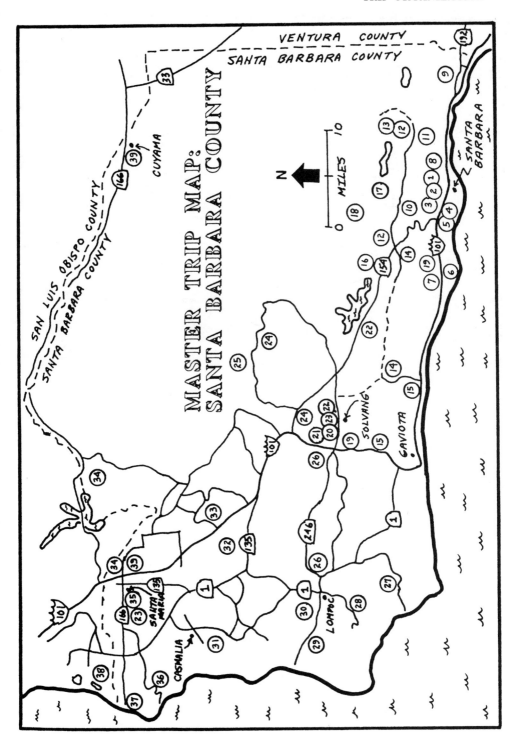

MASTER TRIP MAP: SANTA BARBARA COUNTY

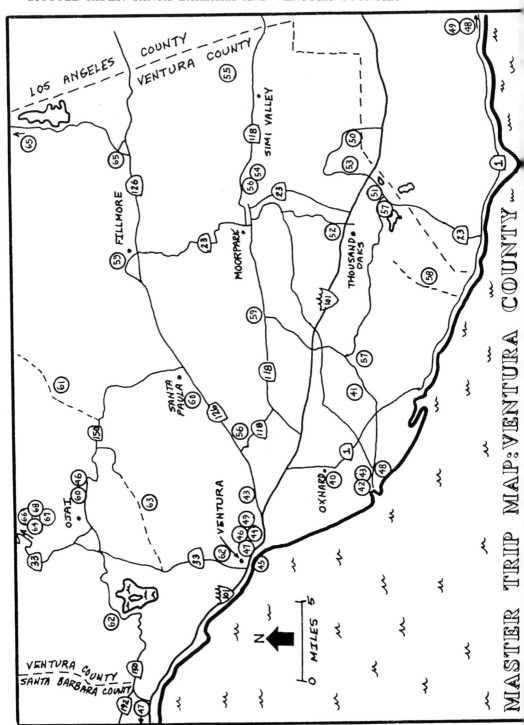

MASTER TRIP MAP: VENTURA COUNTY

MASTER TRIP MATRIX

TRIP NO.	GENERAL LOCATION	LEVEL OF DIFFICULTY			ROUTE QUALITY			TRIP CHARACT.[2]	COMMENTS[3]
		L.O.D.[1]	MILES	ELEV.	BIKE TRAIL (%)	BIKE LANE (%)	OTHER (%)		
1	Santa Barbara, Montecito	M	17.9	Mod	15	30	55	S, N, L, S/A	Eastside Santa Barbara (loop)
2	Santa Barbara, Isla Vista, Goleta	M	26.6	Mod	30	50	20	S, N, L, S/A	Westside (loop)
3	Santa Barbara	M-S	13.0	Mod-Steep	25	45	30	S, N, L, S/A	Central City Tour (loop)
4	Hope Ranch (Santa Barbara)	M-S	9.9	Mod-Steep	-	-	100	S, N, L	Hope Ranch (loop)
5	Santa Barbara, Hope Ranch	M-S	12.6	Mod-Steep	15	60	25	S, N, L, S/A	Southside (loop)
6	Goleta (U.C.S.B. Campus)	E	6.5	Flat	80	-	20	S, N, L, S/A	UCSB Campus Tour
7	Goleta	E	10.4	Flat	60	40	-	S, N, L	Goleta Valley Loop
8	Santa Barbara, Montecito	M-S	23.4	Mod-Steep	-	5	95	S, N, L, S/A, M	Mountain Drive, Bella Vista Dr. (loop)
9	Carpinteria	M	15.5	Mod-Steep	-	60	40	S, N, L, S/A	Carpinteria Runabout + Rincon Beach (loop)
10	Santa Barbara, Santa Ynez Mtns.	S-VS	29.4	Steep	-	20	80	S, N, L, S/A, M, E	Gibralter Road, Chumash Cave (loop)

1,2,3   See footnotes on page 11

5

MASTER TRIP MATRIX

TRIP NO.	GENERAL LOCATION	LEVEL OF DIFFICULTY			ROUTE QUALITY			TRIP CHARACT.[2]	COMMENTS[3]
		L.O.D.[1]	MILES	ELEV.	BIKE TRAIL (%)	BIKE LANE (%)	OTHER (%)		
11	Montecito	S	6.2 (1-w)	Mod-Steep	100	-	-	S, N, E	Romero Canyon Road (off-road)
12	Santa Ynez Mountains	S	17.9 (1-w)	Mod-Steep	-	-	100	S, N, M,E	East Camino Cielo
13	Los Padres National Forest	M	13.4 (1-w)	Mod	100	-	-	S, N, L	Upper Santa Ynez River (off-road)
14	San Marcos & Refugio Passes	S	17.7	Mod-Steep	70	-	30	S, N, L, M, E	West Camino Cielo (Refugio Rd.) (off-road)
15	Solvang, Refugio Pass, Gaviota Pass	S	39.4	Mod-Steep	-	10	90	S, N, L, S/A, M, E	Refugio Pass (Loop) (partial off-road)
16	Santa Ynez River, Mountains	M	8.7	Mod	-	-	100	S, N	Paradise Road
17	Los Padres National Forest	VS	20.3	Steep-Sheer	100	-	-	S, N, L, E	Matius Potrero Loop (off-road)
18	Los Padres National Forest	VS	15.0	Steep	100	-	-	S, N, L, E	Little Pine Mountain Loop (off-road)
19	Santa Barbara, San Marcos Pass, Solvang	VS	77.0	Mod-Sheer	5	10	85	S, N, L, S/A, M, E	Santa Barbara-Solvang Loop
20	Santa Ynez, Los Olivos, Solvang	M	12.0	Mod	-	10	90	S, N, L, S/A	Wine Country Tour #1 (loop) (Santa Ynez Vly.)

1,2,3 See footnotes on page 11

MASTER TRIP MATRIX

TRIP NO.	GENERAL LOCATION	LEVEL OF DIFFICULTY			ROUTE QUALITY			TRIP CHARACT.[2]	COMMENTS[3]
		L.O.D.[1]	MILES	ELEV.	BIKE TRAIL (%)	BIKE LANE (%)	OTHER (%)		
21	Solvang, Foxen & Ballard Canyons	M-S	22.6	Mod	-	-	90	S, N, L, S/A	Wine Country Tour #2 (loop) (Canyon Country)
22	Solvang, Lake Cachuma	M	11.8 (1-w)	Mod	-	40	60	S, N, L	Solvang to Lake Cachuma
23	Solvang, Lompoc, Santa Maria	VS	103	Mod-Steep	-	5	95	S, N, L, S/A, M, E	Solvang-Santa Maria Century Ride (loop)
24	Los Olivos, Happy Cyn., Figueroa Mtn.	VS	39.7	Mod-Steep	-	-	100	S, N, L, S/A, M, E	Figueroa Mountain Workout (loop)
25	Los Padres National Forest	S	14.8	Steep	100	-	-	S, N, L, E	The Catway to Whitehorse Peak (off-road)
26	Buellton, Lompoc Valley	M	34.1	Mod	-	-	100	S, N, M	Santa Rita Hills (loop) (includes Santa Rosa Rd.)
27	Lompoc, Jalama Beach	M-S (1-w)	18.8 (1-w)	Mod-Steep	-	-	100	S, N, M, E	Lompoc to Jalama Beach
28	Lompoc	S (r/t)	18.8 (r/t)	Mod-Steep	-	10	90	S, N, E	Lompoc Hills Tour
29	Lompoc (Ocean Beach)	E	18.0	Flat	-	80	20	S, N, L	Ride to Ocean Beach County Park
30	Lompoc	M	23.0	Mod	-	10	90	S, N, L, S/A	Lompoc City Tour (loop)

1,2,3 See footnotes on page 11

MASTER TRIP MATRIX

TRIP NO.	GENERAL LOCATION	LEVEL OF DIFFICULTY			ROUTE QUALITY			TRIP CHARACT.[2]	COMMENTS[3]
		L.O.D.[1]	MILES	ELEV.	BIKE TRAIL (%)	BIKE LANE (%)	OTHER (%)		
31	Santa Maria, Casmalia, Orcutt	M-S	32.1	Mod-Steep	-	10	90	S, N, L, S/A, M	Casmalia Hills (loop)
32	Mission Hills, Los Alamos	S	34.7	Mod-Steep	-	-	100	S, N, L, S/A, M	Purisma Hills, Los Alamos Valley (loop)
33	Los Alamos, Cat Canyon	M-S	33.7	Mod-Steep	-	-	100	S, N, L, M	Solomon Hills, Cat Canyon (loop)
34	Santa Maria, Los Coches Mountain	S	42.3	Mod-Steep	-	10	90	S, N, M, E	Los Coches Mountain Loop
35	Santa Maria, Orcutt	M	39.8	Flat-Mod	-	20	80	S, N, L, S/A, M	Santa Maria Valley (loop)
36	Point Sal State Beach	S(1-w) VS(r/t)	13.5 (1-w)	Steep	-	-	100	S, N, L, E	State Hwy. 1 to Point Sal State Beach
37	Guadalupe, Guadalupe Dunes	M	29.2	Flat	-	10	90	S, N, L, S/A	City of Guadalupe to Guadalupe Dunes
38	Guadalupe, Oso Flaco Lake	M	27.4	Mod	-	-	100	S, N, L, S/A	Guadalupe, Oso Flaco Lake
39	Santa Maria, Cuyama	M-S	50.4	Mod-Steep	-	-	100	S, L, M	Cuyama River Ride
40	Oxnard	E(1-w) E(r/t)	5.0 (1-w)	Flat	-	100	-	S, L	Oxnard South-to-North City Tour
41	Camarillo, Oxnard	E(1-w) M(r/t)	11.4 (1-w)	Flat	-	-	100	S, N, M	Pleasant Valley Pedal

MASTER TRIP MATRIX

TRIP NO.	GENERAL LOCATION	LEVEL OF DIFFICULTY			ROUTE QUALITY			TRIP CHARACT.[2]	COMMENTS[3]
		L.O.D.[1]	MILES	ELEV.	BIKE TRAIL (%)	BIKE LANE (%)	OTHER (%)		
42	Port Hueneme	E(1-w) M(r/t)	5.9 (1-w)	Flat	20	60	20	S, N, L	Port Hueneme Coastal Tour
43	Ventura-Oxnard -Port Hueneme	E(1-w) M(r/t)	10.4 (1-w)	Mod-Steep	-	90	10	S, N, L	Ventura-Port Hueneme Straightaway
44	Ventura	M	16.6	Mod	-	100	-	S, L, S/A	City of Ventura Loop
45	Ventura	E	17.0	Flat	20	80	-	S, N, L, S/A	Ventura Harbor Loop
46	Ventura-Ojai	M	24.5	Mod	-	30	70	S, N, S/A	Ventura to Ojai, Ojai Valley Trail
47	Ventura-Santa Barbara	M(1-w) S(r/t)	63.1 (r/t)	Mod	20	80	-	S, N, L, S/A, M	Bicentennial Route Coastal Tour
48	Port Hueneme-Santa Monica	S(1-w) VS(r/t)	44.3 (1-w)	Mod-Steep	-	80	20	S, N, L, S/A, E, M	Bicentennial Route Coastal Tour
48A	Port Hueneme-Sycamore Cove	M(1-w) M(r/t)	13.7 (1-w)	Mod	-	100	-	S, N	Northern Segment
48B	Sycamore Cove-Malibu	M-S(1-w) S(r/t)	20.1	Mod-Steep	-	100	-	S, N, L, S/A, E	Middle Segment
48C	Malibu-Santa Monica	M(1-w) M(r/t)	10.5	Mod	10	90	-	S, N, L, S/A	Southern Segment
49	Ventura-Malibu	S(1-w) VS(r/t)	48.3 (1-w)	Mod	-	-	100	S, N, L, S/A, E, M	Coastal Century

1,2,3 See footnotes on page 11

9

MASTER TRIP MATRIX

TRIP NO.	GENERAL LOCATION	LEVEL OF DIFFICULTY			ROUTE QUALITY			TRIP CHARACT.[2]	COMMENTS[3]
		L.O.D.[1]	MILES	ELEV.	BIKE TRAIL (%)	BIKE LANE (%)	OTHER (%)		
50	Agoura Hills	M	8.7	Mod	-	80	20	S, N	Agoura Hills Loop
51	Westlake Village	E	9.2	Mod	10	90	-	S, N, L	Westlake Lake Loop
52	Thousand Oaks	M	18.3 (r/t)	Mod-Steep	-	100	-	S, E	Thousand Oaks City Loop
53	Thousand Oaks-North Ranch	M	10.9	Mod	-	60	40	S, N	North Ranch Loop
54	Simi Valley	M	22.1	Flat	10	80	10	S, N, S/A, M	Simi Valley City Loop
55	Simi Valley	S	11.4	Steep	100	-	-	S, N, L, E	Rocky Peak, Chumash Trail (off-road)
56	Simi Valley, Santa Paula	S	65.0	Mod-Steep	-	-	100	S, N, L, M, E	Ventura Valleys Loop
57	Hidden Valley, Potrero Valley	M(1-w) M(r/t)	11.3 (1-w)	Mod-Steep	-	20	80	S, N, M	Potrero Road Countryside Tour (+ extention)
58	Point Mugu State Park	S (E-M)	16.7 (13.5)	Steep (Mod)	100	-	-	S, N, L, S/A	Sycamore Canyon, Overlook Trail (off-road)
59	Fillmore, Balcom Canyon, Somis	S(2-1p) E(1-1p)	74.8 (2-1p)	Flat-Sheer	-	-	100	S, N, M, E	Fillmore & Somis Loops, Balcolm Cyn. Connector
60	Ventura, Ojai, Santa Paula	S	46.6	Mod-Steep	-	15	85	S, N, L, S/A, M, E	Ojai-Santa Paula Loop

MASTER TRIP MATRIX

TRIP NO.	GENERAL LOCATION	LEVEL OF DIFFICULTY			ROUTE QUALITY			TRIP CHARACT.[2]	COMMENTS[3]
		L.O.D.[1]	MILES	ELEV.	BIKE TRAIL (%)	BIKE LANE (%)	OTHER (%)		
61	Upper Ojai Valley	S-VS	15.8	Steep	100	-	-	S, N, L, M, E	Sisar Canyon (off-road)
62	Ventura, Lake Casitas, La Conchita	S	46.2	Mod-Steep	10	35	55	S, N, L, M, E	Casitas Pass Loop
63	Casitas Springs, Upper Ojai Valley	S	21.8	Mod-Steep	100	-	-	S, N, E	Sulphur Mtn. Rd. (off-road) (+ Ojai Loop)
64	Los Padres National Forest	S	13.5	Steep	50	-	50	S, N, L, E	Pine Mountain, Reyes Peak (off-road)
65	Piru, Lake Piru	M-S	24.0	Mod-Steep	-	-	100	S, N, L, M	Lake Piru (up and back)
66	Los Padres National Forest	VS	85.2	Steep	-	-	100	S, N, L, E	Lockwood Vly., Potrero Rd. & Cuyama Vly. (loop)
67	Lockwood Valley	S	14.4	Steep	90	-	10	S, N, L, E	Mt. Pinos Loop (off-road)
68	Los Padres National Forest	S	12.7	Steep	100	-	-	S, N, L, E	Fishbowls (loop) (off-road)

1 L.O.D. - Overall trip level of difficulty: VS-very strenuous; S-strenuous; M-Moderate; E-easy; 1-w-one way; r/t-round trip

2 TRIP CHARACTERISTICS - General trip features and highlights: S-scenic; N-nature trail or natural setting; L-landmarks; S/A-sight-seeing attractions; E-elevation workout; M-mileage workout

3 (off-road) - Mountain bike trip

11

TRIP DESCRIPTION/TERMINOLOGY

The trip descriptors in the "Master Trip Matrices" are described below in further detail. Several of these same descriptors are also used in the individual trip writeups.

GENERAL LOCATION: The general location of the bike trail is provided in terms of a city, landmark or general area description, as applicable. The "Master Trip Map" may be useful in conjunction with this general locator.

LEVEL OF DIFFICULTY: The rides are rated on an overall basis as *very strenuous*, *strenuous*, *moderate* and *easy*, based on elevation gain, trip distance and condition of the bike route.

A *very strenuous* trip can be of any length, has very steep grades and is generally designed for bikers in excellent physical condition. It should be noted that even on the most strenuous on-road trip, the bike can be walked uphill for bikers in reasonably good condition. However, rather than suffer this fate, it is recommended that bikers start with the easier trips and work up. Alternately, trips are well enough described such that the biker might plan to ride the easier part of a stressing trip and link up with other easier trips. Do not attempt strenuous or very strenuous mountain-bike trips unless you are trail wise and in good condition.

A *strenuous* trip has some steep grades and/or relatively long mileage (on the order of 50 miles total). The trip is of sufficiently long duration to require trip planning and strong consideration of weather, water, food and bike spare parts. Some portions of the trip may be on surfaces in poor condition or on shared roadway.

A *moderate* trip may have mild grades and moderate mileage, on the order of 15-30 miles. The trip is typically of several hours duration and is generally on well-maintained bike route.

An *easy* trip is on the order of 10 miles or less, is relatively flat and is generally on well maintained bike trails or bike paths.

Mountain-bike trips have their own rules. The level of difficulty also will vary with trail condition. Account for a slower average bike speed than for on-road trips, and leave a healthy time pad for contingencies. We have taken off-road trips where a two mile-per-hour pace was pushing it! If you have any doubts, travel with an experienced off-roader. Come well equipped with water, munchies and the necessary bike repair equipment.

TRIP MILEAGE: Trip mileage is generally computed for the one-way trip length for *up-and-back* trips and full-trip length for *loop* trips. *Up and back* is specifically used for trips that share a common route in both outgoing and return directions. *Loop* specifically means that the outgoing and return trip segments are on predominantly different routes. *Round trip* is used without distinction as to whether the trip is an *up-and-back* or *loop* trip. In the trip writeups, the mileage from the starting point or "trailhead" is noted in parentheses to the nearest tenth mile, for example, (6.3).

Obviously, the one-way trips listed can be exercised with a planned car shuttle, ridden as an *up-and-back* trip, or biked in connection with another bicycle trip listed in this book. For convenience, connections with other trips are noted in the trip writeups as "Trip Options."

TRIP ELEVATION GAIN: The overall trip elevation gain is described in a qualitative fashion. *Flat* indicates that there are no grades of any consequence. Steepness of upgrades is loosely defined as follows: 1) *light* indicates limited slope and very little elevation gain; 2) *moderate* means more significant slope requiring use of low gears and may be tens of feet of upgrade; 3) *steep* indicates workout-type grades that require low gears and high physical exertion; 4) *sheer* indicates gut-buster grades that require extreme physical exertion (and a strong will to live!).

The frequency of upgrades is divided into the following categories: 1) *single* for flat rides with a single significant upgrade; 2) *periodic* for flat rides where uphill segments are widely spaced; 3) *frequent* where narrowly spaced or extended upgrades are encountered (e.g., most mountain rides, on- or off-road).

Elevation contour maps are provided for trips with significant elevation change. A reference 5% (*steep*) grade is shown on all such maps. Cyclists in good condition can handle extended 5% grades. Lengthy 10%-and-above grades are extremely taxing, requiring extreme patience (including the possibility of walking your bike) and excellent physical condition.

BIKE ROUTE QUALITY: The trips are summarized with respect to route quality in the "Master Trip Matrices" and a more detailed description is given in the individual trip writeups. The following route terminology (which is similar to that used by Caltrans) is used:

. *Class I* - off-roadway bike paths or bike trails

. *Class II* - on-roadway, separated (striped) bike lanes

. *Class III* - on-roadway, signed (but not separated) bike lanes

If the route is on-roadway and not signed (i.e., not marked as a bike route), it is arbitrarily referred to as *Class X*. All routes are paved unless otherwise noted.

HIGHLIGHTS: The overall highlights of the bike trip are provided in the "Master Trip Matrices" to assist in general trip selection. The trip may be scenic (*S*), with sweeping vistas, exciting overlooks or generally provide views of natural or man-made attractions such as cities. Alternatively, the trip may be a nature trail (*N*) or a path through areas which have an abundance of trees, flowers and other flora. The nature trips or portions thereof are generally on Class I bike routes. The trip may highlight historical or well-known landmarks (*L*) or may have one or more sightseeing attractions (*S/A*). An example of the former is Mission La Purisima near Lompoc (Trip #26) while the latter might be the Seabee Museum in Port Hueneme (Trip #42). Finally, some trips are potentially good workout trips in that there is significant elevation change (*E*) or lengthy mileage (*M*) if the entire trip is taken. The (*M*) designator is also used for trips where there is a noticeable absence of stoplights. Some trips may provide a mix of these characteristics and are so noted.

Several descriptors are unique to the individual trip writeups. Those descriptors are defined below.

TRAILHEAD: The general location of the start of the bike path is provided for a single starting point. Driving directions to that trailhead and/or directions for parking are included where there is a possibility of confusion. Always check to ensure that parking is consistent with current laws.

BICYCLE RIDES: SANTA BARBARA AND VENTURA COUNTIES

Note that for most trails, there are multiple points of entry beyond the primary point listed. For some of the trips in this book (particularly the river routes), alternate bicycle entry points are noted on maps by arrows (✈) along the bike route. Alternate trailheads may be found using information obtained from other bikers, or from state or local publications for more popular routes.

WATER: In the "Trailhead" description, general statements are provided about water availability. In the "Trip Description," available water along the route is noted where water is scarce, although the trip should be planned to assume that water stops may not be operational (or available, for mountain-bike trips). Particular emphasis is placed on public facilities for water and use of restrooms. Stores, shopping centers and gas stations are sometimes noted, although the availability of water or other facilities in these instances is subject to the policies of those establishments. It is vital to take additional water for the more difficult mountain-bike trips--you won't believe the discomfort and biking inefficiency that results from lack of water!

TRIP OPTIONS: Where trips have interesting variants or shortcuts, they are so noted. Particular emphasis is placed on spur trips, which provide scenic beauty, notable landmarks or route extensions.

BIKE TRIP MAPS: Each ride in the book has an accompanying detailed bike map. A summary of symbols and features used in those maps is provided below.

— — — —	Bike trail in trip description (unless otherwise noted).
• • • • • •	Alternate bike route (unless otherwise noted).

SANTA YNEZ RIVER 〰〰	River or creek when it is a point of interest	MAIN ST.	Roadway

1-CITY HALL 2-GRANT PARK	Key trip features. Numbers in key correspond to numbers marked along the mapped route.

OJAI	Nearby City	👟	Park	☐ 5 / 5	Landmark #5
W	Public Water Source	P	Parking	⛺	Camp Site
⊢—•	Locked Gate/ Limited Entry	✕✕✕✕✕	Railroad Crossing or Overcrossing	⌣	Pass or Trip Summit
†	Mission	△ 5%	Reference 5% Grade	Zaca Peak (4341)	Mountain & Elev. (feet)

MAP SYMBOLS AND FEATURES

GENERAL BIKING CONSIDERATIONS

The following is a collection of the thoughts that we've had in the thousands of miles of biking that we have done.

SAFETY: Use common sense when you are biking. Common sense when combined with courtesy should cover most of the safety-related issues. But just to be on the safe side, write to Caltrans (see the chapter on "OTHER BICYCLING INFORMATION SOURCES") for any of their publications and you will get some excellent safety information along with it. The four safety "biggies" are: 1) understand bike riding laws; 2) keep your bicycle in safe operating order; 3) wear personal safety equipment as required (helmet is a must, bright or reflective clothes, sunglasses); 4) ride defensively--always assume that moving and parked car inhabitants are not aware that you are there.

Common courtesy is to offer assistance to bikers stopped because of breakdowns. Point out ruts, obstructions and glass to bikers behind you.

EQUIPMENT: Necessary biking equipment includes a water bottle or two, tire pump, tool kit (typically tire irons, wrench(s), and a screwdriver), patch kit and (sorry to say) bike lock. For longer trips, add a spare tube and bike repair manual as well as a light first-aid kit. Bring sunblock and lip salve for extended tours on sunny days. We recommend a bike light as a contingency for longer trips, even if there are no plans for night biking.

Necessary biking apparel includes a helmet, sunglasses and clothes which will fit pessimistic weather conditions (particularly for longer trips). On all-day, cool or wet winter outings, we carry a layered set of clothes (this includes long biking pants, an undershirt that wicks moisture away from the body, long-sleeve biking jersey, and a two-piece breathable rain suit). Padded cycling pants and biking gloves are a must for long trips. Lycra clothes are light and extremely functional. Invest in a comfortable bike seat. For cool and dry days, we may opt for a windbreaker (look for a windbreaker that folds up into a fanny pack). For other conditions, our outfits are biking shorts, undershirt, short-sleeve jersey and windbreaker.

If you are going to get your money out of this book, get an automobile bike rack! The cost of bike racks is cheap compared to most bikes. Besides, it just doesn't make sense to bike fifty miles to take the planned twenty-mile bike trip.

GENERAL INFORMATION: A collection of seemingly random, unconnected and useless comments are provided which we actually think are "gems of wisdom" based on hard experience:

o Develop and follow a checkoff list for a pre-trip bike examination (tires, brakes, cables, etc.) and equipment (water, food, clothing, tools, spare parts, etc.). A brake check is particularly vital for steep hilly rides. It's embarrassing to start a trip and realize that you've forgotten your bicycle!

o Check the weather before going on an extended trip or any mountain-bike trip of any length. Select trips and plan clothing accordingly.

BICYCLE RIDES: SANTA BARBARA AND VENTURA COUNTIES

o Plan the trip to ensure there is a "pad" of daylight. Night biking just isn't fun when it's not in the original plans. Night biking without the proper equipment is dangerous! Mountain-biking at night is only for the well trained, equipped and adventurous! Overnight exposure in the outdoors can be life-threatening, so bring cold-weather gear as a contingency for remote mountain-bike trips.

o Trip timing should include allowances for finding parking, trailheads or connector routes. Leave a healthy time pad for "surprises" which seem to occur most frequently on mountain-bike tours. You never can fully trust authors of bike books!

o Trip conditions and routing are subject to change because of weather damage, building and highway construction, bikepath rerouting, etc. Especially for long trips, research these key elements before departing.

o Stay out of urban riverbeds when inclement weather threatens, even if marked as part of the route. It may be a very long way to the next exit and it may also rain.

o Some river and creek trails flood during heavy rains. Don't take these trips after heavy rains unless you are willing to plan on route detours or to turn back. Mountain-bike biking in the rain can be dangerous, particularly if the route crosses creeks, rivers or other drainage.

o Always take some water, no matter how short the trip. Having water available provides a feeling of security. Being thirsty creates a bad attitude. Bring enough water to provide for the contingency that "guaranteed" water spots may be dry.

o The best time of day for most on-road trips on busy thoroughfares is before the rush-hour morning traffic. Morning is also best for rides on narrow country roads. With few exceptions, the best time of the week is the weekend, particularly Sunday.

o The best season for some trips depends on the person. If you want comradery, ride the popular routes in the on-season. If your pleasure is free-wheeling and wide-open spaces, save these routes for the off-season.

o Bring snacks for longer trips or any mountain-bike trip. Snacks provide needed energy and attitude improvement when the going gets tough. Having snacks available also allows more flexibility in selecting a "dining out" stop.

o Walk your bike through heavy glass-strewn or across grassy urban areas. Lift your bike onto and off of curbs. Trips are more fun when you can ride your bike!

o Bring a road map for trips that are not on well-marked bike routes (topographic and Forest Service maps for mountain-bike rides). Once off the prescribed route, it is amazingly easy to lose the sense of direction.

o Maintain a steady pace when taking a long bike ride. For pleasure trips, the pace is too fast if you cannot carry on conversation while biking.

o **Additional Mountain-bike Tips.** These trips are best done with an early morning start and on cool days. Overload on water supplies. Bring full repair and basic first-aid kits. Bringing a compass and latest USGS topographic map (USFS maps) and marking trails on these maps ahead of time has been a "life saver" for us a couple of times. Bring a biking buddy! Delay the tour if inclement weather threatens.

SANTA BARBARA COUNTY

Happy Canyon Road

TRIP #1 - EASTSIDE

GENERAL LOCATION: Santa Barbara, Montecito

LEVEL OF DIFFICULTY: Loop - Moderate
Distance - 17.9 miles
Elevation gain - periodic moderate grades

HIGHLIGHTS: From Mission Santa Barbara, this route turns north to State Hwy. 192 and follows the twists and turns 7-1/2 miles to Sheffield Dr. on the eastern boundary of Montecito. There are some interesting natural scenery and a few moderate hill-climbing challenges on the outskirts of the big city. A pleasant downhill through the Valley Club of Montecito on Sheffield Dr. leads to the coast. The course follows the Bikecentennial Bike Route past numerous oceanside attractions west to the Santa Barbara Harbor area, then proceeds on the periphery of the central city back to the mission. There are several side trips off the main route, including a visit to the Santa Barbara Botanic Gardens.

TRAILHEAD: From U.S. Hwy. 101, exit north at Mission St. and drive one mile to Laguna St. Go left and park above Los Olivos St. near Mission Santa Barbara. Explore the mission and plan a picnic at nearby Mission Park.

Mission Santa Barbara

TRIP DESCRIPTION: Mission to Sycamore Canyon. Swing north on Mission Canyon Rd. pass Mission Park, Mountain Dr., Rocky Nook County Park (tree cover, picnic facilities, restrooms, horse trails and scenic views) and the Museum of Natural History. The museum exhibits prehistoric Indian dioramas, plant and animal life, geology of the coastal area, and features a planetarium. Divert east in 0.6 mile on busy Class X Foothill Rd. (State Hwy. 192) and pass Mission Canyon Rd. (entry to the

18

Santa Barbara Botanic Gardens) in 1/4 mile.   Cycle into rolling hills on the tree-lined road, go by the Santa Barbara Tennis Club and begin a serious upgrade beyond. While eying the cactus-dotted hillsides, head uphill past Foothill Ln. and merge with Mountain Dr. in a tree-rich suburban area.   The road crests, then splits to the right on a short segment called Mission Ridge Rd. above the Sheffield Reservoir. (Follow the Hwy. 192 signs.)   Wind past a fire station, head downhill to a flat near El Cielito, and begin a downgrade past Orizaba Ln.   Zip below the homes perched on the hillsides with Sycamore Canyon now appearing to the right.   Cross over a creek on a small bridge to Conejo Rd. and Sycamore Canyon Rd.   (3.2).   An option is to turn south here and do a shortened 6.4-mile tour.   (See trip options described later in this write-up.)

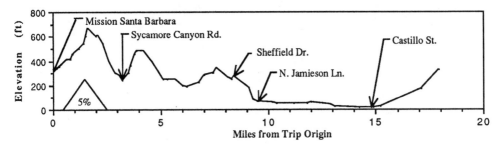

Cruise by lovely rustic homes on a tree-sheltered road and climb 0.7 mile to a flat near Cold Springs Rd.   Skirt the northern edge of Montecito, passing more gated estates so typical here.   Beyond Meadow Wood Ln. is a steady downgrade on a rural lane which becomes East Valley Rd. past Camino Viejo.   Continue downhill into the government/commercial center of Montecito on San Ysidro Rd. (6.0), with a shopping center, gas stations, fast food and several real estate offices.   Not far from the town center, both land development and traffic tail off.   Follow a steady, but modest, upgrade 1.3 miles among a rural setting to Buena Vista Dr.   Pedal 0.8 mile on a mostly flat road to Sheffield Dr.   This treed, two-lane downhill road transits below the plush Valley Club of Montecito and reaches N. Jamison Ln. next to Hwy. 101 in 1.3 miles (9.5).

Stearn's Wharf

19

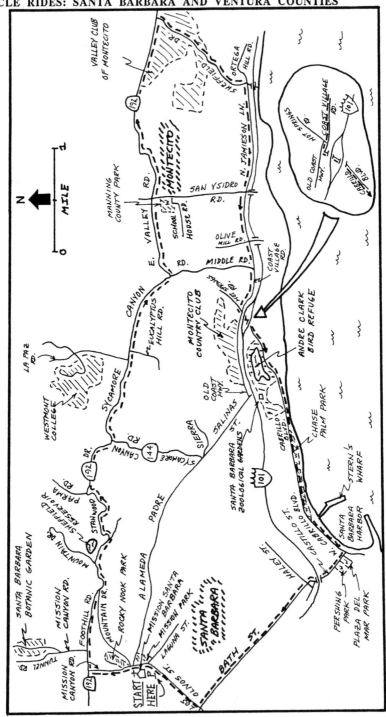

TRIP #1 - EASTSIDE

Coastal Return. The coastal return is similar to the westbound part of the Ventura to Santa Barbara tour (Trip #47-Northern Segment), which chiefly uses the Bikecentennial Bike Route. Follow N. Jamison Ln., a Hwy. 101 frontage road, and proceed 1.7 miles west past Olive Mill Rd. where it changes name to Coast Village Rd. In 0.8 mile, pedal past Hot Springs Rd. to Cabrillo Blvd. (Hwy. 225), duck under Hwy. 101 and pass the Andree Clark Bird Refuge. From here to Castillo St. (14.9), the ride and attractions are identical to those described in the "Oceanside Spin" portion of the All Around the Town tour (Trip #3). Head right at Castillo St. (north), pass Plaza Del Mar and Pershing Park (tree cover, grass, stadium, baseball diamond, tennis courts, restrooms, outdoor theater), dip under the freeway, go right at Haley St., and proceed to Bath St. Head north 1.7 miles on Class II bikeway to Los Olivos St., then beeline 0.8 mile on Los Olivos St. to Laguna St. and return to Mission Santa Barbara (17.9).

There are several good diversion trips off of the reference route, as noted below:

Santa Barbara Botanic Garden/Tunnel Road. A 1/2 mile pedal up lovely Mission Canyon via Mission Canyon Rd. leads to the Botanic Gardens. These 65 acres of gardens in the Santa Ynez foothills contain over 1000 species of rare and indigenous California plants. There are 5-1/2 miles of hiking trails offering the chance for self-exploration or guided tours. Scenic vistas, a picnic area, and the historic Mission Dam are a few of the offerings.

A 1/4 mile off the Mission Canyon Rd. entry is Tunnel Rd., a choice wooded road offering views into the Botanic Gardens. This is a 1.4-mile, 450-foot, climb to the Tunnel Trail trailhead, open to both hikers and off-road bikers. The trail leads to a junction with the Jesusita Trail, where a turn left leads the biker west and south to Stevens Park (see Trip #10 map for more detail).

Westmont College. From State Hwy. 192, bike uphill 0.6 mile and veer left at La Paz Rd. to enter the wooded campus. La Paz Rd. angles right in 0.2 mile and goes to a dead end; the most interesting option is to veer left and follow the rustic campus loop which returns to Cold Springs Rd. The campus is remote, hilly and reminds us of several campgrounds (sans buildings) we have visited.

Sycamore Canyon Shortcut. This trip can be shortened to 6.4 miles by turning south at Sycamore Canyon Rd. The penalty is that the cyclist's best bet to return to Mission Santa Barbara is via the testy and steep Alameda Padre Serra (see Trip #8 for details about this segment).

TRIP #2 ₒ WESTSIDE

GENERAL LOCATION: Santa Barbara, El Encanto Heights, Isla Vista, Goleta

LEVEL OF DIFFICULTY: Loop - moderate
Distance - 26.6 miles
Elevation gain - periodic moderate grades

HIGHLIGHTS: This largely Class II course visits Santa Barbara's west end starting from Mission Santa Barbara and reaching as far west as Ellwood, the site of a WWII

21

BICYCLE RIDES: SANTA BARBARA AND VENTURA COUNTIES

Japanese coastal attack. The initial northern segment follows the contour of the Santa Ynez Mountain's foothills, winds south to visit the UCSB campus and follows the Atascadero Creek Bikeway back into the City of Santa Barbara. The final stretch is a fiendishly clever "backdoor" path to the mission. There are many historical sites and several parks along the way.

TRAILHEAD: The trailhead is at Mission Santa Barbara (see Trip #1).

TRIP DESCRIPTION: Northern Segment. Bike north on a brief downhill on Mission Canyon Rd., rolling by the southern edge of Rocky Nook County Park (tree cover, picnic facilities, restrooms, horse trails, views). Pass the Museum of Natural History which exhibits prehistoric Indian dioramas, plant and animal life and geology of the coastal area, plus a planetarium. In 0.6 mile, turn west (left) on Foothill Rd. (a 0.2-mile diversion right leads to the Botanic Gardens - see Trip #1) and begin an 11.7-mile westward beeline beside the foothills of the Santa Ynez Mountains. The Class X ride is on busy highway via rolling hills for 1.2 miles and reaches San Roque Rd. Cross above Stevens Park and track a sweeping curve into the base of the foothills.

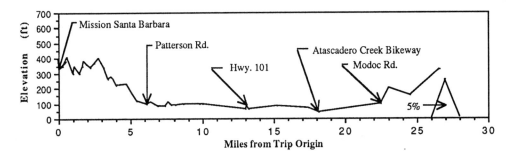

The Class II spin after La Cumbre Rd. traces a gentle rolling contour and crosses State Hwy. 154, where the road becomes Cathedral Oaks Rd. The name "Cathedral" Oaks derives from earlier days when religious meetings were held under them. The rolling terrain is interrupted with a short and steep grade near Camino Remedio. The payoff in 0.4 mile is Tuckers Grove County Park (trees, grass, barbecue facilities, playgrounds, hiking trails, restrooms, water). Bike into a residential area on a Class II road over mild rolling terrain, pass Patterson Ave. (6.1), and reach Stow Grove County Park in two miles. The park, buried in a mixed grove of trees, provides picnic facilities, athletic fields, restrooms and a botanical collection.

The road narrows to two lanes as the north side becomes a bevy of citrus groves. In 0.8 mile is Los Carneros Rd., where a 1/4-mile diversion south leads to the historic Stow House and Horace Sexton Museum, Goleta Railroad Museum and Depot, and Lake Los Carneros County Park. Southern Pacific Legal Counsel, William Stow, built his home in 1882, making this one of the oldest landmarks in Goleta Valley. The old Southern Pacific Depot, uprooted and moved to its current site, has working railroad equipment and a one-man operated station. The expansive tree-covered park around the Stow House encloses serene reed-lined Los Carneros Lake with a circumferential Class I shoreline bikeway.

In 1.1 miles of rural roadway is Glen Annie Rd. Go left on this Class II road to Calle Real in 0.4 mile. (This is the same segmented highway frontage road that hops, skips and jumps as far east as the Earl Warren Showgrounds on Las Positas Rd!)

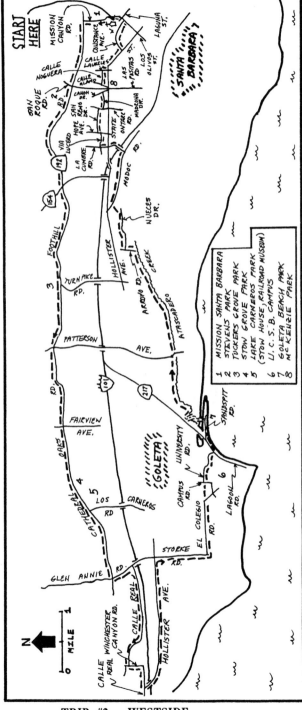

Map labels (clockwise/by area):

START HERE
MISSION CANYON RD.
CONSTANCE AVE.
LAGUNA ST.
CALLE LAURELES
CALLE NOGUERA
LOS OLIVOS ST.
LAS POSITAS
CALLE ALAMAR
SANTA BARBARA
SAN ROQUE RD.
CANON DR.
HOPE AVE.
SAN RAFO DR.
MADRONA DR.
VIA LUCERO
STATE ST.
ONTARE RD.
LA CUMBRE RD.
MODOC RD.
192
154
FOOTHILL
HOLLISTER AVE.
TURNPIKE RD.
ARROYO RD.
CREEK
ATASCADERO
NUECES DR.
PATTERSON AVE.
101
217
STANDSPIT RD.
FAIRVIEW AVE.
OAK
GOLETA
UNIVERSITY RD.
CATHEDRAL
LOS CARNEROS RD.
CAMPUS RD.
EL COLEGIO RD.
LAGOON RD.
STORKE RD.
GLEN ANNIE RD.
CALLE REAL
WINCHESTER CANYON RD.
CALLE REAL
HOLLISTER AVE.

Boxed list:
1 MISSION SANTA BARBARA
2 STEVENS PARK
3 TUCKERS GROVE PARK
4 STOW GROVE PARK
5 LAKE CARNEROS PARK (STOW HOUSE, RAILROAD MUSEUM)
6 U.C.S.B. CAMPUS
7 GOLETA BEACH PARK
8 McKENZIE PARK

N
0 MILE 1

TRIP #2 - WESTSIDE

CITY OF SANTA BARBARA

Continuing south on Glen Annie Rd. cuts 4-1/2 miles off the trip (and misses some scenic attractions). Our reference route turns west on Calle Real and glides over the flat Class III residential area to Winchester Canyon Rd., heading south to again become Calle Real. Cycle onto a freeway overcrossing where the route bends back and returns east (13.1).

Ellwood and Isla Vista. Trace Class II Hollister Rd. east beside the Sandpiper Golf Course. (Location of the famous 1942 Japanese coastal shelling, the first attack on the U.S. mainland since 1812. The target was the extensive Ellwood Oil Fields, now reduced from 30 piers to two piers.) Pass the fence-surrounded Barnsdall-El Rio Gas Station, the last of the Pearl Chase Spanish-style fuel stops. Bike past the Goleta Stables, proceed below a huge eucalyptus stand, then return to urban environs, reaching a cluster of fast-food houses and gas stations at Glen Annie Rd. (15.2).

Turn right on what is now Class II Storke Rd. Just beyond on Phelps Rd., pick up a Class I UCSB path on the east side and pass the multi-story Francisco Torres Dormitories. After the path turns 90 degrees left and parallels El Colegio Rd., head due east on the Class I lighted strip (see Trip #6 for details of the UCSB bike routes). East of the dorms is a convention of parked bicycles. How students find their bikes in this metal maze is a miracle!

View the San Ynez Mountains to the north, go under Los Carneros Rd. and pedal east (to stay on the reference route, ignore spur trails off the main route). Cross Stadium Rd., pass the athletic fields, dip under Mesa Rd. and follow the winding bikepath to its terminus at Lagoon Rd. (1.9 miles from Storke Rd.). At Lagoon Rd., the Class I trail bears northeast along the ocean and passes through the campus gate. Enjoy the downhill while taking in the coastal bluffs and the Goleta Beach County Pier to the east.

Atascadero Creek Bikeway. (Refer to Trip #7 for details on the westernmost bikeway segment up to Patterson Ave.) Near sea level is a fork with the Beachside Bar Cafe to the right and the trail to the left (18.1). Cross the bridge over the Goleta Slough inlet and bear immediately right. The Class I path is sandwiched between State Hwy. 217 with the airport to the west and the marshy wetlands of Atascadero Creek to the east. Cruise 1.6 miles northeast across Patterson Ave. and ride over a bridge above Maria Ygnacia Creek. Bike beside the broad creek plain, enjoy the plentiful vegetation by the waterway, and pass signs announcing exits to Walnut Ln. and Turnpike Rd.

In 1.8 miles beyond Patterson Ave., the path heads onto Class III Arroyo Rd. and turns right at Nueces Dr. (This and the subsequent path are well marked.) Go over Atascadero Creek in an area dotted with trees and horse trails, pass Nogal Dr. and make two more creek crossings. The now Class I path enters a large open area with horse training arenas, then proceeds to a dead end at Modoc Rd. (22.5).

Barnsdall-El Rio Gas Station

Backdoor Return. Eastbound on Class II Modoc Rd. brings a return to car country. A turn north in 1.1 miles at La Cumbre Rd. takes you over Hwy. 101 past a shopping center and across State St. to Via Lucero. Turn right and, in a 1.6-mile series of effective Class II doglegs, bike into suburbia to State St. Pedal another 1/2 mile to Constance Ave., leave the busy roadway and follow a sweeping turn right on what becomes Garden St. Mission Santa Barbara looms directly ahead as you bike Garden St. 0.7 mile to a turn northeast on Los Olivos St. The starting point is in 0.2 mile at the mission (26.6).

Trip Options. 1) Glen Annie Canyon. A turn north on Glen Annie Rd. from Cathedral Oaks Rd. provides a peaceful and flat spin into an agricultural area in a small canyon. After 1/2 mile into the four-mile round trip is the eye-catching Glen Annie Entrance Arch, originally located at the old Hollister/Glen Annie Ranch entrance; **2) El Encanto Heights.** An out-of-the-way family loop is made by using any of the many suburban roads in this area since the only through street is Calle Real to the south. The trick is to link various streets using the Class I path which

El Encanto Heights

connects the dead end of the eastern segment of Padaro Dr. to Brandon Dr. The general area is highlighted in the map labeled "El Encanto Heights"; 3) **Upper San Roque Road.** From Foothill Rd., begin an immediate steep upgrade northward to wide-open spaces, observing the homes perched on the hillsides above. The road levels in 0.3 mile and reaches an area with wide ocean vistas, and a view of Mission Santa Barbara's less-known side. Progress uphill towards the mountains past the Jesusita Trailhead to an overlook of the Lauro Reservoir. In 0.7 mile from Foothill Rd. is a crest with close-up views of the hillside "roosts," the reservoir and the city below. Over the crest is a 0.3-mile downgrade ending at the northern end of the reservoir at a gated private road.

TRIP #3 - ALL AROUND THE TOWN

<u>**GENERAL LOCATION**</u>:   City of Santa Barbara

<u>**LEVEL OF DIFFICULTY**</u>: Loop - Moderate to strenuous
Distance - 13.0 miles
Elevation gain - periodic moderate grades; steep grade at
western entry to Alameda Padre Serra

<u>**HIGHLIGHTS**</u>:   This 13-mile loop provides a condensed look at some of Santa Barbara's most visited attractions. From Mission Santa Barbara, the cyclist is tested by a no-nonsense upgrade on Alameda Padre Serra past Orpet Park, then is treated to a vista-packed downgrade with views of the city below and the Channel Islands. The route skirts the southern periphery of the stately and upscale City of Montecito, then swings toward the ocean to visit such attractions as the Biltmore Hotel, the Andree

25

BICYCLE RIDES: SANTA BARBARA AND VENTURA COUNTIES

Clark Bird Refuge, Chase Palm Park and Stern's Wharf. A Santa Barbara City College transit gives way to a return to the Santa Barbara metropolis as the cyclist threads his way north on historic, attraction-laden, State St. The route returns northeast through residential Santa Barbara to the mission.

TRAILHEAD: The trailhead is at Mission Santa Barbara (See Trip #1).

TRIP DESCRIPTION: Alameda Padre Serra. From Mission Santa Barbara, a short uphill spin alongside Mission Park leads to Alameda Padre Serra, where a challenging uphill awaits. A right turn on Alameda Padre Serra leads uphill past elegant homes where there are numerous looks down into Santa Barbara. The Class X road steepens near Bonita Wy., crests and passes through the center of grassy, shaded Orpet Park, then cruises lazily downhill past the manicured grounds of the Brooks Institute. A gorgeous 180-degree view opens to the ocean and city near Arbolado Rd. The incline steepens, passes Loma Media Rd. and then the scenic and winding road descends to the Five Points Intersection (2.9).

Montecito. Across the intersection, the road changes name to Salinas St. Pump up a short, sharp incline past Mason St. to a flat leading to Old Coast Hwy., where a left turn on a Class II spin leads below the Municipal Tennis Courts. To the east is the exclusive Montecito Country Club with its beautiful golf course. At Hot Springs Rd., go right, then left onto Class III Coast Village Rd. (A shortcut option is to head right, and then immediately left on Cabrillo Blvd. to pass under Hwy. 101 and shave 3.5 miles off the trip.)

At Middle and Coast Village Rds., the cyclist is at the heart of Santa Barbara's Creme de la Creme community of Montecito with its posh shops, upscale homes and groomed neighborhoods. Million-dollar-plus estates are sometimes advertised as "fixer-uppers!" Turn south at Olive Mill Rd. and pedal across Hwy. 101 to the ocean-side estates.

Ocean Spin. The famous Biltmore Hotel is here with its towering palms, abundant floral displays, and open cabanas on dark-green lawns. This grand inn was built in the mid-thirties and has housed many of the rich and famous. A seaside segment leads to a blocked-to-automobiles road, passes the local gated residences, then winds around the woods of the Santa Barbara Cemetery. At E. Cabrillo Blvd., follow the Class I path along the Andree Clark Bird Refuge. The little lake, with its lush islands, has a mixed population of wild and tame ducks, geese and seagulls. On the far side is an entry to the Santa Barbara Zoological Gardens, known for its farmyard petting zoo, botanical gardens, and another zoo with elephants, lions, monkeys and exotic birds.

The beach- and palm-lined Chase Palm Park (athletic fields, barbecue facilities, restrooms, water) open up shortly as the Class I route crosses Cabrillo Blvd. to the park at Milpas St. The pleasant oceanside ride mixes in with other bikers, walkers, skaters, and the ever-present four-wheeled, self-propelled taxis. The breezy route passes the Chamber of Commerce Center and the Chase Palm Park entry at Santa Barbara St. before crossing State St. (8.7), the entry to Stearn's Wharf. This lengthy pier sports concession stands, boat excursion tours, eateries, ice cream stands, tame pelicans and pigeons, the Santa Barbara Sea Center and Nature Conservancy, and plaques describing the wharf's environment and creatures.

Pedal by the protective cover of Santa Barbara Harbor with its shoreline swimming pool, Santa Barbara Yacht Club, marina and several seaside hotels. After Castillo St. is oceanside Del Mar Pool with Plaza Del Mar Park on the inland side (grass, trees, baseball field, tennis courts, restrooms and outdoor theater). The Class I path

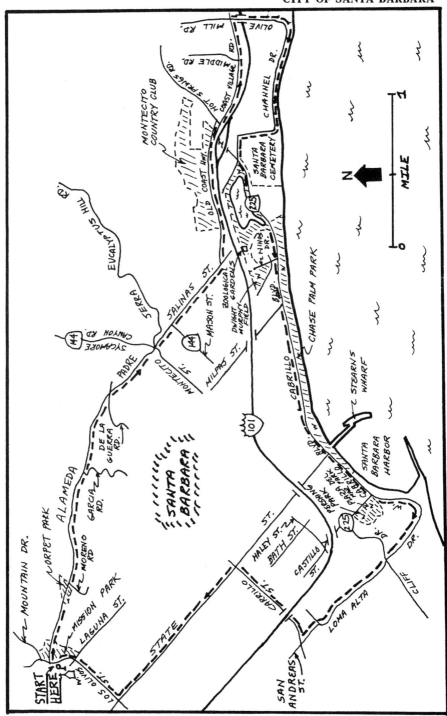

TRIP #3 - ALL AROUND THE TOWN

ends near the Santa Barbara Yacht Club and shifts back over to Class II Cabrillo Blvd. below the bluffs.

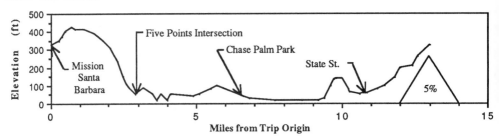

Return through the City. At Loma Alta Dr., head inland and transit the Santa Barbara City College grounds below a pedestrian walkway. Further uphill, cross Cliff Dr. and change from Class II to Class X roadway. Keep uphill along a ridgeline where, after Coronel St., is a 180-degree view taking in the City of Santa Barbara, including the mission. Head downhill for a quick succession of turns at the end of Loma Alta Dr. (right) and San Andreas St. (left), which lead to Carrillo St., then go right (east). A 3/4-mile spin on busy Class X Cabrillo St. leads to State St. Turn north for a ride on this history-filled street.

Chase Palm Park

The route intersects the Red Tile Walking Tour, a distinct sidewalk path circumnavigating some famous historical sites in Santa Barbara (De La Guerra Playa, El Paseo, Museum of Art, County Courthouse, El Presidio State Park and Historical Society Museum to name a few).   This is an interesting Class II path that seems to be unmarked and comingles with traffic until a clearly-marked Class II path appears at each intersection.   Transit on an upgrade near Micheltorena St., site of an Old English style, well-maintained Trinity Espiscopal Church and follow mild rolling hills to Los Olivos St. (12.4).   One mile of a steady upgrade takes you past Laguna St. and back to Mission Santa Barbara (13.0).

Stearn's Wharf

Bath Street Option.   There is an alternative to the busy, historical, and jam-packed State St. segment.   The key is to turn right (northwest) at Castillo St., bike under Hwy. 101 to Haley St., and turn eastward to Bath St.   Once on Class II Bath St., pedal 0.7 mile and go right at Los Olivos St., continuing as described for the reference option.   The trip distance is roughly one less mile than the route described above.

29

TRIP #4 - HOPE RANCH

GENERAL LOCATION: Hope Ranch

LEVEL OF DIFFICULTY: Loop - moderate to strenuous
Distance - 9.9 miles
Elevation gain - periodic moderate grades; single steep grade on Sea Ranch Dr.

HIGHLIGHTS: Enjoy this pleasurable tour into the rolling hills of one of the more upscale communities in Southern California. The trip is but one of many possible routes through Hope Ranch. Much of the cycling is through wooded areas with scattered estates to catch your attention. Lightly used, narrow rural roads are the rule. This would be a moderate tour but for the no-nonsense climb on Sea Ranch Dr. The payoff for this workout is a scenic multi-mile glide back to Las Palmas Dr. from the crest on Campinil Dr. and a short tree-shaded return segment.

TRAILHEAD: From U.S. Hwy. 101, exit south at Las Palmas Dr. Once across the freeway, turn right at the first intersection onto Modoc Rd. and drive west to Nogal Dr. Park along this street beneath the large palms. Bring water to the trailhead or buy some other thirst-quencher at the nearby market.

Laguna Blanca

TRIP DESCRIPTION: **West of Las Palmas Drive.** Bike south on Nogal Dr., cross Cieneguitas Creek and pass Hope House. This historical landmark was built in 1875 by Thomas Hope of Ireland and served as the headquarters for a 4500-acre sheep ranch. The house was restored to its near-original condition in the late sixties-early seventies. The road becomes Via Tranquila and, upon passing Via Presada, enters the rolling hills so characteristic of Hope Ranch.

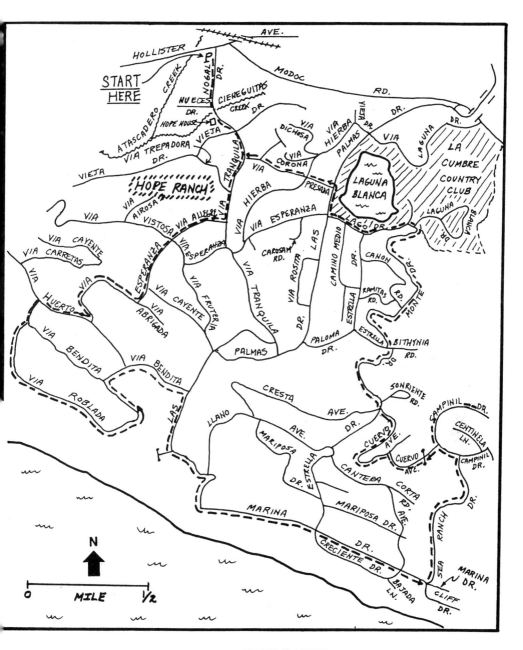

TRIP #4 - HOPE RANCH

The counterclockwise loop is on narrow and rural two-lane roads under a periodic tree mantel. The classy, widely-separated estates are on landscaped lots commonly set back from the road. On Via Esperanza catch views of the lower ranch section with occasional ocean and Santa Ynez Mountain scenes. A series of jig-jogs on various

31

streets (see map) lead to a sweeping turn on Via Roblada and a steep downhill on Via Bendita below Via Huerto. This swift descent leads to Las Palmas Dr. (3.3).

East of Las Palmas Drive. A short spin under overhanging trees on this busier road leads to a light upgrade which continues past Estrella Dr. Soon the street bends right (becoming Cliff Dr.) and the cyclist must cross the on-going traffic lane to stay on Marina Dr. Hang left on Sea Ranch Dr. and tackle a steepening 1/2-mile upgrade that flattens at Campinil Dr. Enjoy the sweeping suburban and ocean vistas, as well as the picture-postcard Santa Barbara views from the north side of the Campinil Dr. arc.

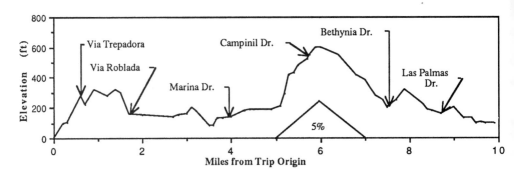

Return to the first (unmarked) street west of Sea Horse Dr., pass around the auto barrier that separates Hope Ranch from the City of Santa Barbara (6.4), and freewheel down Cuervo Ave. East. This switchbacking downhill provides excellent alternating ocean and inland panoramas. A hard right at Estrella Dr. and more winding downhill, with numerous views into lower Hope Ranch, leads to Bethynia Rd. A short jog west (left) brings you to Monte Dr. and a modest uphill, followed by another winding downgrade, then to an overlook of Laguna Blanca (a small reservoir with surrounding bird- and duck-filled wetlands, and the exclusive La Cumbre Country Club). Return to Las Palmas Dr., then zig-zag 1.2 miles through more woodlands to the start point, with one modest upgrade on Via Presada (9.9).

TRIP #5 - SOUTHSIDE LOOP

GENERAL LOCATION: Santa Barbara, Hope Ranch

LEVEL OF DIFFICULTY: Loop - moderate to strenuous
Distance - 12.6 miles
Elevation gain - periodic moderate grades;
steep grade on Miramonte Dr.

HIGHLIGHTS: This trip leaves super-scenic Shoreline Park and traces a steep climb from the Ledbetter Beach area to Honda Valley. After checking the 360-degree vistas from this plateau, return to Santa Barbara proper and enter Hope Ranch from the north. After cutting through the heart of one of America's most luxurious residential communities on Las Palmas Dr. and Marina Dr., the route finale is a bluff-side pedal on Cliff Dr. and Shoreline Dr. An option to use the flatter city streets, as opposed to climbing up to Honda Valley, is described. This is a moderate-level trip option as opposed to the strenuous-level option described.

TRAILHEAD: From U.S. Hwy. 101, exit south at Castillo St. (State Hwy. 225) and drive 0.4 mile to road's end at W. Cabrillo Blvd./Shoreline Dr. Go right onto Shoreline Dr. and trail that winding road one mile to Shoreline Park (picnic benches, barbecues, grass, children's playground, restrooms, water, spectacular coastline views both east and west). The inviting Shoreline Beach below is reached from the east through Ledbetter Beach and Park via Santa Barbara Point.

TRIP DESCRIPTION: **City Segment.** Follow vista-laden Class II Shoreline Dr. 0.9 mile down to Loma Alta Dr., pedal below the Santa Barbara City College pedestrian overcrossing, cross Cliff Dr. and turn left at Class X Coronel St. After a short prayer stop, turn right at Miramonte Dr. and begin tackling the vigorous 1/2-mile, 250-foot uphill (average 9% grade). There are spectacular over-the-shoulder views on the ascent and another visual payoff at the summit in Honda Valley above Via Del Cielo. Cyclists are treated to a 360-degree view that ranges from Honda Valley's panorama to majestic ocean views. A refreshing descent leads across Carrillo St. (2.6) and sees the road name change to Mountain Ave. A view of Santa Barbara opens up that is unrivaled.

Shoreline Park

A steepening downhill leads to Victoria St. where the cyclist must steer left to stay on Mountain Ave. The downgrade ends shortly and, beyond Pedregosa St., bikers encounter a short and steep upgrade which lets out below at road's end at Portesuello

33

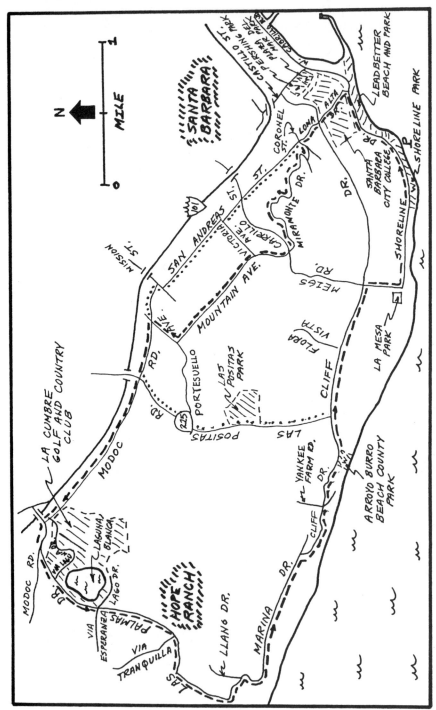

TRIP #5 - SOUTHSIDE LOOP

Ave. A turn right (northeast) on the Class X residential street leads to busier Class II San Andreas St. A 1.9-mile mainly flat cruise on this road, which becomes Modoc Rd. beyond the road "hitch" at Mission St., leads to Las Palmas Dr. (6.1).

Hope Ranch. Go south under the fancy grillwork gateway announcing "HOPE RANCH" to a Class III palm tree-lined road. To the left and in 1/2 mile is the upscale La Cumbre Country Club and lush Laguna Blanca. Lined up at varying offsets from the road are scattered gated estates on impressively-landscaped grounds. Upscale homes are also built into the rounded hills which dot the territory. The curvy road stays under rows of towering palms on rolling terrain, becomes Marina Dr., then turns sharply right and becomes Cliff Dr. as Marina Dr. continues straightahead (9.4).

Cliff Drive/Shoreline Drive. Now within the city limits, Cliff Dr. narrows and heads downhill to highly visible Arroyo Burro Beach County Park (benches, barbecue pits, restrooms, snack bar, Brown Pelican Restaurant, and a cozy beach). The road climbs from sea level, passes a shopping center/fast-food mecca and reaches Meigs Rd. in 1.3 miles from the park. The Class II road leads downhill past La Mesa Park (benches, restroom, playground, grass, scenic ocean vistas) and bends east to become Shoreline Dr. In a little over a mile along the bluffs is the trip start point.

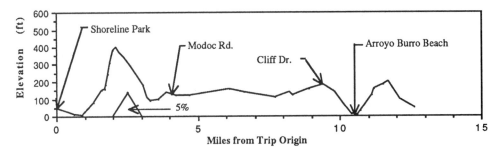

Moderate-Level Trip Option. At Coronel St. and Loma Alta Dr., stay on the latter Class X street along the ridgeline, enjoying the 180-degree Santa Barbara City panorama. A brief descent leads to the end of Loma Alta Dr. where a sharp right turn is followed by a quick left at San Andreas St. A 1.3-mile flat spin on this Class II leads to Portesuello Ave. The rest is as described above (trip length for this option is 12.1 miles).

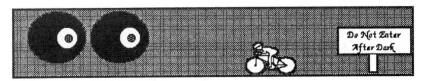

TRIP #6 - UCSB CAMPUS TOUR

GENERAL LOCATION: Isla Vista

LEVEL OF DIFFICULTY: Loop - easy
Distance - 6.5 miles
Elevation gain - essentially flat

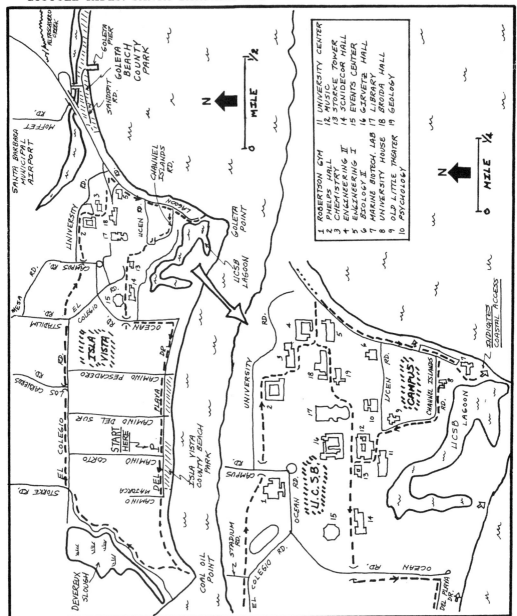

TRIP #6 - UCSB CAMPUS TOUR

HIGHLIGHTS: This easy campus tour is primarily on Class I bikeway. The route visits a secluded beach below Coal Oil Point and the Devereux Slough before returning to the campus section at El Colegio Rd. The next several miles involves a tour into and on the eastern periphery of the main campus. This includes the UCSB Lagoon and cozy Campus Beach, as well as a final segment through bustling, student-filled, Isla Vista.

36

TRAILHEAD: From State Hwy. 101, exit at Storke/Glen Annie Rds. and go south 1-1/4 miles to road's end at El Colegio Rd. Turn left and then right at Camino Del Sur, heading to road's end across from Isla Vista Beach Park.

TRIP DESCRIPTION: **Coal Oil Point and Devereux Slough.** Cycle west on Del Playa Dr. past little Isla Vista Beach Park and, at road's end, follow the right junction of a fork into a packed-dirt path that is bikable with both skinny- and balloon-tire bikes. A short tour on this meandering path leads past a gated entry to several abandoned structures and the newer, better-maintained, caretaker's facility at Coal Oil Point. There are excellent coastal views and a westside access to a surfer's beach. Return to the packed-dirt path and seek a dirt roadway circle to the west. Follow the exit route north past the old Campbell Ranch Manor, now the Devereux School. A little downhill leads past the Devereux Slough, a shallow mud flat teeming with animal and floral wildlife, which is also an ecological study area. Further pedaling places you at El Colegio Rd. and the student dormitories which dominate the area (1.7).

UCSB Campus

UCSB Campus. Cross El Colegio Rd. and trace the Class I path paralleling that street. Cruise by a northbound Class I connector, duck under Los Carneros Rd. (where there are more northbound Class I connectors), then pass south of the soccer field and stadium. Cross Stadium Rd., go by a restroom and the La Crosse and baseball fields, dive under Campus Rd. and meet the campus' western edge. The asphalt-ribbon parallels University Rd., where the Santa Barbara Municipal Airport comes into view to the north. A hard right along Phelps Hall gives way to a zig-zag path between the campus buildings to a confluence with the central campus path. Turn left toward the ocean.

At Lagoon Rd. (3.7), take in the view, then retrace the path to the junction point, head west and eventually south, paralleling Lagoon Rd. The path ends at UCEN Rd., where you bike to Lagoon Rd. to its end. Pedal by the lush Pearl Chase Garden beside the scenic UCSB Lagoon, pass the Marine Lab and visit the beach below (reached by going to the end of the asphalt path). There is excellent off-road biking on the lagoon's south edge and on the southern bluffs above the lagoon (haul your bikes up the eroded stairway to get there).

Return to Lagoon Rd., then Channel Islands Rd. (4.8) and follow a serpentine route into the campus to yet another bikepath confluence. Stay on the westbound trail beneath stately Storke Tower and continue to the Ocean Rd. underpass. An immediate left on a Class I path guides you to a terminus at Del Playa Dr. in 1/4 mile. Return 0.8 mile, passing privately-owned student homes on a street jammed with autos, bicyclists, skateboarders, walkers and joggers (at least during the school operating session) (6.5).

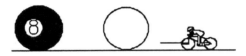

TRIP #7 - GOLETA VALLEY LOOP

GENERAL LOCATION: Goleta

LEVEL OF DIFFICULTY: Loop - easy
Distance - 10.4 miles
Elevation gain - essentially flat

HIGHLIGHTS: This easy-going tour circles Goleta Valley starting from Lake Los Carneros County Park. A visit to the northern edge of the UCSB campus follows, then a fun four-mile Class I tour along Atascadero and Maria Ygnacia Creeks. The return segment plies lightly-traveled suburbia and makes four creek crossings on bridges that are barricaded to motor traffic. There are excellent Santa Ynez Mountain vistas throughout the tour.

TRAILHEAD: From U.S. Hwy. 101, exit north at Los Carneros Rd. and drive 0.3 mile to the entrance to Lake Los Carneros County Park. At the park is the Stow House, built in 1872 by a Southern Pacific Railroad lawyer, which is open for weekend tours. Also at this beautifully landscaped site is the South Coast Railroad Museum at the historic Goleta Depot. This landmark is a Victorian-styled 1901 Southern Pacific freight-passenger station, with a museum that features refurnished rooms and informative displays. Miniature train rides are available for the young or the young at heart.

TRIP DESCRIPTION: To Goleta Beach County Park. Turn south onto Class II Los Carneros Rd., make an over-the-top passage of Hwy. 101, and take an easy 2.7-mile spin to El Colegio Rd. and the UCSB campus' western extreme. South of Hollister Ave. is Class I biking on a path that turns left and fuses with the Class I path along El Colegio Rd. Keep to the lighted path into the UCSB campus proper, cross Stadium Rd., cruise by several athletic fields, and pass under Campus Rd. Parallel University Rd., bend south after Phelps Hall and follow a serpentine route south and east (see Trip #6 for details) to Lagoon Rd. (3.0). After enjoying the view of Campus Beach below and the distant coastline to the east, parallel Lagoon Rd., pass the campus' east gate and coast downhill to Goleta Beach County Park (barbecue facilities, play area, benches, grass, restrooms, pier, coastal views). On the eastern edge is one of our favorite local eateries, the Beachside Cafe.

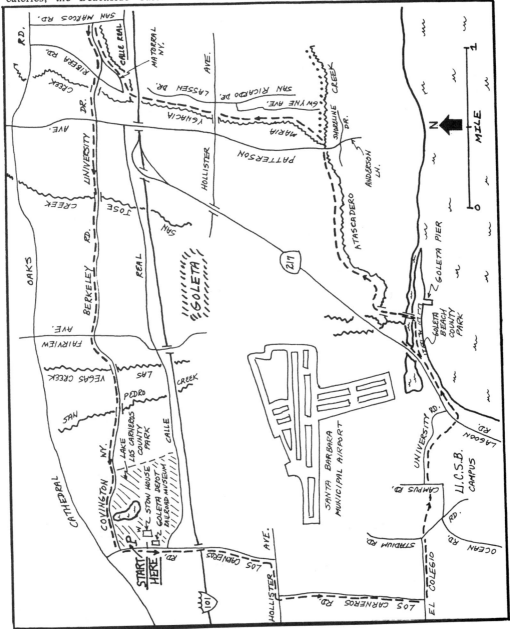

TRIP #7 - GOLETA VALLEY LOOP

The Creek Trails. Bike along Sandspit Rd. to a signed junction. Left is a route which crosses under County Hwy. 217 while the sign proclaims "The Atascadero

39

Goleta Beach Future Great
(Susan Cohen Photo)

Bikeway" (our route) to the right. Stay along the park on this sandspit to the Class I path's end at a road that passes over the small lagoon. Go left (north) and pedal the signed route over the bridge, immediately joining the Class I bikeway that lies nestled between the highway and the wetlands of Atascadero Creek. Follow the bikeway past signs for the Ward Dr. and Patterson Ave. outlets, passing under the Santa Barbara Municipal Airport flight path. After Patterson Ave. is a bridge crossing over Maria Ygnacia Creek and a trail fork. Turn north along the creek, paralleling Gwyne Ave. and reach the first residential tract in about 0.3 mile from the junction.

A teeter-totter ride under Hollister Ave. (5.7) passes below Hwy. 101, where we observed a rock climber scaling a freeway concrete abutment. Once under the freeway, take the left fork at the first trail junction and make an almost immediate right at the next fork. This Class I trail traces San Antonio Creek on a fun mini-roller coaster 0.6 mile through the tree-studded environs. This can be an impressive segment in autumn when the leaves change color. Parallel University Dr. to a dead end at San Marcos Rd. (7.1).

Goleta Depot and Railroad Museum

40

The Residential Beeline Return. At San Marcos Rd. return east on University Dr. The 3.1-mile, nearly straight, path follows University Ave./Berkeley Rd./Covington Wy. via a lightly-traveled suburban area. What makes this segment most interesting (and keeps the traffic light) is the creek crossings over small bridges, which are barricaded to motor traffic. Crossings are at Ribera Dr. (Maria Ygnacia Creek), Murida Dr. (San Jose Creek), Suellen Ct. (Las Vegas Creek) and Carlo Dr. (San Pedro Creek). The Covington Wy. segment passes beside the hedgerows and varied tree cover at the northern edge of Lake Los Carneros Park. A southward turn on Los Carneros Rd. leads back to the park's entry (10.4).

Lake Los Carneros Loop. From the Stow House, there is an entry to a paved walkway/bikeway which circuits Lake Los Carneros. The restful loop offers a variety of plant life, shade trees and an abundance of aquatic wildlife.

TRIP #8 - MOUNTAIN DRIVE +

GENERAL LOCATION: Santa Barbara, Montecito

LEVEL OF DIFFICULTY: Loop - moderate to strenuous
Distance - 23.4 miles
Elevation gain - steep grades on Mountain Dr. above Rocky Nook County Park, on Park Ln. above East Valley Rd., and on Alameda Padre Serra above the Five Points Intersection

HIGHLIGHTS: This is one of our favorites in the City of Santa Barbara. There are three gritty, short-to-medium length uphills with some of the most scenic vistas in the area. Just doing an up-and-back on Mountain Dr. (15 miles total) is rewarding. Traffic is light and slow due to the sinuous street contour and narrow path. The ridge ride is mostly flat. Bella Vista Dr. provides a similar opportunity to ply the ridgeline of the frontal Santa Ynez Mountains and to gander at some of the plush estates, though the climb is tougher. The return weaves across scenic Ortega Ridge, wanders onto the light-use streets of Montecito, then climbs Alameda Padre Serra to a crest before returning to the start point at Mission Santa Barbara.

TRAILHEAD: The trailhead is at Mission Santa Barbara, as described in the Eastside tour (Trip #1).

TRIP DESCRIPTION: Mountain Drive. Above Mission Park, turn right onto Mountain Dr. and follow the steep and winding upgrade over Rocky Nook Park, keeping left at the first junction. The adjoining ridge immediately begins to block

41

the view into the City of Santa Barbara.   A brief respite above Tremonto Rd. follows a more challenging uphill past Foothill Rd.   Beyond is the filtration plant at Sheffield Reservoir where Mountain Dr. veers left.   Mountain Dr. breaks to the right after Las Canoas Rd. (keep your eye on the road sign), flattens and narrows to less than two lanes.   The next four flat miles is on a small, winding, ridge-hugging road offering frequent and varied views of both land and sea -- one of the trip highlight segments!

Mountain Dr. Mailbox

Pass Cold Springs Rd. and the trailhead to East and West Fork Cold Springs Canyon Trails just beyond.   Begin a three-mile downhill which lets out at East Valley Rd. (8.5). Two miles of this segment is continually scenic, but less curvey than before.   The last mile is a weaving route southward through an exclusive neighborhood at the northern reaches of Montecito.   Tree cover overhanging the road characterizes this segment, where the Mercedes run so thick that you can swat them like flies.

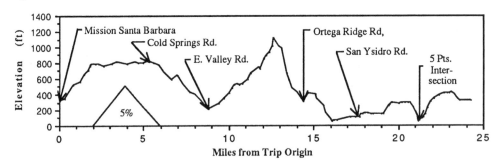

Park Lane/Bella Vista Drive. Pedal eastward 0.6 mile on East Valley Rd. to Park Ln., turn north and bike under an impressive mantle of eucalyptus trees. The flat gives way to a two-mile upgrade through an area of mixed groves and palacial estates. To the left and above are homes perched on the mountainside. Views to the south abound near the two-mile point. Past Romero Canyon Rd. is an 0.8-mile gritty uphill to the trip's zenith. A 0.3-mile rolling-hill segment gives way to a varying downgrade which steepens at Bella Vista Dr., bends south and becomes Ladera Ln.

The Return Maze. A turn west at East Valley Rd. (13.4) begins a circuitous return through Montecito and eastern Santa Barbara. A scenic 1.3-mile over-the-top ride on Ortega Ridge Rd. dumps out at shaded Ortega Hill Rd. The subsequent downhill leads to Sheffield Dr., with an ensuing flat patch-work ride to Manning County Park (lush mixed greenery, picnic facilities, walking trails, restrooms, water) near the heart of Montecito (17.5). Along the way are fenced estates, horse trails and plentiful tree cover.

Continue on a ride of flat connecting "back roads" into "millionaire heaven," which leads to Class II Hot Springs Rd. and Alston Rd. Tracking the latter road leads to the first (short) upgrade in a spell, then a mile of level travel before reaching Eucalyptus Hill Rd. This busier road splits in 1/4 mile, where you veer left onto Alameda Padre Serra and follow a steep downhill past Overlook Ln. to the Five Points Intersection. Below Overlook Ln. is a distant view of our destination, Mission Santa Barbara.

TRIP #8 - MOUNTAIN DRIVE +

43

Veer right to stay on Alameda Padre Serra and begin a testy upgrade which becomes a "lung-buster" above Cota St. While pushing the pedals, catch a few glimpses of the city and ocean below. The contour flattens somewhat after Arbolado Rd. Alameda Padre Serra passes Orpet Park with its many scenic overlooks. The crest is reached near Pedregosa Ave. and the biker is treated to an exciting downhill to Mission Canyon Rd. The mission is reached in a short distance south (23.4).

Estate Below Ortega Ridge Road

TRIP #9 - CARPINTERIA RUNABOUT

GENERAL LOCATION: Carpinteria

LEVEL OF DIFFICULTY: Loop - moderate
Distance - 15.5 miles (base loop plus side trip to Rincon Beach)
Elevation gain - moderate-to-steep grades on Toro Canyon Rd.

44

Santa Claus Lane

HIGHLIGHTS: The basic 11-mile loop provides a brief tour of Carpinteria, an uphill challenge on Toro Canyon Rd., and a pleasant rural pedal on Foothill Rd. through citrus groves and nurseries. The latter "lazy" segment is very popular with cyclists. You can add 4-1/2 miles by heading south on Carpinteria Ave. to the scenic bluffs of Rincon Beach County Park. Finally, there is a moderate-to-strenuous 3.2-mile diversion to a hidden gem, Toro Canyon County Park.

TRAILHEAD: From U.S. Hwy. 101, exit south at Casitas Pass Rd. and drive 1/4-mile to road's end. Go right at Carpinteria Ave. for 1/4 mile to Linden Ave. and head left towards the ocean. Drive to Carpinteria State Beach and park. There are picnic facilities, restrooms, concession stands and a wide sandy beach.

TRIP DESCRIPTION: Carpinteria and Toro Canyon Road. Return 0.6 mile to Carpinteria Ave. and go left (northwest) on that busy Class II road. In 0.5 mile of flat biking through a mix of commercial and industrial areas, turn right at Santa Ynez Ave. and proceed over Hwy. 101. The first left turn leads to Via Real, where 2-1/4 more miles of freeway frontage road and continuous views northward of the Santa Ynez Mountains steer you to Santa Claus Ln. (interesting shopping and numerous eateries on the other side of the freeway) and Nidever Rd. Pass the Santa Barbara Polo and Racquet Club, pedal along the groomed hedgerows and reach Toro Canyon Rd. in 3/4 mile (3.9). Bike a 0.7-mile upgrade through a mix of citrus groves and scattered homes before reaching Foothill Rd. (State Hwy. 192).

Foothill Road Return. An immediate steep upgrade provides the reward of a seaward view out to the Channel Islands. Cruise three miles in a rural, rolling-hills setting among a mix of citrus orchards and nurseries (mostly flowers). The Stewart Orchards are 1.2 miles from Hwy. 192 where the road bends sharply right. Return to the Carpinteria City limits 4.1 miles from the Hwy. 192 junction and reach Linden Ave. just beyond.

Options are to continue on Hwy. 192 to Casitas Pass Rd. or divert to cozy El Carro Park (restrooms, playground, playing field). Either option leads to the intersection of El Carro Ln. and Class I Casitas Pass Rd. (9.7). A southward pedal on the latter road leads back over Hwy. 101 to Carpinteria Ave. The fast-food establishments and gas stations nearby start looking better and better on the return leg. All that awaits is the return to the start point at Carpinteria State Beach (11.0) or add the fun diversion trip below.

Rincon Beach and Back. Spin eastward 1-3/4-mile on Class II Carpinteria Ave. to the Carpinteria outskirts, pass Bailard Ave. and the Rincon overpass. Off Bailard Ave. is an access to a dirt path which off-roaders can use to parallel the railroad

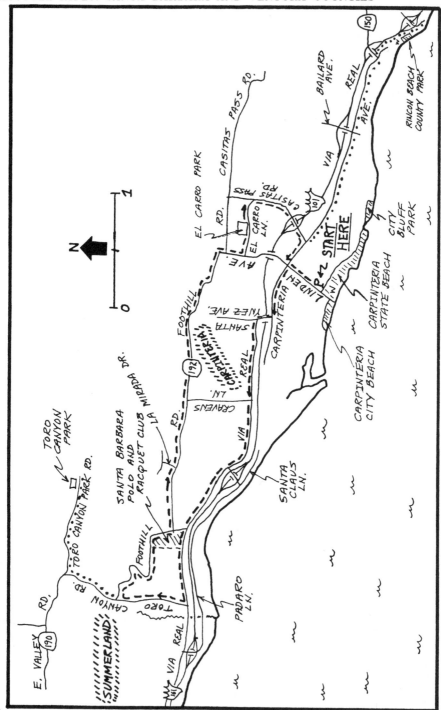

TRIP #9 - CARPINTERIA RUNABOUT

tracks between Carpinteria State Beach and Rincon Beach County Park. Follow the extension of Carpinteria Ave. to an elevated, scenic parking area on the bluffs that hang-gliding enthusiasts use as a jumping off point. However, our route follows the on-ramp to Hwy. 101 south and exits at Bates Rd. A short jog seaward leads to a junction with Rincon Point to the left and Rincon Beach County Park (restrooms) right. Hike to the beach from either area or simply enjoy the views. Return to the trip's origin; the up-and-back tour to Rincon Beach County Park adds 4-1/2 pleasant miles (15.5).

Beach Below Bailard Ave.

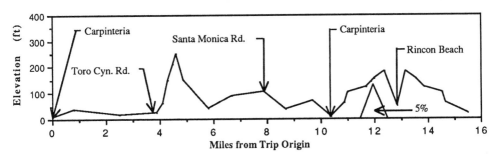

Toro Canyon County Park. There is an excellent 3.2-mile (up-and-back) diversion tour which visits serene Toro Canyon County Park, tucked away in the shaded reaches of the canyon. To get there requires a 0.6-mile, 225-foot, pumpathon on Toro Canyon Rd., followed by an equally tough 0.7-mile, 200-foot, upgrade on Toro Canyon Park Rd. The reward is a nice 0.3-mile downhill runout on a tree-covered country road before reaching the park. This pleasant site offers trees, grassy meadows, picnic areas, restrooms, water, creek with walking bridges and hiking trails. It is sufficiently removed from development to be blessed with Mother Nature's version of peace and quiet.

TRIP#10-GIBRALTER ROAD/CHUMASH PAINTED CAVE

GENERAL LOCATION: Santa Barbara, Santa Ynez Mountains

LEVEL OF DIFFICULTY: Loop - strenuous to very strenuous
Distance - 29.4 miles
Elevation gain - steady steep upgrades on Gibralter Rd.;
periodic steep grades on E. El Camino Cielo

HIGHLIGHTS: Only about 30 miles, but what a 30-mile workout! A warmup stretch on Cathedral Oaks Rd. past Tucker's Grove County Park gives way to a steady climb on Las Canoas Rd. up to Skofield Park.   The subsequent flatter segment gives way to a northbound six-mile uphill on Gibralter Rd., which takes you past the Mt. Calvary Monastery and eventually up to the small settlement at Flores Flats.   There are spacious city, mountain and canyon vistas during the climb.   Once on E. Camino Cielo, ride the sharp Santa Ynez Mountains crest for nine miles to Painted Cave Rd.   Along the upper shaded portions is the Chumash Painted Cave.   This road swoops down to meet San Marcos Pass Rd., continues downhill on Old San Marcos Rd. and returns to Goleta Valley.   This set of final downhill segments offers a myriad of sights, ranging from close-up mountain and canyon vistas to distant city and ocean panoramas.

TRAILHEAD: From U.S. Hwy. 101 east, exit north at Patterson Ave. and drive 3/4 mile to Cathedral Oaks Rd.   Head right 1-1/4 miles to Turnpike Rd. and the Tucker's Grove County Park entry.   The park has trees, barbecue facilities, grass fields, playgrounds, hiking trails, restrooms and water.   Westbound traffic should exit at State Hwy. 154 and continue 3/4 mile to Cathedral Oaks Rd.   The park entry is 1-3/4 miles west.

TRIP DESCRIPTION: The Warmup.   From the park, pedal a westbound warmup stretch into rolling hills on Class II Cathedral Oaks Rd. (State Hwy. 192).   Bike through residential areas with an undercrossing of State Hwy. 154 (1.7) and pass the south segment of Mission Canyon Rd.   Hwy. 192 veers right, but our route goes left on the north segment of Mission Canyon Rd. (4.9).   Cycle to the Tunnel Rd. junction, stay right and follow the signed turnoff to the Santa Barbara Botanic Gardens.   A eucalyptus-shaded road and small bridge crossing leads to winding, uphill Las Canoas Rd.   Bike 1.8 miles of variable workout grades on a partially-shaded road in an upscale rural area.   On the way is Skofield Park (trees, picnic tables, water), followed by a wide swing to the south and a left on El Cielito Rd. (7.2).   This two-lane country road winds between estates and follows a short downhill to Gibralter Rd. in 0.3 mile.

Gibralter Road.   A turn north leads to the start of a six-mile, 1450-foot, steady climb to E. Camino Cielo.   This narrow corridor to the Santa Ynez Mountains' ridgeline goes below the Monastery of Mt. Calvary in a mile.   Turn sharply right on a winding stretch of exposed road with continuous views into Sycamore Canyon.   Ahead and

48

above is a radio tower; view with caution because of the scattered potholes along the remaining road segments.

Chumash Painted Cave

Veer east and begin a series of switchbacks that provide varying mountain and Santa Barbara views. Skirt below and near the radio tower (10.7), then traverse alongside and well above Rattlesnake Canyon in the heart of the mountain range. A short flat, then downhill reprieve, leads past little Flores Flats, followed by a workout back into the upper reaches of Rattlesnake Canyon. Views to the crest appear and, in 1/2 mile, you reach the road terminus at E. Camino Cielo. A sign announces that Big Caliente Hot Springs is 17 miles east (right) and State Hwy. 154 is 11 miles west (13.5).

E. Camino Cielo. Our mistake was not remembering that "it ain't over till it's over!" We envisioned a modest pedal along the ridgeline. Another uphill on the totally-exposed crest provides great canyon views south. On a refreshing, sometimes steep, downhill past Tunnel Trail (at Angostura Pass) is a clear look at an upcoming challenging upgrade.

49

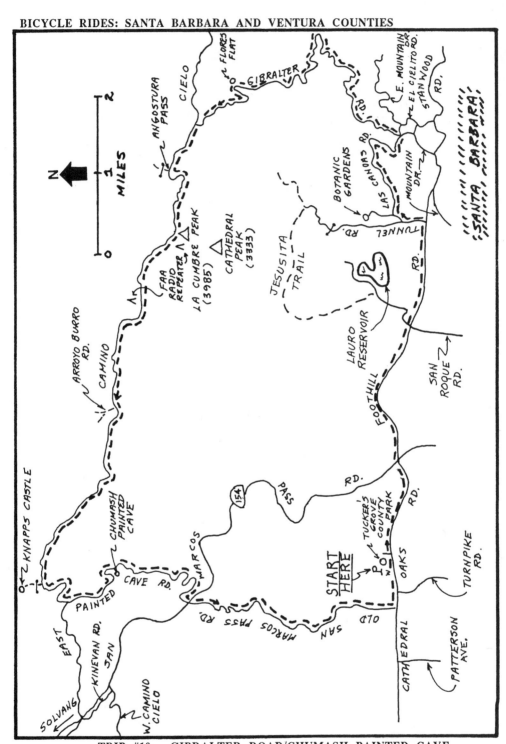

TRIP #10 - GIBRALTER ROAD/CHUMASH PAINTED CAVE

This uphill leads to the trip's crest at La Cumbre Peak, the location of an FAA radio repeater station and La Cumbre Vista Point. This two-mile stretch on the spiny crest presents alternating views south to Santa Barbara and north to the Santa Ynez River; Gibralter Reservoir is clearly outlined well below.

Skirting alongside precipitous drops, the road dips down past a second repeater station and follows the crest on a downhill to a saddle at Arroyo Burro Rd. (18.2). Stop and enjoy the picture-postcard view back to La Cumbre Peak, then bike a 1-1/2-mile upgrade to a crest with the first peeks into the westward canyons that envelope Painted Cave and San Marcos Pass Rds.

Breathe easy and coast 1-1/2 miles between the ridgeline crest to a trail which leads to Knapp's Castle. George Knapp, a wealthy retired industrialist, had his dream home carved from thick sandstone blocks, decked with illuminated waterfalls and featured a room housing a huge pipe organ. Stone walls, part of the foundation, and a few chimneys are the sole remnants of a disastrous fire in 1940. One mile beyond the trail junction is Painted Cave Rd. (22.4).

Painted Cave Road. A turn here leads downhill past the Laurel Springs Ranch into a wee community with a Painted Cave souvenir shop and onto a narrow asphalt strip with some one-lane stretches. Past two very sharp and steep downhill switchbacks, enter densely-treed terrain and come to the Chumash Painted Cave. A few uphill steps lead to this 22-foot deep cave, with its magnificent rock art (complex with vividly-colored designs), found within the gated cave and in the overhead formations. The paintings date back at least a thousand, and possibly 1500, years. Maria Ygnacia Creek flows through the lush forest on the opposite side of the road and below.

The road widens, passes under several homes buried within the tree cover and drops to an area with a clear ocean vista. In just over a mile from the cave, the downhill steepens and begins an exposed traverse, hugging the western mountain slopes. A sheer drop via a couple of sharp switchbacks brings Santa Barbara City views into focus and lets you out at Hwy. 154 (25.6).

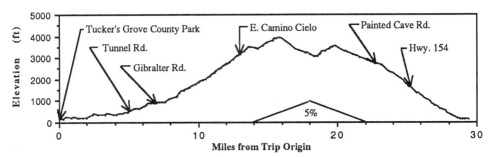

Old San Marcos Road. Carefully cross the busy highway and follow Old San Marcos Rd., staying left at the first intersection. Glide by the San Marcos Trout Club (now a private residence) and enjoy the Goleta Valley overlook. After a couple of low-speed, sharp switchbacks, take in the panorama from the Santa Ynez Mountains to Santa Barbara and Goleta. Across the canyon is Hwy. 154 sliced into the mountainsides. After 2.3 miles of variable downhill and a milder set of switchbacks, the path flattens near Twin Ridge Rd., the site of scattered upscale homes. Cross Maria Ygnacia Creek, enter another residential area and return to Cathedral Oaks Rd. Turn left (east) and pedal 0.3 mile to the comforting shade of Tucker's Grove County Park (29.4).

51

TRIP #11 - ROMERO CANYON ROAD (Mountain Bike)

GENERAL LOCATION: Montecito, Romero Canyon

LEVEL OF DIFFICULTY: Up and back - strenuous
Distance - 6.2 miles (one way)
Elevation gain - continuous moderate-to-steep grades

HIGHLIGHTS: One of the few routes in the Santa Ynez Mountain's frontal range, this former road has eroded somewhat and is more trail than road beyond the initial Romero Canyon Creek crossings.   The road was closed to automobile traffic in the late seventies when heavy rains caused massive slides which blocked it.   This is a steady (average 6-1/2%) workout upgrade which moderates after 5.5 miles, then drops down to E. Camino Cielo.   This all-dirt road access to the Santa Barbara backcountry climbs in and out of Romero Canyon, crosses a couple of cement bridges and winds its way to Romero Saddle and E. Camino Cielo.   The exposed south-facing slopes provide little shade, although the coastal breezes and scenic ocean vistas moderate the discomfort on hot days.

Romero Canyon Below Toro Canyon Road

TRAILHEAD: From U.S. Hwy. 101, exit north on Sheffield Dr., then turn west (left) on State Hwy. 192 (East Valley Rd.) in 1-1/2 miles. Turn north (right) almost immediately on Romero Canyon Rd., and turn right again at road's end onto Bella Vista Rd. In 0.3 mile is the gated entry to Romero Canyon Rd., Trail 5N15.

TRIP DESCRIPTION: **To Toro Canyon Road.** Beyond the gate, the first 1/2 mile seems steeper than it really is as a result of the loose surface and severe rutting. The route crosses Romero Canyon Creek on a bridge near the 0.3-mile point, turns east and passes a power-line access road junction and recrosses the creek near the Romero Canyon Hiking Trail junction (not suited for cycling). The grade moderates as the overgrown road/trail heads east and leaves the canyon. Continue about a mile as the trail loops east and then north under a low frontal range peak. Enjoy the Montecito and Toro Canyon views below. On the northward swing, the trail crosses a saddle with a water tower, overhead power lines and the gated Toro Canyon Rd. junction (1.9).

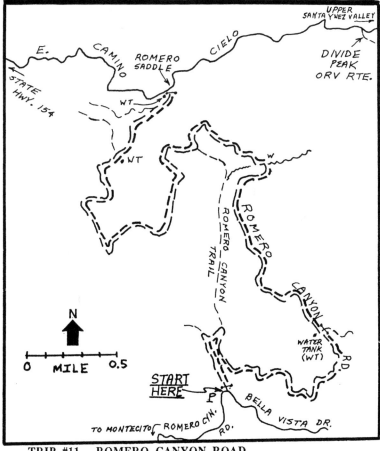

TRIP #11 - ROMERO CANYON ROAD

To E. Camino Cielo. Stay to the left at the junction and return to Romero Canyon on a traverse well above the canyon floor. A small horseshoe bend takes the roadie across a year-round, spring-fed creek (3.1). The path makes a full sweep above

53

and to the north of the canyon on a smooth, crushed-shale surface. Another creek crossing leads to a traverse of the slopes on a sweeping 1.5-mile southerly circumnavigation of a clumped group of frontal peaks, before returning north.

Just below the most northern peak, the trail transits another saddle, passes a second water tank (5.5) and returns to the upper reaches of Romero Canyon. The last 3/4 mile is mostly level, with the end segment dipping down to and ending near a concrete tank and cistern near the junction with paved E. Camino Cielo (6.2).

Connector Options. There are several options to connect the Romero Rd. ride with other trails which branch off E. Camino Cielo. Most require a car shuttle or strength, stamina, experience and a strong will to live (well, almost!). A return to Santa Barbara can be made via **Gibralter Road** (5.8 miles west). Backcountry options are to connect with **Angostura Pass Road** (6.6 miles west), **Cold Springs Trail** (2.8 miles west), **Divide Peak Off-Road Vehicle Route** (1.5 miles east), or to continue on E. Camino Cielo down into the **Upper Santa Ynez River** drainage. (Consult other mountain-bike sources for all except Gibralter Rd., Upper Santa Ynez River and E. Camino Cielo options above.)

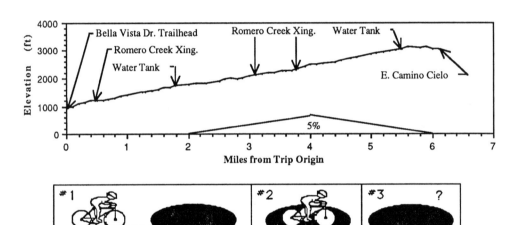

TRIP #12 - EAST CAMINO CIELO ("SKY ROAD")

GENERAL LOCATION: Santa Ynez Mountain Crest

LEVEL OF DIFFICULTY: Loop - strenuous
Distance - 17.9 miles
Elevation gain - frequent moderate-to-steep grades

HIGHLIGHTS: The paved eastern section of "The Sky Road" provides about 18 miles of alternating views to the Santa Barbara area and the Santa Ynez River drainage. The one-way tour described leaves the Cielo Store and works along the Santa Ynez Mountains ridgeline 8.7 miles to a super-scenic summit near La Cumbre Peak. In two miles is Gibralter Rd., followed by a roller-coaster 7.2 miles (mostly downhill) along the ridgeline to the end of the paved section at Romero Saddle.

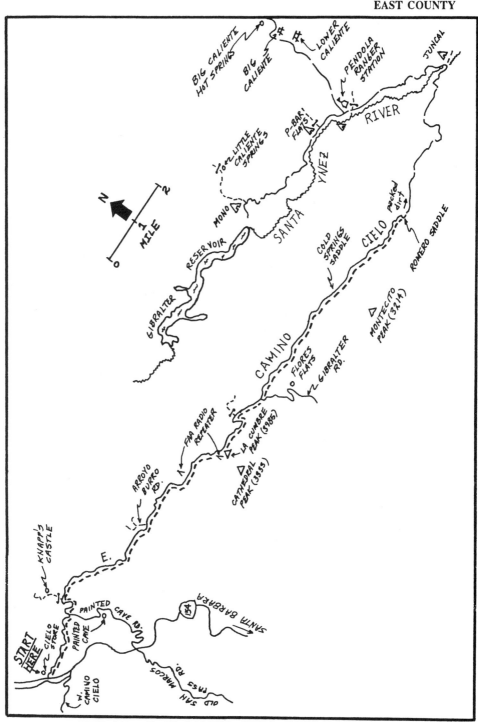

BIG CALIENTE HOT SPRINGS

BIG CALIENTE

LOWER CALIENTE

PENDOLA RANGER STATION

JUNCAL

LITTLE CALIENTE SPRINGS

TO

P-BAR FLATS

RIVER

SANTA YNEZ

N

MILE
0   1   2

MONO

RESERVOIR

COLD SPRINGS SADDLE

CIELO

PACKED DIRT

ROMERO SADDLE

GIBRALTER

CAMINO

MONTECITO PEAK (3214)

FLORES FLATS

GIBRALTER RD.

FAA RADIO REPEATER

LA CUMBRE PEAK (3985)

ARROYO BURRO RD.

CATHEDRAL PEAK (3333)

KNAPP'S CASTLE

E.

PAINTED CAVE RD.

SANTA BARBARA

START HERE

CIELO STORE

PAINTED CAVE

154

W. CAMINO CIELO

OLD SAN MARCOS PASS RD.

TRIP #12 - EAST CAMINO CIELO ("SKY ROAD")

55

Mountain bikers can continue on graded dirt to the Upper Santa Ynez River area (see Trip #13). Pendola Ranger Station is eight miles downhill and the Big Caliente Hot Springs are 2.8 miles further. These springs are Santa Barbara County's finest.

TRAILHEAD: From either Santa Barbara or Solvang, follow State Hwy. 154 to San Marcos Pass. Turn east at E. Camino Cielo and go to the Cielo Store near San Marcos Ranger Station. The store offers mouth-watering sandwiches and other munchies which can be pocketed for later use. The route is waterless, so on hot days, bring several quarts of water for this one-way trip. For off-roaders extending the trip past Romero Saddle, the next reliable water source is at Pendola Ranger Station.

East Camino Cielo Near Painted Cave Road

TRIP DESCRIPTION: **To La Cumbre Peak.** The two miles to the Painted Cave Rd. intersection involve a steady climb on a tree-covered winding road that passes several gated estates and proceeds into open exposed countryside. The first of many views down into Santa Barbara and the Santa Ynez drainage opens beyond the first mile of the crest (morning riders may see no more than the top of thick coastal clouds, depending on weather). After Painted Cave Rd. is a trek across a broad ridge. Navigate a saddle crossing (3.6), and follow a thin ridgeline to a crest in an uphill mile. A look ahead and above brings into focus the first of two FAA radio repeater towers that the route will pass.

The exposed ridge ride drops almost 500 feet in 1-1/2 miles, crosses another saddle, creeps closer to the repeater station, and bottoms out at graded-dirt Arroyo Burro/Santa Ynez River Rds. junction (6.1). Just to the north are the historic Knapp's Castle ruins (see Trip #10). A view-laden 2.6-mile upgrade leads across a saddle below the peak and the westernmost repeater, passes into some welcome tree cover, then reaches the trip's summit alongside the La Cumbre Peak radio repeater

(8.7). To the north and below is one of the outstanding looks at Gibralter Reservoir. (The best Santa Barbara viewpoint from the peak is reached via a dirt road about 0.2 mile from the repeater.)

To Romero Saddle. Follow along a thin ridgeline, carefully taking in the alternating precipitous drops off the northern and southern slopes. Yet another saddle crossing leads to a broader area of the Santa Ynez Mountains spine and Gibralter Rd., two miles from the summit. Beyond are the more isolated stretches of E. Camino Cielo, with only an occasional passing vehicle returning from the Santa Ynez River basin playground. The ridgeline roller-coasters 2.6 miles to a crest and follows a downhill past several above-ground water tunnel entry towers on the way to Romero Saddle. Parts of the road are on a thin asphalt ribbon with stark drops on either side. (Like hiking, some trips require watching the trail at the expense of the nearby scenery!) The road condition degrades as the route arrives at the paved eastern reaches, where the northern landscape dominates the scenic vistas. The paved section terminates at Romero Saddle, 7.2 miles from Gibralter Rd. (17.9).

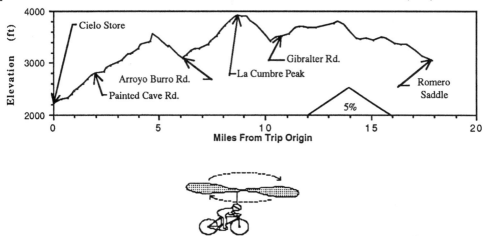

TRIP #13 - UPPER SANTA YNEZ RIVER (Mtn. Bike)

GENERAL LOCATION: Los Padres National Forest, Juncal

LEVEL OF DIFFICULTY: One-way - Romero Saddle to hot springs - moderate
Distance - 13.4 miles (to Little Caliente Hot Springs)
Elevation gain - periodic moderate grades

HIGHLIGHTS: This trip leaves Romero Saddle and drops down to Juncal Campground within the upper Santa Ynez River drainage. The swift downhill is scenic, although the highlight segments for most mountain bikers are those trails which fan out in all directions from the river plain. A sample of these roads and trails is provided in terms of trips to two of the best hot springs in the county, Big and Little Caliente Hot Springs. To get there involves a mostly flat ride along the Santa Ynez River. Big Caliente Hot Springs is reached via a 2-1/2-mile sojourn up Agua Caliente Canyon. Little Caliente Hot Springs is accessed via an extension along the river, a short segment along Mono Creek, and a one-mile ride into the lower reaches of Little Caliente Canyon.

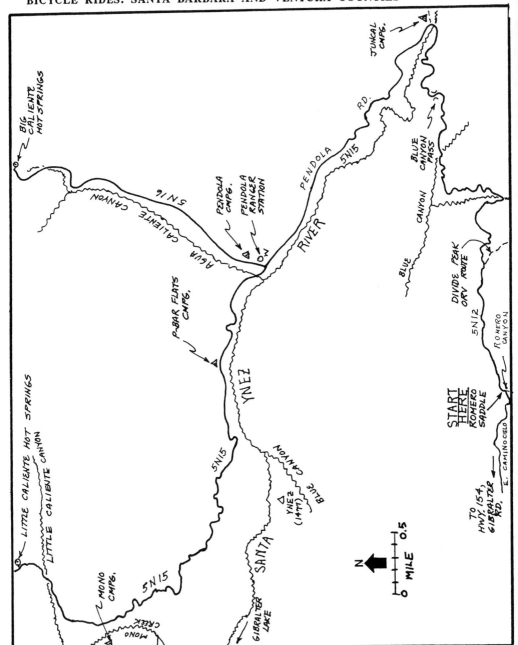

TRIP #13 UPPER SANTA YNEZ RIVER

TRAILHEAD: Follow the on-road tour on E. Camino Cielo to Romero Saddle as described in the E. Camino Cielo ("Sky Road") tour (Trip #12). The described trip drops from the saddle and follows along the Upper Santa Ynez River--it assumes a return car shuttle. The round trip is very strenuous. Pendola Ranger Station has water, but there is none at the drive-in campgrounds or picnic areas in the Upper Santa Ynez River area. Bring water or plan to treat water from natural sources.

The graded dirt road past Romero Saddle is open, except during periods of heavy rain. Check with USFS Pendola Ranger Station before doing this trip during periods of stormy weather. The road is used by off-road vehicles (ORV's) and cars, so keep your eyes/ears open.

TRIP DESCRIPTION: **Romero Saddle to Juncal Campground.** Starting at the point where E. Camino Cielo transitions from asphalt to graded dirt (there is a concrete water reservoir here), pass the Romero Canyon Rd. junction and enjoy the views down into the Santa Ynez River drainage. The junction with the Divide Peak ORV route is just beyond. The road dives downhill with route quality degrading to sections of mixed rougher surface and gravel. Bikers wind eastward before taking a sharp turn south, crossing Escondido Canyon (2.3) and swinging north. In a mile, go under seemingly out-of-place power lines. There is a view into Blue Canyon to the west as you cross a concrete bridge and head uphill at Blue Canyon Pass (one of the few workouts on this tour) (3.6). After the pass are vistas of the Santa Ynez River drainage, once the road transitions to the north side of the ridge. Watch for rock slides across the road which we encountered in May of 1994. A downhill leads across the river on one of the concrete fords so typical of the west side of the Santa Ynez River entry (see Trip #16). To the right is shaded Juncal Camp and the Juncal Rd. junction (5.1), the easternmost point of the trip.

Near the Divide Peak ORV Junction

Juncal Campground to Agua Caliente Canyon. What is now Camuesa Rd. (the same road referenced as a junction on the Little Pine Mountain Loop, Trip #18), stays above and north of the Santa Ynez River on packed dirt. This is a great ORV and mountain-biker playground area with inviting swimming holes scattered along the river. Bike a 1-1/2-mile roller-coaster that descends modestly 1-1/2-miles to Agua Caliente (Spanish for "the place of warm water") Canyon. There are a few feeder creek crossings and a transition from the nearly continuous scrub and spotted-tree zone to a broad, barren region on both sides of the river near the seven-mile point. At this juncture are two particularly interesting options.

Option 1-On To Agua Caliente Spring. Turn north into Agua Caliente Canyon and, in a few hundred yards, bike past Pendola Ranger Station. The almost-level dirt road passes Pendola Campground and enters a rapidly-narrowing canyon in one mile. After several creek crossings, there is a parking area, which announces that Big Caliente Hot Springs is near. Past the parking area, take the trail further into the canyon and look for a trail across the creek about 100 feet above on the side of a mountain. Cross the creek to the access trail. If you reach Big Caliente Debris Dam, you've gone 1/2 mile too far. The hot springs are actually a cement pool with piped-in hot water. Take time to enjoy!

Option 2-On To Little Caliente Spring. Cross Agua Caliente Creek and trail the Santa Ynez River on the north bank heading into the Middle Santa Ynez Campground. On a continued flat, pass a marker listing distances to various destinations and meet with P-Bar Flats Campground (9.2). Both camps have some tree cover, which make them candidate rest stops. In a little over 1/2 mile, meet the Blue Canyon Trail coming in from the south and leave the riverbed heading northwest and up.

A short climb on what is still Camuesa Rd. and a rolling traverse of the frontal hills leads to a high point 4.5 miles from the Agua Caliente Canyon entrance (11.5). A downhill follows with a final modest ridge traverse, where Mono Campground is visible. At the signed road junction, bear right towards Mono Campground and the large trees, passing the short western spur leading to this site (12.2). An option is to divert on a short loop which passes into the campground and returns to the main road. Bike north under an awning of overhanging trees (this is a heavenly stretch!) for 0.3 mile. Camuesa Rd. bears left, but turn right and bike one mile up along Little Caliente Canyon to a locked gate and the Little Caliente Hot Springs. The springs (a cement tub similar to that at Big Caliente Springs) are on a short footpath off a car turnaround loop (13.4).

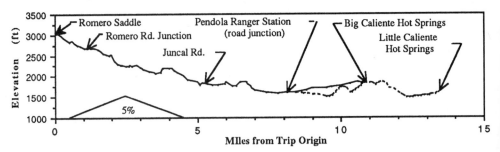

Other Options. This trek could be used to connect with a significant number of mountain-bike trails along the way to either hot springs. In order, the route passes: 1) Romero Canyon Rd., Divide Peak ORV Route, Blue Canyon Trail, Murietta Divide Trail, Pendola Jeepway and Hildreth Jeepway (applies to either Big or Little Caliente Hot Springs); and 2) Gibralter Trail, Mono Trail, Cold Springs Trail and Camuesa Rd. (trip to Little Caliente Hot Springs only).

TRIP #14 - WEST CAMINO CIELO (Mountain Bike)

GENERAL LOCATION: San Marcos Pass, Refugio Pass

LEVEL OF DIFFICULTY: One-way - strenuous
Distance - 17.7 miles (State Hwy. 154 to Refugio Pass)
Elevation gain - periodic moderate-to-steep grades

HIGHLIGHTS: This challenging mountain-bike trip takes the cyclist into the "outback" of the Santa Ynez Mountain's crest.   The one-way tour described starts at Hwy. 154, climbs to a summit in four miles to the Winchester Gun Club area and plummets on a rock-strewn dirt road into the bowels of the range.   A tenuous six-mile ascent to the crest at Santa Ynez Peak provides numerous Santa Barbara and Lake Cachuma views.   Shortly beyond is a return to paved road and the start of a rewarding six-mile downhill adventure which ends at Refugio Pass.   An option to bike down Refugio Rd. to Refugio Beach State Park (25.0 total miles) is also described. We recommend that W. Camino Cielo be transited from east to west if the rider is inclined to get the hard work done early.

TRAILHEAD: Drive on San Marcos Pass Rd. (State Hwy. 154) to the W. Camino Cielo turnoff (southbound motorists) or the Kinevan Rd. turnoff (northbound).   In the latter case, follow Kinevan Rd. 1/4-mile north to W. Camino Cielo and park near the W. Camino Cielo/Kinevan Rd. intersection, well off the road.

The "Switchback"

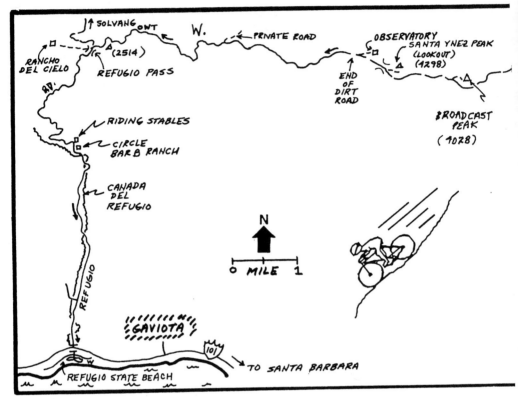

SOLVANG ⟶ OWT   W.   ← PRIVATE ROAD   OBSERVATORY
SANTA YNEZ PEAK
(LOOKOUT)
(2514)   (4298)
RANCHO
DEL CIELO   REFUGIO PASS
END
OF
DIRT
ROAD
RIDING STABLES   BROADCAST
PEAK
CIRCLE
BARB RANCH   (4028)
CANADA
DEL
REFUGIO   N
REFUGIO   0 MILE 1
GAVIOTA
101
TO SANTA BARBARA
REFUGIO STATE BEACH

TRIP #14 - WEST CAMINO CIELO

TRIP DESCRIPTION: **To the Winchester Gun Club.** The beginning segment lets you know your "ticker" is working, with an almost four-mile uphill to the Winchester Gun Club. All paved road, this average 5%-grade goes through mostly wooded terrain past several homes and an interesting naturally-sculpted boulder (0.7). There are short level segments interspersed amid the long climb. The winding road passes the turnoff to the Goddard Picnic Grounds just beyond the two-mile point and keeps climbing to a crest before reaching the shooting range. Glide past the scattered shell casings on the flat road past the gun club's entrance, after which the road transitions to dirt in 1/4 mile (3.9).

To the Northernmost Trip Point. The road dives downhill on a rocky, packed-dirt surface for 1/2 mile before reaching a smoother section. This is representative of the road's mix for the next 7.8 miles, with the rock-strewn surfaces being far more common. A mile on the dirt pack leads to a wild switchback, "The Switchback," with an abundance of shale and a steep drop. Near the bottom-out point is a water tower and the start of a six-mile pull to the trip's high point at Santa Ynez Peak. We got "buzzed" by two off-road motorcyclists early in the climb, one of the rare times we met traffic. There are a few flats and shallow downhills to keep the spirits up along this grade. After 6-1/2-miles, leave the forested surroundings and enter open scrub areas.

Start a long traverse up the northside ridgeline where there were hide-and-seek views of Lake Cachuma on the fog-bound October day that we rode. Rock, shale and

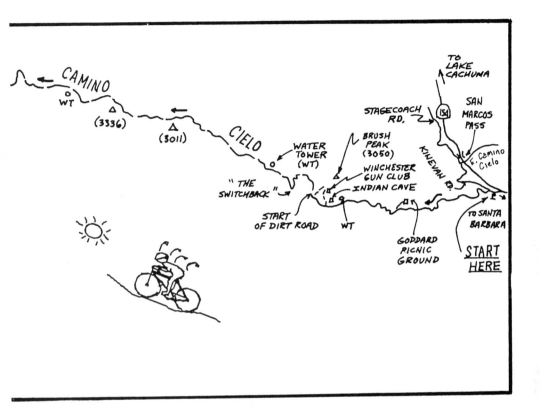

TRIP #14 - WEST CAMINO CIELO

smooth surfaces, and more rock (you get the idea), take off-roaders past a second water tower. Another mile-plus of this scenic ride leads to a wide swing north below a summit outcropping, the most northerly point (9.2).

The Push to Santa Ynez Peak. Around the bend is a vista across a deep canyon to Broadcast and Santa Ynez Peaks. Cross an exposed saddle and pass a subtle jeep trail junction that plummets down the northern slopes to Hwy. 154. Pump a steepening upgrade below the TV tower of Broadcast Peak on the mountain's southern flank. Bikers are treated to the first view of the road's summit (almost) on the southern side of, and below, Santa Ynez Peak.

An exposed climb across another saddle leads to an area where the grade mercifully lightens. The trip's summit is reached in 1/4 mile on the west side of the peak (11.1). The views west and south are spectacular, so we've heard--we saw thick layers of coastal fog and the Santa Barbara Observatory to the north. A flat traverse leads past the observatory and returns to paved road in another 1/4 mile (11.7).

The Downhill "Blowout." What remains is a six-mile downhill which starts with a straight ridgeline traverse and changes to a winding dive through the lower mountain range. In 2.5 miles from the observatory is a private road to a ranch. The route reenters a lovely forested area and, in 1/2 mile, reaches Refugio Rd. at Refugio

Pass. Across Refugio Rd. is the gated entry to Rancho del Cielo, President Reagan's domain (17.7).

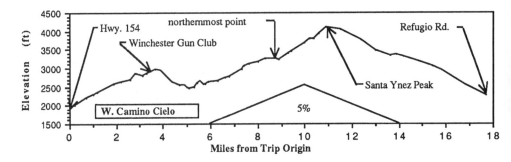

West Camino Cielo/Santa Ynez Mountain Backdrop

Trip Options. 1) We set up a car shuttle and rode another "hang-it-out" 7.3 miles down to our transportation, waiting at Refugio Beach State Park. This is a wild 2250-foot switchbacking downhill through dense forest which dumps out into a shallow canyon beside Canada del Refugio (see Trip #15 for details). It took one fifth of our total trip time to finish the last roughly 14 miles of our 25-mile tour (Santa Ynez Peak to the park); 2) Pedal an up-and-back from Refugio Pass to the end of the paved section below the Santa Barbara Observatory; 3) true "animals" can do the 4000-foot climb from Refugio Beach State Park to the paved road terminus and return.

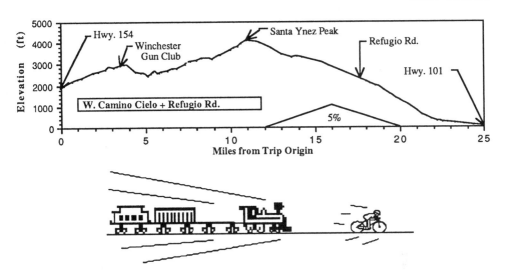

TRIP #15 - REFUGIO PASS LOOP (Partial Mtn. Bike)

GENERAL LOCATION: Solvang, Refugio Pass, Gaviota

LEVEL OF DIFFICULTY: Loop - strenuous
Distance - 39.4 miles
Elevation gain - steep grade to Refugio Pass

HIGHLIGHTS: Few tours offer this kind of variety mixed with physical challenges. The route leaves the picturesque environs of Solvang and heads east to Refugio Rd. A 7.5-mile demanding climb on this mixed paved/dirt road leads through the magnificent forested slopes of the Santa Ynez Mountains to the trip's summit at Refugio Pass. A 3.5-mile scenic "bomb run" down Refugio Rd. leads into rural Refugio Canyon and Refugio State Beach. A lengthy stint on State Hwy. 101 takes you past Gaviota Beach State Park and through the Gaviota Pass tunnel. After a stiff climb to Nojoqui Pass, cruise Old Hwy. 1 and return to Solvang via pastoral Alisal Rd., passing Nojoqui State Park and the Alisal. A nifty option is to arrange a car shuttle and confine the trip to the fantastic Refugio Rd. segment.

TRAILHEAD: From U.S. Hwy. 101, exit east at State Hwy. 246 and go three miles to the edge of Solvang, where the road is named Mission Dr. Drive into the heart of this tourist mecca 3/4-mile to Solvang Park, just past Atterdag Rd. This beautiful treed and grassy park has restrooms, water, picnic tables, a bandstand, a bust of Hans Christian Anderson and a large rock showing the mileage from Solvang to Copenhagen. From State Hwy. 154, turn west on State Hwy. 246 and drive four miles to Alamo Pintado Rd. In 3/4 mile, just beyond Alisal Rd.,is the park. Be sure to explore the park either before or after this trip. An alternative is to start from Santa Ines Mission, 1/4 mile east as described in Trip #20.

TRIP DESCRIPTION: **Mission Drive.** Cycle east into the heart of the Solvang shopping district (see Trip #20), pass Mission Santa Ines, and pedal the rolling hills 2.7 miles to Refugio Rd. On the way are views north to the "gentlemen" horse ranches and farms perched along the hillsides. Enjoy the mountain vistas both north and south on this Santa Ynez Valley segment.

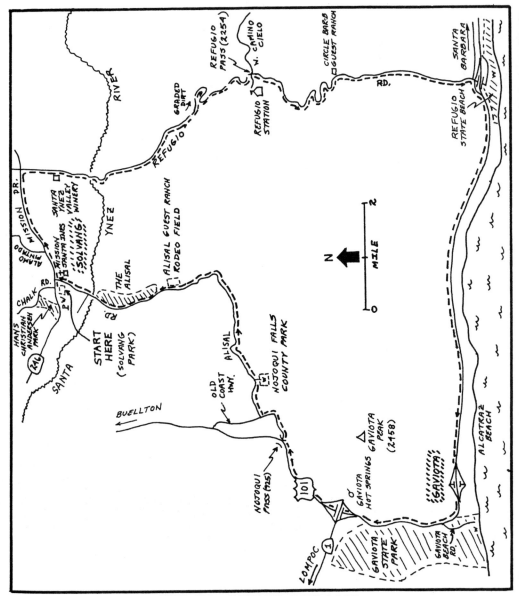

TRIP #15 - REFUGIO PASS LOOP

Refugio Road to Refugio Pass. The trip highlight is the 14.4 miles on this road. Turn south onto Refugio Rd. and cruise into a valley, pass scattered farms and cattle-grazing lands, the Santa Ynez Winery, then cross the Santa Ynez River. The destination pass is high in the mountains ahead and southeast. The road narrows and starts a mild climb, passing an "Impassible in Wet Weather" sign. Heed this warning as there are several crossings of Quiota Creek in the next two miles past the river, which can have very treacherous flows during rainy periods. The road conditions on the upper reaches of the south side of Refugio Pass can also get <u>very</u> nasty!

More grazing land gives way to rolling hills and increasingly dense tree cover. This forest entry portends the inspiring tree-covered rise through the Santa Ynez Mountains that lead to the pass. In four miles from Mission Dr., the road transitions to packed dirt, ranging in conditions from smooth to downright rocky and rutted. The climb gets serious and progresses higher above a steep canyon off to the east for the next 1.4 miles. A sharp switchbacking climb to the right transitions the rider to an area above a canyon to the west, then the road cuts back again above the original canyon. Another 1-1/2 miles of winding traverse along the mountain slope leads past a gated road entry, a sharp left bend in the road, a creek crossing, and a final short uphill assault to Refugio Pass (10.2). At the pass is the W. Camino Cielo junction, La Sherpa Conference Grounds (private), and a gated entry to Rancho Del Cielo (to the west or right), also called the Reagan Ranch (private).

Refugio Road South of West Camino Cielo

Refugio Pass to Refugio State Beach. The payoff for all of the hard work is a 3-1/2 mile (average 7% grade), 1600-foot "bomb run" down the mountain, followed by a nearly-flat run through a scenic shallow canyon of nearly equal length. The outlet is at State Hwy. 101, just north of Refugio State Beach. The transit from the pass is on wider paved highway which takes the bicyclist through another mile of dense tree cover. The tree canopy thins and bikers return to exposed mountain terrain. Along the way are entries to large ranches (Rancho Dos Vistas and Castello Gandolpho stand out), scattered residences, and grand ocean vistas. (We observed Santa Barbara Channel oil rigs poking out of a low fog the day we passed through.)

Follow a precipitous downhill toward Refugio Canyon which enfolds the watercourse of Canada Del Refugio. In 3-1/2 miles below the pass is a steep downhill and turn south which drops to the flatter canyon floor. Pass the Circle Bar B Guest Ranch, which features a stable of riding horses, private cabins and swimming pool.

The next 2.2 relaxing miles follows Canada Del Refugio south past citrus orchards and scattered homes to the State Hwy. 101 on-ramp (17.1).

Highway 101. The next 6.6 miles on this busy oceanside highway provide a steady diet of rolling hills. Before the highway swings north toward Gaviota Pass is the Mariposa Reina exit to Gaviota (population-94) and its massive oil refinery. After the northerly transition is an entry to Gaviota Beach State Park (see Trip #19), a traveler's rest area (trees, water and restrooms), and the impressive northbound tunnel which was blasted through the mountain bedrock. This is Gaviota Pass (26.4). A steady 3.6-mile climb through the foothills beside Canada de la Gaviota takes cyclists past the Hwy. 1 turnoff (to Lompoc) up to the Nojoqui Summit.

Alisal Road Return. The turnoff east at the Nojoqui Falls sign guides you down the rough Old Coast Hwy. (There is no southbound access to Hwy. 101 here if should you do the trip in reverse.) We saw two small deer cross the road below. In a mile from the summit, go right (northeast) onto Alisal Rd. (The straightahead continuation of the Old Coast Hwy. does provide southbound access to Hwy. 101.) The exit to Nojoqui Falls Park is in 3/4 mile (see Trip #19). Leave the flat and pedal up into hilly cattle-grazing country.

Tree cover returns in abundance as the road follows Nojoqui Creek to a summit 1.8 miles from the park entrance. Wind eastward and jog north, picking up Alisal Creek below a nearly hidden reservoir. The treed arch thins and Alisal Rd. passes horse stables, showground and cabins of Alisal Creek Guest Ranch (36.4). The next two miles follows beside the Ranch Course at Alisal, a lush north-south golf course which sees Alisal Creek passing through its bounds. The clubhouse parking lot sported a Rolls Royce and several other fine motoring machines which caught our attention as we cycled by. Alisal Rd. recrosses the Santa Ynez River, passes the Royal Scandanavian Inn (Solvang Century start/end point), and reenters Solvang proper. Turn left at Mission Dr. and return to Solvang Park. (39.4).

Trip Option. Arrange for a car shuttle to drop you off at Refugio Rd. and Mission Dr. (State Hwy. 246). Cycle the mixed Santa Ynez Valley/Santa Ynez Mountain segment, with the last 3.5-wooded uphill miles to Refugio Pass being on mixed quality dirt road. Take the "blowout" winding downhill into Refugio Canyon, then share hot dogs and "cold ones" with your trusty shuttler at Refugio State Beach.

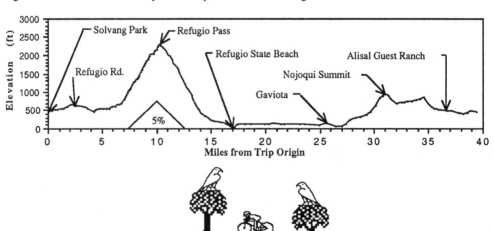

TRIP #16 - PARADISE ROAD (Mountain Bike Option)

GENERAL LOCATION: Santa Ynez Mountains and River

LEVEL OF DIFFICULTY: Up and back - moderate
Distance - 8.7 miles (one way)
Elevation gain - periodic moderate grades

HIGHLIGHTS: This sojourn is a river rat's delight! Leave the Paradise Store and Grill and bike 4.8 miles past campgrounds and picnic sites through a mix of open and treed areas. Past the Los Prietos Boy's Camp are no less than ten river crossings of varying width, all ridable with either on- or off-road bikes. This latter stretch is in a narrowing, mostly wooded canyon. The tour ends at a point where pavement turns to graded dirt, beyond which off-roaders can bike a few more miles to the Gibralter Reservoir. An option to divert and visit the Rancho Oso Resort is also provided.

TRAILHEAD: From Santa Barbara, follow State Hwy. 154 over San Marcos Pass. In three miles, turn right (north) at Paradise Rd. and drive 0.1 mile to the Paradise Store and Grill. From Solvang, head east on State Hwy. 154, pass Stage Coach Rd. and drive 1-1/2 miles to Paradise Rd. Go left to the store, which offers soft drinks and other brews, picnic supplies, great sandwiches, and other goodies.

If you plan to drive to the "high" road/"low" road trailhead (see Trip Option-Gibralter Reservoir) at the end of the paved road, check the river level by watching a few other vehicles cross before proceeding on. We watched two different motorists stall when making the last motor vehicle crossing to the parking area beyond the Live Oak Picnic Area. If you have doubts, park near the picnic area or further downstream.

Water Hole Just Beyond Live Oak Picnic Area

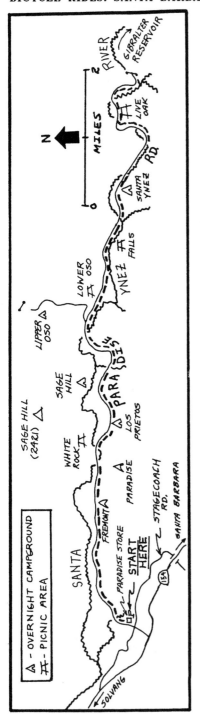

TRIP #16 - PARADISE ROAD

TRIP DESCRIPTION: To the First River Crossing. From the store, coast downhill, cross the creek in Los Laureles Canyon, then proceed on a mildly winding road into rolling hills. Fremont Campground is reached in 2.1 miles, the first of an array of overnight campgrounds and day-use picnic areas. Beyond is the Paradise Campground, the Community Hall and Los Prietos Campground. This is a heavily treed area with a shaded road. Near a southbound dirt road junction (the road leads uphill to Knapp's Castle) is the Sage Hill Campground and a ranger station, followed by a crossing over the creek in Lewis Canyon. Paradise Rd. splits, with the paved road to the right leading to private Rancho Oso Resort (see "Trip Option" below). Stay left and pass Los Prietos Boy's Camp. The "Slow to 5 MPH" sign provides a warning that the first of several Santa Ynez River crossings is around the bend (4.8).

And Beyond. In July 1993, there were 4-6 inches of water above the first and longest (approximately 150-foot) crossing. We watched the auto traffic pass before "diving in." This is a typical, one-at-a-time, crossing and motorists were polite about the order. The road splits and we stay right, heading toward the Lower Oso Picnic Area. The road narrows and stays north of, and above, the river in a semi-exposed area, passes the graded-dirt Santa Ynez River/Arroyo Burro Rds. junction, then returns to tree-shaded environs and the Falls Picnic Area (5.5)

After the Santa Ynez Campground, climb above and south of the river, recross the watercourse, and return to a long wooded stretch In the next two miles, pedal into an ever-narrowing canyon, with no less than seven more crossings. Buried within is the Live Oak Picnic Area. Past the last crossing is a car barrier and graded dirt road (8.7)

Trip Option-Rancho Oso Resort. This is a 5.0-mile round-trip diversion, mostly unshaded, leading to a fancy dude ranch. To get there, follow a narrowing road across several cattle guards and up a few short, steep winding switchbacks. The final stretch is a steep coast down into the valley, which nestles the large resort within, to the Rancho Oso Resort gate.

Rancho Oso Resort

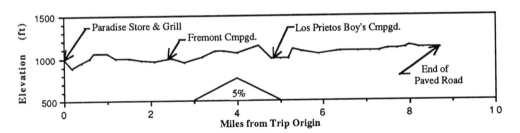

Trip Option-Gibralter Reservoir. From the end of the paved road, the cyclist can take an off-road (loop) tour to Gibralter Reservoir. (Refer to the Trip #17 map for the described loop.)

"High" Road. Cross the river on a concrete ford, pass the entry to the parking area, and stay to the right. Follow the fire road, pass beyond a locked gate and start an immediate upgrade on the side of an unnamed peak. Follow the good-quality bikeway (this is characteristic of this entire "high"-road segment) as it tracks the Santa Ynez River to a river viewpoint, then switches back and carves out a continuing traverse below the peak's summit. More river views appear, now below and to the east. The river is backdropped by a series of rugged frontal peaks. One mile from the parking area, the road flattens and moves away from the river, providing a look at the maintenance station above Gibralter Lake.

River Crossing in Red Rock Area

Cycle east on several ups and downs (mostly "ups") to the trip's high point 500 feet above the trailhead (1.8). From here are the first views of Gibralter Lake and the eastbound Gibralter Trail beyond. A nearly flat traverse leads to the North Portal area, where the road stairsteps, then bombs steeply downhill. Pass the marked Devil's Canyon outlet (27W21), cruise along its namesake creek, travel under a welcome tree canopy and return to an exposed section near the "high" road/"low" road junction. Directly in front of you is the stately and massive Gibralter Dam!

Following the road east (right) leads, in 0.7 mile, to the Angostura Rd. and the Gibralter Trail junctions. These paths lead you to Matias Potrero Trail and the Gibralter Mine (see Trip #17). However, our route takes the left fork (2.5).

"Low" Road Return. The "low" road is an easily seen, but unmarked, trail which crosses the river below the Gibralter Dam. There is only 130-feet elevation loss for the 3.3-mile riverside transit which returns you to the starting point. The path follows the Santa Ynez River contour with a continuous mix of rock fields, smooth bikable trail, numerous river crossings and scattered tree-sheltered sections.

The trail connectors at river crossings are reasonably easy to find. There are several deep swimming holes in the lower sections of this segment; they were filled with swimmers, sunbathers and people using rope swings to jump into the river on the 90-degree day in July 1994 when we biked through (5.8 miles total loop).

Note that some crossings on the "low" road are 2-3 feet deep (deeper in the winter) that should discourage you from using panniers to haul your paraphernalia. A day-pack or fanny-pack is a better bet (we carry spare water, maps, altimeter, camera and munchies, thus the need for a carrying pack of some type).

72

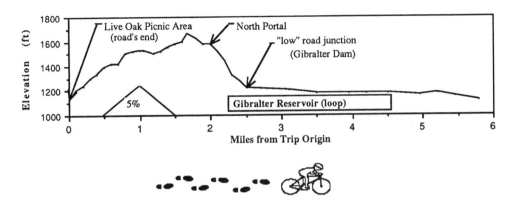

TRIP #17 - MATIAS POTRERO LOOP (Mountain Bike)

GENERAL LOCATION: Los Padres National Forest

LEVEL OF DIFFICULTY: Loop - very strenuous
Distance - 20.3 miles (loop)
Elevation gain - periodic steep-to-sheer grades
(sheer grade to Angostura Pass Rd.)

HIGHLIGHTS: This single loop provides an outstanding variety of scenic trails, breathtaking vistas and both natural and man-made landmarks. From Lower Oso Campground, the route samples a short segment of the Santa Ynez River, climbs Arroyo Burro Rd. and tracks the Matias Potrero Trail along the grass-laden Santa Ynez Fault. This traverse is followed by a rugged climb to the Angostura Rd. summit and a several-mile downhill to Gibralter Rd. above the Gibralter Reservoir. The return is via the dirt "high road" above the Santa Ynez River and paved Paradise Rd. Two less-stressing shortcut options, and a side trip to the Gibralter Mine, are also provided.

TRAILHEAD: From San Marcos Pass Rd. (State Hwy. 154), go right (north) on Paradise Rd. and follow the directions to Lower Oso Campground described in the Paradise Road ride (Trip #16).

TRIP DESCRIPTION: Arroyo Burro Road. From Lower Oso Campground, bike one mile east on Paradise Rd. to the signed White Oaks turnoff. Drop down to river level and cross over to the Arroyo Burro Rd. origin (or terminus). A short breather on the dirt road gives way to a steep and winding uphill. At a sharp bend to the left (east), about one mile from the road's origin, is the junction with the northern end of the Arroyo Burro Trail. The road winds in a series of arcs upward and along the mountain contour before reaching the western terminus of the Matias Potrero Trail (3.4).

Matias Potrero Trail. This trail is actually an old power-line service road which has become so overgrown that certain sections are seemingly buried in tall grass. It tracks the Santa Ynez Fault on the lower northern slopes of the Santa Ynez Mountains, mainly below La Cumbre Peak. Meander east, cross no less than five canyons, each with a downhill and a return steep uphill. There are frequent vistas into the Santa Ynez River drainage and the distant northern mountains. At the end of

73

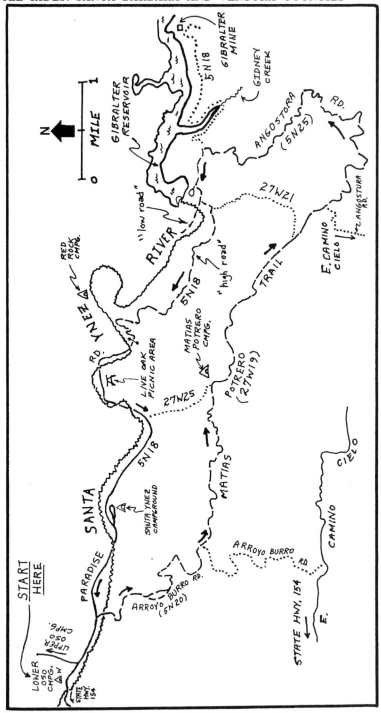

TRIP #17 - MATIAS POTRERO LOOP

this segment is a junction with a southbound power-line access trail (27W25) (5.4). Pedal 1/4 mile to a signed marker for Matias Potrero Trail Camp.

Following the trail through the camp requires a steep climb on the outlet side. An option is to take the more level high trail a few yards past the marker and skirt above the camp. Progress upward and cross a ridge in over 1/2 mile from the marker. Pause and take in the north-oriented vistas with the Santa Ynez River below, backdropped by a stacked series of mountains. The roller-coaster downhill/uphill across a large canyon returns to a very steep climb along a ridge, leading to a junction with the Devil's Canyon Trail (27W21) (7.6).

Gibralter Dam Near the High-road/Low Road Junction
(Sam Nunez Photo)

For our reference route, off-roaders pedal east on Matias Potrero Trail to its terminus, enduring a brutal one-mile, 1000-foot, climb to Angostura Rd. (5N25), the trip summit. Count on pushing your two-wheeler through sections of the ascent. Once stopped, it is difficult to point uphill and get restarted. A right turn here takes you on a sheer two-mile climb west and north to Angostura Pass.

Angostura Road. Head left (east) instead for a well-deserved downhill. This dirt road access to the Gibralter Reservoir winds west and south below, and roughly paralleling the Santa Ynez Mountain's ridge crest and E. Camino Cielo. Reach the southernmost extremity on a modest downhill, head north and traverse a wide canyon (9.7). A saddle is reached in about a mile, after which Angostura Rd. goes northwest below a ridge, then "bombs" 0.4 mile down to the Gibralter Rd. junction near a water tank (12.4). The tour leaves the vegetated slopes in 3/4 mile from this intersection. A turn right (east) takes you along the Gibralter Reservoir to the Gibralter Mine; see the trip option below.

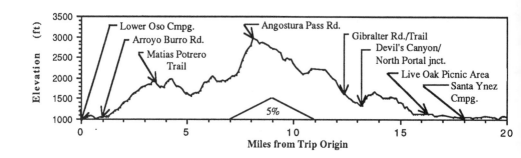

Gibralter Reservoir and the "High" Road Return. Our tour heads left (west) on a parched stretch close to the reservoir where the dam is visible. The first major road junction left winds back 180-degrees and trails the Santa Ynez River above its south bank to another junction (13.1). Here the right (north) fork crosses the river and follows the north bank (the "low" road), but our described route on the "high" road forks left, crosses Devil's Canyon (the 27W21 trail outlet), and climbs to the North Portal area. The next steep-to-sheer 1/2 mile leads to a one-mile slanted downhill bench well above the river. A junction to the right (14.9) drops into the river and meets the "low" road. Continue on the "high" road and follow a 180-degree switchback that takes you, in 0.3 mile, past a gate to the river at the western split of the "high"-road"/low"-road (15.6), where there is a large dirt parking area here.

Above Gidney Creek on Gibralter Trail

76

Santa Ynez River Return. Cross the river and proceed west along the wide river bed and cross again to the south bank. A short flat segment brings you to the shaded Live Oak Picnic Area on paved Paradise Rd. Follow Paradise Rd. four miles back to Lower Oso Campground, with several concrete river fords to enhance your pleasure (20.3). At 0.6 mile from the Live Oak Picnic Area is the 27W25 trail outlet (look to the east of a small canyon coming in from the south). The roads and campsites along the way are described in detail in the Paradise Rd. tour (Trip #16).

Shortcut Options. To reduce mileage and elevation gain, divert north on the **power-line access trail (27W25)** (5.4) and reduce total trip distance to 9.5 miles. Follow a steep northern ridgeline and drop down to paved Paradise Rd. in less than one mile. Skirt the eastern edge of a small canyon near the outlet, about 0.6 mile west of the Live Oak Picnic area. Another less-stressing option is to return to the Santa Ynez River via the **Devil's Canyon Trail (27W21)** (7.6). Follow an arcing ridgeline east for about 0.3 mile, then north for another 0.4 mile, descending into Devil's Canyon and dumping out at the west side of Gidney Flat and Gibralter Rd. (5N18). The shortcut is about 1-1/2 miles in length and lessens total trip distance to 15.9 miles.

Side Trip to Gibralter Mine. Divert east at the Angostura Rd. junction (12.4) at the water tank. Look for the Gibralter Trail sign and a locked gate. This dirt road was built to service the mercury mine (called "quicksilver"), which is the trip's destination. Drop down on a winding road, follow a 180-degree switchback, and parallel a reservoir finger leading to the Gidney Creek outlet (0.6 mile--mileage now measured from the junction). Swing back toward the reservoir, follow the finger on an exposed, 1/2-mile, steep upgrade, then bend back east (1.0). Enjoy the continuous overlook of the Gibralter Reservoir, as well as an easier up-and-down, 0.9-mile, ride to the mine.

Exploration of the structures is not encouraged, as with any long-closed mine site, but also because there may be high levels of dangerous mercury in the area. Past the mine structures, the road curves east around a hill for 0.2 mile and splits. The right (east) fork follows a series of switchbacks to other mine sites, while the left fork meanders southeast into the surrounding mountains. That trail returns to the Santa Ynez River inlet and the reservoir in several miles, and is an access to the excellent biking areas in the Upper Santa Ynez River drainage (see Trip #13).

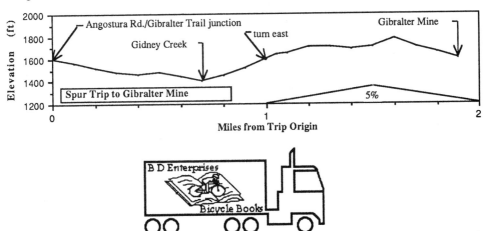

77

TRIP #18 - LITTLE PINE MOUNTAIN LOOP

GENERAL LOCATION: Los Padres National Forest, Little Pine Mountain

LEVEL OF DIFFICULTY: Loop - Very strenuous
Distance - 15.0 miles
Elevation gain - steady, steep upgrade to
Happy Hollow Campground

HIGHLIGHTS: This scenic loop takes hearty cyclists from Upper Oso Campground 10.1 miles on Camuesa-Buckhorn Rd. (Road #6N13) to the southern flank of Little Pine Mountain. The 3260-foot trek is graced with views of the Santa Barbara backcountry and panoramic vistas near the summit which include the distant Channel Islands and Mt. Pinos. A short climb to the Little Pine Mountain summit from Happy Hollow Campground provides more spectacular scenery. The return is via the Santa Cruz Trail on a steep, technical, single-track downhill, providing more unique vistas, interesting geologic features and a pleasant pedal in Santa Cruz and Oso Canyons alongside shaded creeks. There are many options off this route, including shorter mileage, less-stressing tours.

TRAILHEAD: Follow Paradise Rd. five miles, cross the Santa Ynez River and turn left (north) past the Lower Oso picnic area. Follow the signs to the day-use Upper Oso Camp parking lot. (Refer to the Trip #16-Paradise Rd. map.) The trailhead is near the northeastern corner of the lot.

Camuesa-Buckhorn Road Near the Camuesa Trail Connector

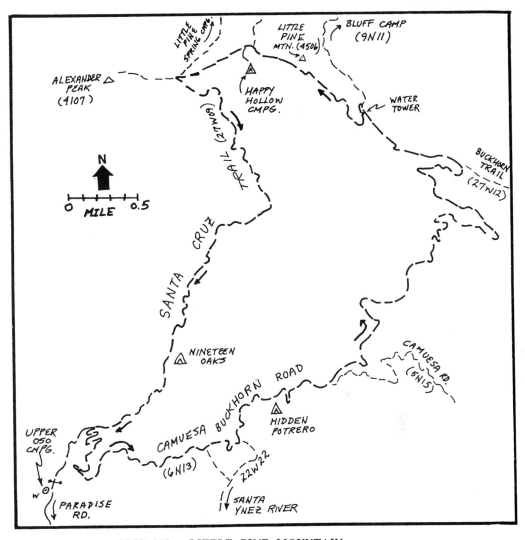

TRIP #18 - LITTLE PINE MOUNTAIN

<u>TRIP DESCRIPTION</u>: **Camuesa-Buckhorn Road.** Pass around a locked gate and follow Oso Creek into narrow, shaded Oso Canyon. After an easy 3/4 mile, pass the Santa Cruz Trail (27W09) junction and start the first of many switchbacks. The segment below the Camuesa Rd. junction (4.1) has switchbacks under scattered oaks and a ride along the south side of Oso Canyon. Along the way are the Camuesa Trail Connector (22W22) (within in a big grassy meadow) (2.9), and Hidden Potrero Campground (fire grates, piped-in spring water). The next few miles on what is now Buckhorn Rd. are below and on the northwest side of a series of peaks with some easy downhill. Cross a couple of saddles and return to a very steep section that signals the start of a four-mile+ uphill assault to the southern flank of Little Pine Mountain. A series of linked switchbacks take you below a peak on the trip's most easterly point (6.8), followed by a circumnavigation of that peak to a long, and more barren, northwesterly ridgeline. Begin a series of stairstep uphills along the southeastern

ridge extension of Little Pine Mountain. There were abundant grassy fields intermixed with large flowered areas when we visited in late spring. A wide swing east and uphill leads to a crest and the Buckhorn Trail (27Wl2) junction (7.9).

Little Pine Mountain. Pass the junction and pump the last (steep) uphill mile to the Little Pine Mountain junction (next to a concrete water tank). Among the many lookout points on the ascent, this is one of the best. South is the coastline and the distant Channel Islands, while Mt. Pinos and the sister peaks loom to the north. Turn left onto the smaller road and proceed southwest. The road soon levels and passes into a manzanita, pine and oak forest to the south flank of Little Pine Mountain.

Head downhill toward Happy Hollow Campground, a campsite situated within a large forested depression with picnic tables, firepits and a short trail (at the south end) to one of the summits of Little Pine Mountain. The nearest water is roughly one (very steep) downhill mile northwest at Little Pine Spring Camp. About 200 yards short of the Happy Hollow Campground, follow a trail right (southwest). This 1/2-mile steep spur trail leads down a ridgeline to Alexander Saddle. Portions of this spur trail leave the treed areas, providing vistas of the Santa Ynez Mountains. Turn left onto the Santa Cruz Trail at the saddle (10.7).

Santa Cruz Trail. The first several hundred yards are steep and on narrow trail with severe drop-offs. Varied geological features are highlighted by the multi-colored rock formations on this treeless, south-tending trail section. There are scattered slides here and the trail is shared with hikers and horsemen, which should encourage cyclists to maintain a controllable speed on this dynamite downhill! Enjoy views of the frontal Santa Ynez ranges and peeks down into Oso Canyon, while keeping an eye on the trail.

A mile past the spur junction, the Santa Cruz Trail crosses the upper reaches of Santa Cruz Creek, levels and bends southwest entering the like-named canyon above creek level. Switchbacks in the treed canyon bring the biker into Nineteen Oaks near the like-named campground (13.4). Drop down to Santa Cruz Creek, follow its course back into Oso Canyon and cross several spur creeks. In a mile along the creek is a short and steep ascent to Camuesa-Buckhorn Rd. and a 3/4-mile return to the gate (15.0).

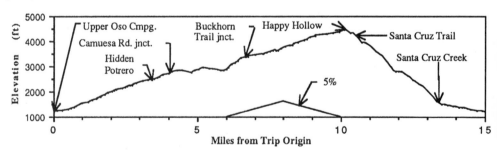

Trip Option 1-Camuesa-Buckhorn Road, Up and Back. Follow the route described to a suitable turnaround point within your abilities and coast back to the start point.

Trip Option 2-Camuesa Connector Shortcut. A 12-mile loop can be formed by biking from Upper Oso Campground to the signed connector route and following this excellent, but lightly used, single-track downhill to the Santa Ynez River above Santa Ynez Campground, then returning via Paradise Rd.

Extended Trip Options - Extended daytime or overnight routes can be made by linking **Camuesa Rd., Buckhorn Trail** or **Big Pine Rd.** trips to the described route (consult other mountain bike sources for Option 2 and extended trip options).

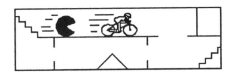

TRIP #19 - SANTA BARBARA - SOLVANG LOOP

GENERAL LOCATION: Santa Barbara, Solvang, Gaviota

LEVEL OF DIFFICULTY: Loop - very strenuous
Distance - 77 miles
Elevation gain - steep-to-sheer grades to San Marcos Pass

HIGHLIGHTS: Don't even think about the full tour unless you are a well-conditioned, long-distance cyclist!   From Stow Grove Park in Goleta Valley is a murderous, but scenic, trip up to San Marcos Pass with a rolling-hills workout past Lake Cachuma to Solvang.   A countryside tour heads back uphill to Nojoqui Falls County Park and eventually up Nojoqui Grade, followed by a downhill to Gaviota Beach State Park.   Past the park is an extended seaside return through more rolling hills to the trip origin. Sightseeing along the way is great!   The views of Cold Springs Arch from Stagecoach Rd., Nojoqui Falls and Gaviota Pass are three excellent examples.

TRAILHEAD: From U.S. Hwy. 101 in Goleta, exit north at Los Carneros Rd. and drive 3/4 mile to Cathedral Oaks Rd. Turn right and travel 3/4 mile to La Patera Ln. Turn right again and park within day-use Stow Grove County Park (grass, barbecue pits, tables, restrooms baseball fields, showers. restrooms, water). Stow Grove (see Trip #2) is the name given to the band of oaks which fronted the northeast edge of the original Stow property. If there is any doubt about your return time, park on the local residential streets.

Cold Springs Arch Bridge

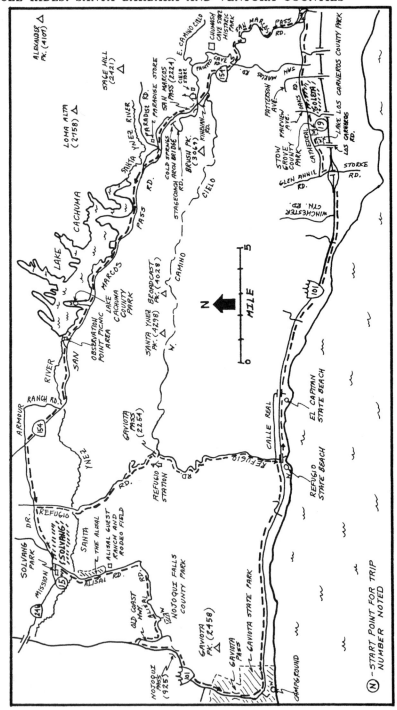

TRIP #19 - SANTA BARBARA-SOLVANG LOOP

Bring two or three quarts of water. There are long stretches without any water sources.

<u>TRIP DESCRIPTION</u>: **Outbound to San Marcos Pass.** Steer east on Class II Cathedral Oaks Rd., aptly named since religious ceremonies were once conducted under the sweeping oak branches. Follow the rolling hills on an uphill past Old San Marcos Rd., an alternate route which is discussed later (2.7). Pass lush Tucker's Grove County Park and go left (north) onto State Hwy. 154/San Marcos Pass Rd. (4.8).

The access to San Marcos Pass Rd. is uphill, signalling just a small measure of what is to come (2000 feet in seven miles--an average 5-1/2% grade). The busy, four-lane, divided highway flattens as the Santa Ynez Mountains beckon directly ahead, plummets downhill, then crosses San Antonio Creek and proceeds on a righteous upgrade. Begin the first of several sweeping arcs that climb into the heart of the forested mountains and then crosses the boundary of the Las Padres National Forest (6.6).

Look across a broad canyon and glimpse the road as it cuts into the mountainsides at higher elevations. In a little over one mile, reach that mountain-hugging piece of road with over-the-shoulder views to Santa Barbara and the ocean. Three miles from the forest boundary is the southernmost San Marcos Rd. intersection (Painted Cave Rd. to the right) and the northern intersection 0.2 mile beyond.

Nojouqi Falls

About 260 feet and 0.8 mile below San Marcos Pass is W. Camino Cielo (13.7) and a couple of interesting choices: 1) follow busy Hwy. 154 over the pass and ride on the Cold Springs Arch bridge down into Cachuma Valley; or 2) turn onto W. Camino Cielo and, just past the San Jose Creek crossing, go right on Kinevan Rd. and take the slower winding-mountain road under the arch, returning to Hwy. 154 at the northern Stagecoach Rd. intersection with the main highway.

On to Solvang. Surprise, surprise! Our route takes the second option. Kinevan Rd. rejoins the main highway before San Marcos Pass, but the trick is to turn left onto Stagecoach Rd. prior to the Hwy. 154 intersection. (An option is to visit the rustic Cielo Store, with a wide array of munchies and hiking/biking publications, reached by crossing Hwy. 154 and biking less than a hundred yards on E. Camino Cielo.) Stagecoach Rd. winds downhill through surrounding forest, providing some scattered views down into the Santa Ynez River basin, and reaching the Cold Springs Tavern, once a stagecoach stop. Not only is this a sometimes rowdy tavern (with guest bands outdoors on some weekends), but also a fine restaurant with a rustic atmosphere that we have visited more than a few times.

More winding downhill leads to a vista area in Cold Springs Canyon, with views of the Cold Springs Arch high above. Stagecoach Rd. goes under the bridge, roughly parallels Hwy. 154, crosses Paradise Rd. and meets the main highway and proceeds through rolling hills alongside the easternmost arms of Lake Cachuma. Pass Camp Whittier, Lake Cachuma County Park, and a vista point near the lake's western end at the Observation Point/Picnic Area (30.2).

Cycle on rolling terrain into the Santa Ynez Valley; the main highway passes Armour Ranch Rd. and follows an upgrade to State Hwy. 246/Armour Ranch Rd. (north branch). Head mostly downhill on a 4.8-mile countryside spin into Solvang with the first stop light in ages at Alamo Pintado Rd. Pass the Gainey Winery, the backside of historic Santa Ynez, the Chumash Bingo Hall and the Santa Ynez Winery. Turn south at Alisal Rd. in 0.7 mile (40.1).

Gaviota Beach State Park

On to Gaviota Beach State Park. Alisal Rd. cuts through the heart of Solvang (see Trip #20), passes the Royal Scandinavian Inn (start/end point for the Solvang Century), and crosses the Santa Ynez River. This puts you outside the city and alongside the plush Alisal Golf Course, which stretches along the road for over a mile before giving way to the Alisal Guest Ranch (a dude ranch with rodeo grounds and an assortment of horses and cows). The now-winding road narrows and enters an area of dense tree cover, continuing for two miles from the ranch to a crest.

The route threads its way through an extended patch of tree cover on a high plateau, crosses Nojoqui Creek and, in 1.7 miles from the crest, reaches the Nojoqui Falls County Park turnoff (46.3). This grand hideaway has trees, picnic tables, barbecues, playground, restrooms, water, and is a great place for a short family bike ride. On the south end is a maintained path to majestic Nojoqui Falls, a ten-minute hike away. Make a sharp turn left in 0.7 mile within a small valley, then a hard right onto Old Coast Hwy. (Do not go left as there is no direct access to U.S. Hwy. 101.) The little highway heads up to Hwy. 101, where you must negotiate a challenging crossing against high-speed traffic.

A steep 300-foot climb up Nojoqui Grade leads past a welcoming sign announcing "Steep 6% Downgrade Next Two Miles," followed in two miles by the State Hwy. 1 turnoff (51.1). In over a mile, within a canyon below Gaviota Peak, is Gaviota Pass. The northbound lane goes into a tunnel that has been blasted through the mountainous rock. Beyond is a rest area with shade, restroom and telephone (just thought we'd mention the latter), followed by the turnoff to Gaviota Beach State Park. This fine site has an inviting beach front, overnight camping, water, general store, restrooms, large pier, remnants of Old Post Oxford, and an overhead railroad trestle.

Return to Santa Barbara. A short upgrade leads to panoramic vistas and a rolling-hills route past "sprawling" Gaviota (population-94) and Alcatraz State Beach. The busy highway chases the ocean with the Southern Pacific railroad tracks on the bluffs in between. In 9.4 miles from Gaviota Beach State Park is the Refugio State Beach/Park exit (63.0). Stay on Hwy. 101 or divert toward the beach on a Class I path along the bluffs 2-1/2 miles to El Capitan State Beach (campground, general store). Proceed on rolling hills and move further inland, staying nestled between the ocean and the foothills of the Santa Ynez Mountains. At Hollister Ave./Winchester (72.1), exit Hwy. 101, pass the Sandpiper Golf Course and transition back into a residential/commercial area. In two miles, head north onto Storke/Glen Annie Rds., and cross over the freeway to Cathedral Oaks Rd. Ride to the start point at Stow Grove County Park (77.0).

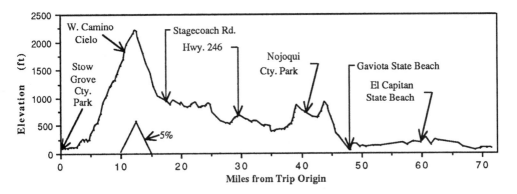

Trip Options-Old San Marcos Pass Road. Old San Marcos Pass Rd. is an option for reducing mileage on busy State Hwy. 154. Veer left (2.7) in the reference trip write-up to exercise this alternative which reduces trip distance by three miles. There is a misleading several-hundred yard flat stretch before this road crosses Maria Ygnacia Creek and heads skyward, providing a 3.5-mile, 2000 foot, air-sucking workout which has little auto traffic. This is the Old Santa Ynez Toll Rd., which the stage line used in the late 19th century to cross the mountains. As with Hwy. 154, there are dynamite views back into the Goleta Valley to help take the pain out of the couple miles of climb. Just after the San Marcos Trout Club turnoff, take the left (north) of two forks to Hwy. 154 and continue as described in the reference tour.

Refugio Pass Shortcut. An option which reduces the total trip by about 11 miles is to take Refugio Rd. south just prior to entering Solvang. The climb to Refugio Pass is strenuous and requires a mountain bike. South of the pass is an exhilarating downhill on paved road which lets out near Refugio State Beach (see Trip #15).

TRIP #20 - WINE COUNTRY TOUR #1 (Santa Ynez Valley)

GENERAL LOCATION: Santa Ynez, Los Olivos, Ballard, Solvang

LEVEL OF DIFFICULTY: Loop - moderate
Distance - 12.0 miles
Elevation gain - periodic moderate grades

HIGHLIGHTS: Grapes were introduced to the Santa Barbara area in the late 1700's by Padre Junipero Serra. Wine was first made by the Franciscan Friars, carrying on homeland traditions and easing the pain of living on the rugged frontier. The 1800's saw plentiful winemaking. Prohibition devastated the business in the early 1900's, then came a revival surge starting in the mid-sixties. Modern-day production began in the mid-seventies. Rincon Point to Point Conception is the only east/west shoreline segment from Alaska to Cape Horn. The east/west orientation of the mountains ensures the vineyards will get warm days with ocean breezes and cool nights, conditions similar to the major grape growing regions of France. Best time to visit the 10,000 acres of vineyards is in the spring when the hills and valleys are in full bloom, and the fall when the area is abuzz with grape harvesting.

This tour visits the heart of the Santa Ynez Valley, a region of lazy oak-sprinkled rolling hills, horse ranches and wineries. The counterclockwise tour visits historic Santa Ynez, skirts picturesque Los Alamos, passes teeny tucked-away Ballard and returns to eastern Solvang. Modest rolling hills and "gentlemen" ranches are the order of the day. Numerous wineries along the route provide varied services or facilities to the public, including wine-making tours, tasting and picnicking facilities. Information on wineries can be obtained from brochures found in most hotels in the area or the Santa Barbara Chamber of Commerce.

TRAILHEAD: From U.S. Hwy. 101, exit east at State Hwy. 246, and drive three miles to the edge of Solvang, where the road name is Mission Dr. Drive into the heart of Solvang one mile to the Santa Ines Mission just past Alisal Rd. From State Hwy. 154, go west at State Hwy. 246 and motor four miles to Alamo Pintado Rd. The mission is in 1/2 mile.

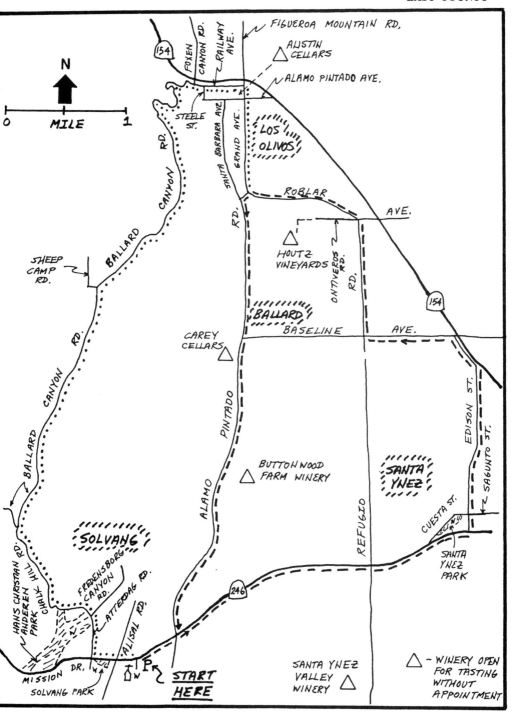

TRIP #20 - WINE COUNTRY TOUR #1 (Santa Ynez Valley)

BICYCLE RIDES: SANTA BARBARA AND VENTURA COUNTIES

Mission Santa Ines

Solvang, with its eateries, shopping, sightseeing, parks, and entertainment, was founded in 1911 by a Dutch group in search of a site for a Danish school. Solvang, which means "Sunny Field," was the location selected and Atterdag College opened in 1914. The Village, as it is called, retains its old charm and quaintness and is visited by thousands yearly from all over the world. Old Mission Santa Ines, founded in 1804 by the Franciscan Fathers, became the 19th in a chain of 21 missions, and is one of the best preserved. Visitors can enjoy tours, a gift shop and museum.

TRIP DESCRIPTION: **Santa Ynez to Los Olivos.** Bike onto busy Class X Hwy. 246 on wide bike shoulder, enjoying the surrounding Santa Ynez Valley views with a distant mountain backdrop. After Alamo Pintado Rd. is a long uphill that peaks near Refugio Rd. Enjoy a transition into mostly open country with scattered upscale homes on large lots and horses behind every white picket fence.

Beyond the Chumash Bingo Hall is Edison St. (3.3) where you go north into Santa Ynez. In the 1880's, this town swelled in anticipation of the arrival of the Pacific Coast Railway that never came. The sleepy town has a pocket of buildings near and on Sagunto St., some left over from the old days and some which are excellent modern-day replicas. Tour this street, if time permits, and visit the Santa Ynez Valley Museum and Carriage House (restored stagecoaches, wagons, buggies, carts) at the corner of Sagunto and Faraday Streets. Other interesting structures on Sagunto St. are the Pony Express Horsemen's Supply, Longhorn Coffee Shop (coconut cream pie a specialty), and the Cota Market (excellent sandwich menu).

Northbound, enter a treed, rural-suburban area built on rolling terrain and see the properties melt into large abuted horse ranches. At narrow Baseline Ave., bike another mile of horse ranches and other fenced properties before heading north again on Refugio Rd. Zig-zag north and west into vineyards and horse ranch country, entering the outskirts of quaint Los Olivos on Roblar Ave. at Grand Ave. (7.3). To the north, this picturesque locale has a dozen art galleries and is totally absent of traffic lights, fast-foods or a supermarket. The five-star Grand Hotel proudly displays a 100-bottle wine list. However, our reference tour heads west on the frontage road and veers south on Alamo Pintado Ave. past the Side Street Cafe (a local favorite) and classic Los Olivos Market which began business in 1889.

Baseline Ave. is 1-1/4 miles south from the Roblar Ave. intersection. Consider a diversion east into Ballard, the valley's oldest and smallest town, with the Ballard Inn (a "spoil-you rotten" bed and breakfast) and Ballard Country Store, noted for its continental style food and fancy box lunches. Our tour continues south on Alamo Pintado Ave. on a Class II bikeway and passes Carey Cellars Winery. A short downhill

Solvang Proper

Stylish Los Olivos Mansion

gives way to a two-mile flat stretch with an estate seemingly perched on every hill. After Village Ln., proceed south to Mission Dr., turn west and return to Mission Santa Ines (12.0).

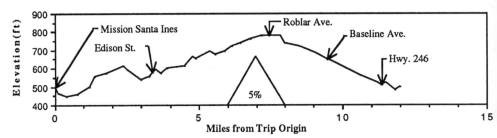

Solvang Tour. Solvang is a nifty place to bike at a leisurely pace in spite of the traffic. Stay off Mission Dr. and you will find that traffic is slow and watchful for the many horse-drawn carriages, trolley cars, people-powered pedal carriages that ferry tourists through the area, and the ever-present pedestrians. A favored cycling and browsing area is south of Mission Dr. between Alisal Rd. and Atterdag Rd. Keep a watchful eye for autos and pedestrians while checking out the shops (and shoppers!).

TRIP #21 - WINE COUNTRY TOUR #2 (Canyon Country)

GENERAL LOCATION: Solvang, Foxen Canyon, Ballard Canyon

LEVEL OF DIFFICULTY: Double loop - moderate to strenuous
Distance - 22.6 miles miles
Elevation gain - periodic moderate grades;
            steep grade at Ballard Canyon entry

HIGHLIGHTS: This exciting double-looper ranks as one of our favorites. Start at the beautifully-restored Mission Santa Ines and bike into vineyards and horse ranch country to picturesque Los Olivos with art shops and Victorian-era homes. A super segment on Foxen Canyon Rd. through rolling hills, peppered with coastal oaks, leads to a scenic ridge-top overlook, followed by a swooping downhill to Zaca Station Rd. This is "The Wall" of Solvang-Santa Maria Century fame. The Ballard Canyon Rd. segment offers a 1/2-mile test-of-will upgrade, followed by a leisurely several-mile pedal through the countryside outback, "undiscovered" by city motorists. Plan to visit the many wineries along this rural ride.

90

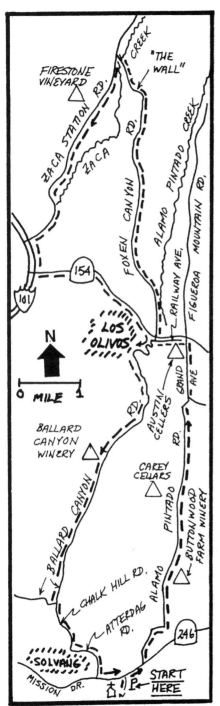

TRAILHEAD: The trailhead is at Mission Santa Ines, described in the Wine Country tour #1 (Trip #20).

TRIP DESCRIPTION: To Los Olivos. Leave the mission and bike east on busy Mission Dr., going north in 0.6 mile at Alamo Pintado Rd. Drop down to Village Ln., pick up a Class II path and pedal a modest grade into a ranch-filled valley with small hills. Pass an apple orchard, the Carey Cellars Winery, and continue slowly uphill through farming country to a road split one mile past Baseline Ave.

Head right, follow the "To Los Olivos" sign, turn left on Grand Ave. (4.5) at a "T" intersection just beyond and cruise into Los Olivos. Observe the modern-day reproductions of Victorian-era homes on the way into town and the "real thing" in Los Olivos. Grand Ave. is lined with a series of look-alike flat store fronts, mostly art galleries, although Clausen's Deli is sandwiched in (ha!). Go left (west) at Railway Ave. and pass behind Los Olivos' best-known attraction, Mattie's Tavern. This watering hole and restaurant, built in 1886 at the terminus of the Pacific Coast Railroad, boarded passengers bound for Santa Barbara by stage.

Foxen Canyon and Zaca Station Roads. Stay west and turn north on the first road which crosses State Hwy. 154. Across the highway is a sign announcing Foxen Canyon Rd., a scenic and serene countryside stretch for which "Wine Country" is so well known. Keep north on this flat two-lane road (rough in spots) through spotty tree-covered rolling hills, sporting vineyards and horse ranches. A "side-splitter" upgrade in two miles goes to a ridgeline with open vistas and a great view below and paralleling Zaca Station Rd. An exhilarating 0.7-mile winding downgrade leads across Zaca Creek and down its namesake road (9.9). This is "The Wall," the formidable upgrade encountered near the end of the "Solvang-Santa Maria Century" ride (see Trip #23). The lazy spin into a small valley passes the Texaco Oil Field, Firestone Vineyard, and road's end at U.S. Hwy. 101 (13.1).

TRIP #21 - WINE COUNTRY TOUR #2 (CANYON COUNTRY)

91

Misplaced Horse on Railway Ave.

Lower Ballard Canyon Road (Susan Cohen Photo)

Return to Ballard Canyon. Rather than cross busy Hwy. 101, stay to the northbound shoulder a few hundred yards, cross State Hwy. 154 to the far lane and head eastward. Tackle a 1.2-mile workout, coast back to Los Olivos and go right at the first street. A quick right on an unmarked road leads, in 0.3 mile, to where the road veers left and becomes (unsigned) Ballard Canyon Rd. The road narrows, enters horse and sheep country and proceeds on a 1/2-mile steep, switchbacking road to a crest near Los Olivos Meadows Rd. There are exceptional views of the scattered ranches in the valley below.

A winding downhill on sometimes rough pavement leads to a transit just above valley level. The still-unmarked road tracks the contour of the hillsides to the valley's west side, then enters a region of rolling hills and the return of the first of several estates. This serene country lane passes Tapadero Rd. (17.7), several large cattle ranches with their extensive grazing lands, and enters a large valley with the Ballard Canyon Winery near its northern edge. After two miles on rolling terrain, veer left and follow Chalk Hill Rd. Return to a residential area near Holmstead Dr. and enjoy views of Solvang proper, pass Hans Christian Anderson Park (52 acres with a plaza, lawn, restrooms, water, tennis courts, creek and a large unimproved area), then intersect Hwy. 246 in 1/2 mile. Pedal east on Mission Dr. past Solvang Park (see Trip #15) and return to the mission (22.6).

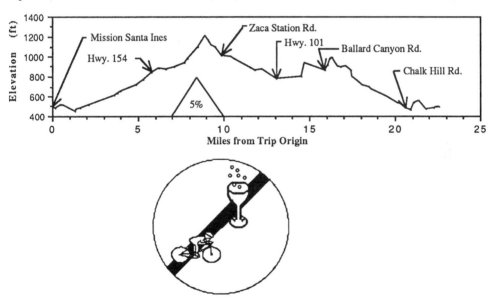

TRIP #22 ‑ SOLVANG TO LAKE CACHUMA+

GENERAL LOCATION: Solvang, Armour Ranch, Lake Cachuma

LEVEL OF DIFFICULTY: Loop - moderate; up and back - moderate
Distance - 11.8 miles (one-way)
Elevation gain - periodic moderate grades

HIGHLIGHTS: There are several fun rides starting from Solvang. Two are Wine Country tours (Trips #20 and #21), and another is a scenic and sometimes-shaded

93

country tour to Nojoqui Falls (see "Solvang to Nojoqui Falls" at the end of this write-up). The described tour departs from the eastern tip of Solvang through rolling hills on a general uphill to Lake Cachuma. The end point is the camper's/fisherman's haven at Lake Cachuma Recreation Center. On the way, cyclists are treated to mountain views both north and south, an interesting "backside" view of the Victorian section of Santa Ynez, a peaceful pedal through the Armour Ranch and a visit to Bradbury Dam's Vista Point.

Bradbury Dam

TRAILHEAD: From Santa Barbara, follow State Hwy. 154 over San Marcos Pass to State Hwy. 246. Turn west, drive 4-1/2 miles to Alamo Pintado Rd. and park at the shopping center (Nielsen Center). This puts the rider at a Solvang start point, but limits the amount of travel through that crowded tourist town. An option is to start at Santa Ynez Park 2-1/2 miles east at Cuesta St. The park has hiking and equestrian trails, no water or restrooms and biking is prohibited. There is limited tree cover in the park. From Buellton and points west, exit U.S. Hwy. 101 at State Hwy. 246 and continue east about 4-1/2 miles to Alamo Pintado Rd. (or seven miles to Santa Ynez Park).

TRIP DESCRIPTION: Solvang to Lake Cachuma. Once on Class II Hwy. 246, eastbound, bikers immediately get the feel of returning to more open countryside. A moderate roller-coaster ride travels alongside the "Land of Gentlemen Farms" to the north with a backdrop of the San Rafael Mountains. Beyond Refugio Rd., the route creeps towards Santa Ynez and reaches the city limit in 2-1/2 miles. The busy road passes the Chumash Bingo Hall and Edison St. The "backside" of Santa Ynez comes into view, providing a unique look at the many and varied Victorian structures along Sagunto St.

Pass the Santa Ynez Airport (exciting and scenic glider rides originate here), the Gainey Vineyard and transit open country uphill to Hwy. 154 (4.3). Bike straight across the highway, leave busy Hwy. 246 behind, and cycle onto more serene Armour

94

Ranch Rd. From here, proceed 2.8 miles through the rolling hills of this huge ranch which brings you to road's end at Class X Hwy. 154.

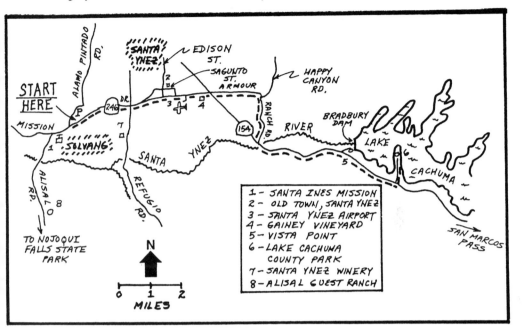

TRIP #22 - SOLVANG TO LAKE CACHUMA

Cross the Santa Ynez River on an upgrade to the Vista Point turnoff (10.3), where bikers can take a break and view the 1/2-mile wide Bradbury Dam, a 206-foot earth and rock structure that holds back Lake Cachuma. Back on Hwy. 154, you are treated to a flat, a short upgrade and a pleasant 0.3-mile downgrade which leads to the entrance to the Cachuma Lake Recreation Center (11.8). This oasis is home to tree cover, restrooms, barbecues, overnight camping, boat ramp, and fishing for bass, trout, catfish, bluegill and crappie.

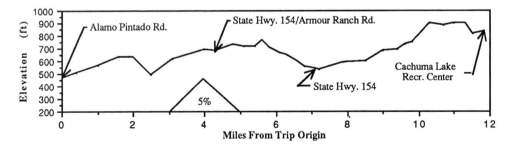

Solvang to Nojoqui Falls. An option out of Solvang is to bike south on Alisal Rd. to Nojoqui Falls County Park. The best bet is to start from Solvang Park (1st St. in Solvang which is one intersection west of Alisal Rd.) and follow the route described in the Santa Barbara-Solvang Loop (Trip #19), starting from the 40.1-mile point. The tour is 5.2 delightfully-hilly miles to the Nojoqui Falls County Park turnoff.

95

TRIP #23 - SOLVANG - SANTA MARIA CENTURY

GENERAL LOCATION: Solvang, Lompoc, Santa Maria

LEVEL OF DIFFICULTY: Loop - very strenuous
Distance - 103 miles (loop)
Elevation gain - periodic moderate-to-steep grades

HIGHLIGHTS: If there is a finer century ride in the U.S.A., we'd like to hear about it! This exciting, but grueling, 103-miler goes west from Solvang to Santa Rosa Rd. into serene countryside. (The circuit can vary from year to year; the 1993-1994 version, starting from Solvang, is described.) It continues into Lompoc and the first of five strategically-placed SAG (rest) stops. The route north introduces the biker to the Vandenberg Grade, a three-mile workout that is the first of several tests of grittiness and humility. Ten more miles brings you to the half-way point at the Santa Maria Airport and the beginning of an adventure into the more scenic part of the course.

Past the U.S. Hwy. 101 crossing, return to open country, eventually following a winding road at the base of the Solomon Hills. Past the tiny town of Sisquoc is an introduction to the enticing backcountry. Foxen Canyon Rd. is a steady, but moderate, ten-mile upgrade. A steeper incline signals the start of "Heartbreak Hill," a nasty 1-1/2-mile surprise to first-time riders who have only heard about "The Wall." A hang-it-out downgrade leads to the final SAG stop at the Fess Parker Winery, followed by a 3/4-mile "chain-braker" on the famed Wall. A long downhill leads across State Hwy. 154 to a short gut-wrencher (on "95-mile legs") on Ballard Canyon Rd. and an "its-all-downhill-stretch" to Solvang. (OK, there is one more small nagging climb past the Chalk Hill Rd. intersection!)

TRAILHEAD: From U.S. Hwy. 101, turn east onto State Hwy. 246 and proceed three miles to Solvang. Park on the Solvang periphery and bike to the starting point, the Royal Scandinavian Inn; parking is hard to find on ride day. To get a hotel in Solvang on ride day requires about a one-year advance reservation for the more popular hotels. The Solvang Century takes place the first weekend in March, regardless of weather. The full century has five well-equipped rest stops and is supported by bike-repair assistance crews and SAG wagons. Bring 2-3 quarts of liquid for use between rest stops.

TRIP DESCRIPTION: The excitement begins as riders prepare for a 6-9 am start in either Solvang or Santa Maria; the Solvang-Santa Maria Century (or Solvang Century, as it is frequently called) has two start points to accommodate the roughly 6000 participants on what has become our country's most popular century bike ride. This used to be a century-only ride; that is, no short tours, unless one arranged a drop-off at Solvang or Santa Maria and a shuttle at the 50-mile end point. Now, cyclists can bike 50 "big ones" and catch a shuttle back to home base (advance arrangement needed).

This well-known event is the unofficial "kick-starter" of the "century" season. Weather can vary from the rain-and-scattered-hail of 1992, to the "sunscreen special" of 1993, to the overcast ride of 1994. The ride described is on the 1993-1994 route starting from Solvang. Author Don Brundige and book reviewer Susan Cohen biked the more scenic eastside Santa Maria-Solvang segment on century day 1993, while Don biked the full century in 1994.

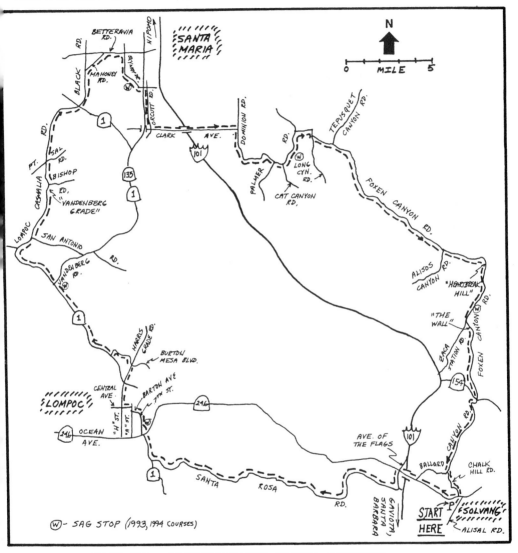

(W) – SAG STOP (1993, 1994 COURSES)

TRIP #23 - SOLVANG-SANTA MARIA CENTURY

Solvang to Lompoc. Starting from the Royal Scandinavian Inn, a short meander through Solvang leads to State Hwy. 246 and a five-mile westward spin to Buellton (5.7). As with most major intersections, the CHP controls the traffic flow on century day, giving cyclists the general right of way. (It is paramount that you observe traffic laws on the tour; non-compliant cyclists have been ticketed in the past.) A turn south at Avenue of the Flags, a bridge cross-over and the entry to Santa Rosa Rd. follows. A roughly 16-mile spin on this pleasant country road provides a few mainly flat/downhill miles along the northern base of the Santa Rosa Hills. This

Centurians on Foxen Canyon Road (Susan Cohen Photo)

is followed by a bevy of rolling hills along the Santa Ynez River plain. Cross the river to the valley's north side and proceed on a testy uphill to California Hwy. 1 (23.5) (See Trip #26 for a detailed description of Santa Rosa Rd.) A short upgrade is followed by a long runout into Lompoc and a "surprise" stop light at State Hwy. 246, the first in about 18 miles. The route works its way to a "fuel" stop near San Julian Rd. and Chestnut Ave.

Lompoc to Vandenberg Air Force Base (VAFB). After enjoying power bars, fruit, cookies and overloading on water and "superjuice," the mainly flat route goes north, crisscrossing several roads before leaving Lompoc on "H" St (Hwy. 1). Pass Lompoc Airport, the Santa Ynez River, Purisima Rd. and veer right onto Harris Grade Rd. (28.5). A left turn (west) on Burton Mesa Blvd. takes centurions into Vandenberg Village on a deviating route which deposits them back onto Hwy. 1 and a return to hilly terrain. Continue northwest past the VAFB main gate at California Blvd./Vandenberg Rd. to a more informal rest stop on what is now Lompoc-Casmalia Rd. (37.3).

VAFB to Santa Maria. A northbound downhill takes bikers just past the 40-mile mark to be greeted by the "terror" of the western century segment, the three-mile, roughly 800-foot, climb up the infamous Vandenberg Grade (average 6% grade). This is time for "granny-gears," patience and some soul-searching regarding cosmic reasons for doing this ride. After a crest is another (but lesser) uphill, followed by a cooling downhill and a reasonably flat stretch leading to the Santa Maria SAG stop near the halfway point. To get there, bear right at Black Rd. off Lompoc-Casmalia Rd. and follow the quilt-work path into the Santa Maria Airport Hilton parking lot, arriving southbound on Skyway Dr. (53.4).

Santa Maria to Sisquoc. Load up on munchies and enjoy a little lunch-time music, then depart on Skyway Dr. south, veering left on a narrow road to reach State Hwy. 135. Across that intersection, go immediately right onto Orcutt Rd. and parallel Hwy. 135 through a residential area to Clark Ave. (61.4). Bear east, cross U.S. Hwy. 101 and reenter the world of farms, horse and cattle ranches. A climb near Telephone Rd. gives way to a nice runout to Dominion Rd. where the route goes south. These are wide-open spaces with views of the valleys and distant ranges to the north and west. A right turn and steady climb brings the entourage of centurions into an exposed area of winding roadway with the Solomon Hills and Cat Canyon Oil Fields to the south. Dominion Rd. makes a gradual swing to the east and deposits bikers at Palmer Rd. after about three miles and a memorable winding downhill (68.7). East and beyond the intersection is a small roadside rest stop with all the amenities that mad cyclists dream about. Load up and then cycle through a small canyon (see Trip #21 for details on the next two miles) to the town of Sisquoc.

Up the "Wall"

Sisquoc to Fess Parker Winery. A turn east on Foxen Canyon Rd. leads the winding line of cyclists on one of the premier countryside stretches in Southern California. This 18-mile stretch on the southern edge of the Santa Maria Valley dips into Foxen Canyon below the oak-studded Solomon Hills and passes a bevy of vineyards. There are a solid ten miles of gradual upgrades when, near the 83-mile mark, is "Heartbreak Hill." We were well prepared for "The Wall" (more later), but this 1-1/2-mile, nearly 10% grade, was a total surprise to newcomers (try the shade near the base or the roadside shrubbery on the way up). Once at the top, there is a brief flat, then a let-it-out downgrade to the final SAG stop at the Fess Parker Winery (85.0).

On to Solvang. Susan Cohen made a good case for an eat, drink and be merry rest break (plus a short rest on the grass for Don) before we tackled "The Wall," a 3/4-mile steep pumpathon. The good news is that cyclists can see the top of the grade from the point where the road seems to go "vertical." This is at the 86-mile point, beyond which bikers are famous for making bicycle adjustments, taking advantage of photo opportunities, or praying for deliverance. Beyond the summit is one super "hang-ten" downhill through tree-studded, rolling farmland to the State Hwy. 154 junction (91.3).

On the "Wall"

Across the highway make a quick right (south) onto unsigned Ballard Canyon Rd., follow a sharp right curve and tackle a 1/2-mile steep uphill that would be just interesting under other circumstances, but is a real tear-jerker for 95-mile "old" legs. A several-mile series of gradual downgrades leads into open hills with grazing cattle, farms and open country to Chalk Hill Rd. Veer left to a nagging upgrade (it was supposed to be all downhill after the Ballard Canyon Rd. workout!), then coast into the northern outskirts of Solvang. Another downhill funnels the weary hoard onto Atterdag Rd., across Mission Dr. (State Hwy. 246) and into Solvang. A series of turns within town take the wheeled-serpentine to the **103-mile** mark at the Royal Scandinavian Inn.

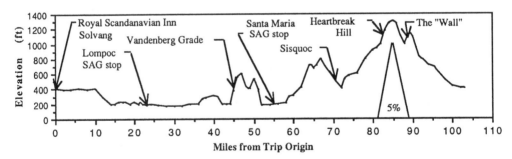

The Welcome Aftermath. Here at last, "fresh-as-daisy" bikers (great actors!) pass under the finish line and beeline for friends, congratulations and (probably) a couple of free beers. Relish the many booths (which generally focus on cycling wares), gobble some munchies and/or enjoy a well-deserved massage. And don't forget to pick up that testimonial T-shirt! It's party time, and time to maybe think about the next one!!

TRIP #24 - FIGUEROA MOUNTAIN WORKOUT

GENERAL LOCATION: Los Olivos, Happy Canyon, Figueroa Mountain

LEVEL OF DIFFICULTY: Loop - very strenuous
                         Distance - 39.7 miles
                         Elevation gain - steady moderate-to-steep grades
                                        (Happy Canyon Rd. to Ranger Peak)

HIGHLIGHTS: Almost 40 miles of back-road heaven, this mountain loop is only for the hearty.   From Mattie's Tavern in Los Olivos, follow an eight-mile, hilly-warmup stretch into farmland and grape vineyards.   Once onto Happy Canyon Rd., transit six miles through a pastoral setting of farms, pastures and horse ranches with an abundance of large oaks providing shade.   This latter stretch is a fun foray for those seeking a moderate, but rewarding ride.   Following is a challenging 6.1-mile, 1325-foot, climb through the upper reaches of Happy Canyon, which includes a visit to Cachuma Camp.

After Cachuma Saddle at Happy Canyon's terminus is Figueroa Mountain Rd. and a grueling 3.3-mile, 1340-foot, workout along the slopes to the forested backside of Ranger Peak.   Precipitous drops, with compelling valley and canyon views below, are numerous.   A downhill takes the bicyclist past Figueroa Campground, Figueroa Mountain Lookout turnoff and Figueroa Station.   A long runout through the frontal hills of the San Rafael Mountain range dumps into a large valley with Alamo Pintado Creek.   All that remains is a steady, modest seven-mile glide back to Mattie's.

Happy Canyon Road

BICYCLE RIDES: SANTA BARBARA AND VENTURA COUNTIES

This loop is best taken in the direction described to take advantage of well-paved Figueroa Mountain Rd. and a worry-free downhill finish. The upper reaches of Happy Canyon Rd. have numerous spots where creeks running across the highway have deposited dirt and rocks. There is also a one-mile graded dirt section that must be navigated with care by on-road bikers.

TRAILHEAD: From State Hwy. 154, exit south at Grand Ave. in Los Olivos. Turn right almost immediately onto Railway Ave. and parallel the highway. Park at Mattie's Tavern, a friendly "watering hole" and restaurant best saved for after the trip.

Bring water to the start point as there are no public water sources or gas stations in town. This is a tour best suited for a cool day or else started early in the morning. Cycle in the described direction; Happy Canyon Rd. has some unpaved road in spots and rough road where creeks drain across it. Figueroa Mountain Rd. is well paved and provides a smooth runout back to the start point. Check with the Cachuma Saddle Ranger Station after rains to ensure that Happy Canyon Rd. is open and passable.

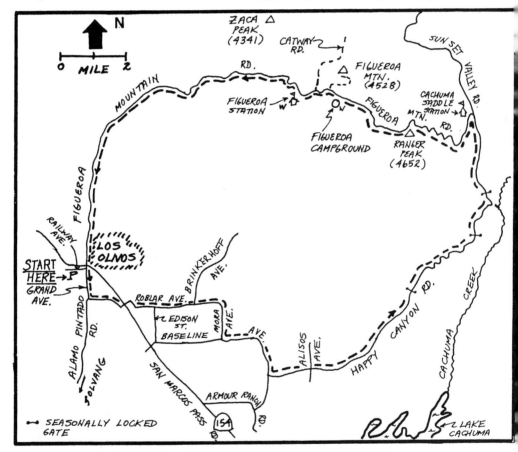

TRIP #24 - FIGUEROA MOUNTAIN WORKOUT

TRIP DESCRIPTION: The Warmup. The first eight miles serve as a pleasant warmup before ascending Happy Canyon Rd. The journey proceeds through quaint

Los Olivos with its tall ship's mast in mid-road presented by the Needlecraft Society in 1927, and enters open countryside once you cross Hwy. 154. The miles fly by as the rider is treated to unobstructed valley views, with the distant Santa Ynez Mountains to the south and a set of peaks looming north. The entire segment is in rolling hills with the widely-separated ranches growing ever larger. Reach a high plateau near Brinkerhoff Ave. on Roblar Ave. and follow a gentle rolling downhill to Happy Canyon Rd. (8.0).

Happy Canyon Road. A turn left (east) leads through rolling hills and across a couple of creeks on a sporadically rough road. The now narrow path goes into a euphoric country setting, passes between scattered large oaks and skirts the base of the foothills to the east. Wind steadily uphill into shaded farm and ranch lands, cross one of several cattle guards and cruise past the spruced-up Running Springs Ranch (12.8). With the San Rafael Mountains looming ahead, cross several brief dirt-and-rock-strewn sections of road, a sample of the work done by the creeks which run across it during rainy periods. A sign on the steepening road proclaims "Paved and Dirt Road Next 3 Miles" (14.1). Turn radically left, and pass another of the gates which are used to seal off sections of road during flooding conditions.

Switchbacks announce the upcoming climb as the steep and now-exposed road heads toward the visible San Rafael Mountain ridgeline. Climb higher above Happy Canyon and cross a saddle in 1.3 miles where another cattle guard is passed. The road transitions to graded dirt in 0.6 mile, returning to pavement in just under one mile, where there are views into the Cachuma Creek drainage below. Coming up is a 300-foot downgrade into a tree-shaded area with Cachuma Camp (overnight camping, fire pits, picnic tables) nestled beside Cachuma Creek (18.0). (We observed a happy camper staring at us from within a doorless porta-pottie. The chuckles trailed off as we started another climb to make up for the free-wheeling downhill and subsequent flat.)

Figueroa Mountain Road Above the Westside Frontal Hills

A couple of creek crossings on the tree-shaded road lead to a more exposed upper canyon, with a short section of unpaved road. One thousand feet and 2.4 challenging

103

miles past the campground is the Sunset Valley Rd. junction and the Cachuma Saddle Ranger Station (20.2). To the right is graded-dirt Cachuma Mountain Rd. The posted sign board provides bear warnings, hiker's rules, identifies horse trails and states the merits of each camping facility. The sign also boasts of the heavy chaparral, large big-cone fir, and both ponderosa and jeffery pine at the higher elevations of Figueroa Mountain and Ranger Peak, plus the blue oak and digger pine at lower elevations. Finally, there are notices of road closures in January and February (when snows occur) and during winter rainy periods.

Figueroa Mountain Crest. A turn left and uphill places the biker at Figueroa Mountain Rd. Wind back southward for an ever-steepening and more scenic view back down into Happy Canyon. Swing west and hug the southern edge of the San Rafael Mountains' ridgeline with periodic distant views into the canyons and valley below. Pump uphill to a saddle, then follow a climb to the backside of Ranger Peak, where there are views of the canyons to the north. Another wide swing around a peak north of Ranger Peak leads to a summit (23.5), followed by a downhill entry into a small shaded forest.

Overview of the Frontal Hills

Leave the dense shade in 0.4 mile and follow Figueroa Mountain Rd. onto a broad plateau with precipitous drops and continuous unobstructed views south. Pass a small turnout to Junction Camp and coast on a forested flat below Figueroa Mountain, reaching the Figueroa Campground (tree cover, water, picnic facilities, overnight camping) in one mile (26.4). The last upgrade along the crest passes the Figueroa Mountain Lookout turnoff (1-1/2 miles on graded dirt with vistas near the lookout). After the crest comes Catway Rd. (dirt) and a sign announcing that Los Olivos is 13 miles distant. (Catway Rd. is a great mountain bike tour as described in Trip #25.) Tunnel Rd. and the Figueroa Station (27.8) are passed in alternating exposed and treed sections before the road begins the eastward passage off the mountain range.

Figueroa Mountain Road-Downhill Return. More steady downhill leads through the last switchback, becoming a less winding road with some exposed sections. Birbent Canyon below parallels the road as you begin traversing the frontal hills of the range. Scattered trees dot the hillside beyond. Make a wide hairpin turn in 4.4 miles from Figueroa Station, bike north and dump out at the mouth of Birbent Canyon. Enter a wide valley, cross Alamo Pintado Creek and start the seven-mile return along the valley floor. The valley has large farming tracts and scattered residences, including striking Rancho Los Potreros (36.5). A steady moderate downhill leads past Acampo Rd. and the Los Olivos Equestrian Center to State Hwy. 154. Cross the highway, turn right at Railway Ave. and "crash" at Mattie's Tavern (39.7).

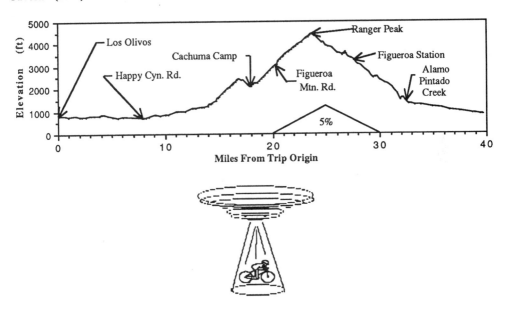

TRIP #25 - THE CATWAY

GENERAL LOCATION: Los Padres National Forest

LEVEL OF DIFFICULTY: Up and back - strenuous
Distance - 14.8 miles
Elevation gain - steep-to-sheer grades from Cedros Saddle
on return segment

HIGHLIGHTS: Think of this as the ride on top of the world! From Figueroa Mountain Rd., Catway Rd. transits open road and pine forest for 2.2 miles to a saddle and the first of many backcountry vistas. Remnants of the November 1993 fire are clearly evident in this and part of the subsequent ridgeline segment. The entire remaining route follows a prominent ridge where bikers are treated to multi-directional, picture-postcard views. Cyclists are treated to a 1-1/2-mile "bomb run" from the trip's summit (and cursed by the steep-to-sheer return segment) to Cedros Saddle. The ridgeline road leaves the last forested segment at this saddle and rides the exposed mountain spine up and down 1-1/2 miles to a final superb vista point at Whitehorse Peak.

TRAILHEAD: Drive up Figueroa Mountain Rd. from Los Olivos to Catway Rd., 1/2 mile below and west of Figueroa Mountain Campground. Park at the campground or at the Catway Picnic Site on Catway Rd. Bring 2-3 quarts of liquid for this waterless trip.

TRIP DESCRIPTION: **Trailhead to Zaca Peak Trail Junction.** From Figueroa Mountain Rd., follow Catway Rd. (known as "The Catway") and pass through a gate that is closed in rainy weather. Pass the Catway Picnic Site on a steady, 2.2-mile, moderate-to-steep grade. Patches of pine fill the landscape as you bike around and

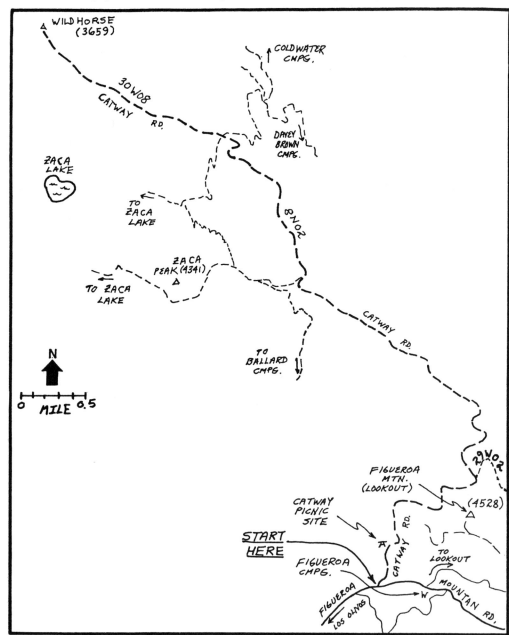

TRIP #25 - THE CATWAY

below the Figueroa Mountain summit for the first 1.5 miles. This peak has a lookout station reached via an alternate dirt road south of Catway Rd. Loop northwest, cross above Birbent Canyon and below an unnamed low peak.

At a saddle (2.2) is the Figueroa Jeepway (29W02) that dives eastward to Davey Brown Campground. This is the first of many backcountry 180-degree vistas that include Willow Spring Canyon, Fir Canyon and the San Rafael Wilderness. The Catway flattens, heads northwest and tracks a narrow, exposed and rolling ridgeline. After a return to pine forest in 1.7 miles, Catway Rd. reaches a shaded saddle. The last 1/2 mile to the saddle requires low gears and inspired pedaling. Reach a second saddle in 0.3 mile with junction 30W10 on the left; that diversion leads to Zaca Peak, the dominant mountain west. A later junction off of 30W10 leads north and steeply down to privately-owned Zaca Lake and the Zaca Resort.

The Zaca Lake Resort is 80 years old and all the building are originals, including the 14 cabins situated directly along the lake and the restaurant that is open for breakfast, lunch and dinner Thursday through Monday.

Catway Road with San Rafael Mountains Backdrop

On to Wildhorse Peak. The trail tops the ridge at the trip summit and drops steeply (about 600 feet in a mile) to exposed Cedros Saddle (5.8). Think long and hard before committing to this downgrade, which now is shadeless, but has 360-degree views, including Zaca Lake, west and below. A marked junction notes the trail to the west heading steeply down to Zaca Lake, and to the east leading to Sulphur Springs and Manzana Creek. Stay on the Catway and you are now "on top of the world!" Follow this northwest-aligned ridge on the San Rafael Mountain crest and view Zaca Lake from this vertically undulating road section. Whitehorse Peak is 1-1/2 miles from Cedros Saddle with a heart-stopping look into the Sisquoc River drainage north

107

and a succession of peaks and valleys west. After reveling in nature's scenery, tackle the return uphill past Cedros Saddle (a very tiring climb on hot, sunny days) and follow The Catway back to the start point (14.8).

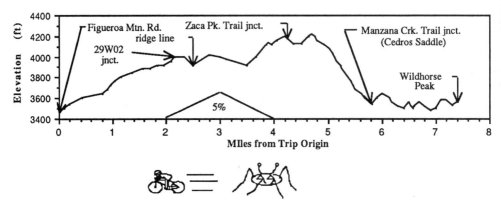

TRIP #26 - SANTA RITA HILLS

GENERAL LOCATION: Buellton, Lompoc

LEVEL OF DIFFICULTY: Loop - moderate
Distance - 34.1 miles
Elevation gain - periodic moderate grades

HIGHLIGHTS: Santa Rosa Rd. is a back-road delight, a lightly-used roadway through farming valleys, with an occasional hill climb for spice. This is part of the "moderate 50-miler" in the Nov. 1993 Solvang Prelude. The route follows the course of the Santa Ynez River before reaching State Hwy. 1, crosses the river and returns to Buellton on busy State Hwy. 246. The return is by way of scenic Santa Rita Valley, filled with farms and fields of flowers. Although Class X, there is wide shoulder on Hwy. 246 and the scenery does more than offset the nuisance of traffic.

TRAILHEAD: From U.S. Hwy. 101, exit west at Hwy. 246 and drive to Avenue of the Flags, a separated road with a wide, grassy median strip, and a series of standards bearing international flags. Go right to visit famous Andersen's Pea Soup Restaurant or left and park where convenient. There is a market on the southwest corner. Private water sources are in Buellton and at River Park in Lompoc--that's it for water.

TRIP DESCRIPTION: **Santa Rosa Road.** Bike south over the Santa Ynez River to road's end near the Hwy. 101 on-ramp (do not enter the freeway). Veer right as the road becomes Santa Rosa Rd. and start a 16-mile segment of enchanting country charm. The road ripples through mostly-flat terrain with miles of horse ranches and farms, bends south (3.7) and leaves behind Hwy. 246, previously visible across the valley. Bike a few more miles along a valley of variable width that cuddles the Santa Ynez River. The road hugs the southern valley edge following the Santa Rosa Hills contour.

More farms and ranches pass before you must tackle a tough grade, pedal by the dirt road entry to Santa Rosa Country Park (8.3) and cycle to a crest. The downhill beyond returns to more valley pedaling, now on Lompoc Valley's eastern edge. The

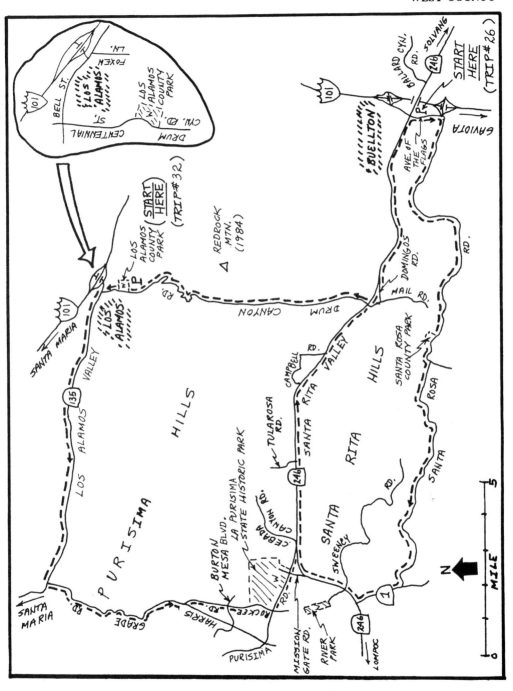

TRIP #26 - SANTA RITA HILLS
TRIP #32 - PURISIMA HILLS/LOS ALAMOS VALLEY

109

Viewpoint from Santa Rosa Road (Susan Cohen Photo)

road rises above and returns bikers to valley level twice in the next six miles. The valley vistas at the high points are interesting and the Santa Ynez River flood plain becomes more evident. Take in the scattered apple farms in this long thin valley, which is otherwise sparsely treed. Dip into the valley, cross over Salsipuedes Creek (16.4), and follow a winding contour among the hills on the opposite valley side. The Hwy. 1 junction is reached after a 1/2-mile uphill.

Highway 246 Return. Ride 1-1/2 miles on busy Hwy. 1 through a short White Hills segment to the Lompoc City limit. Go right on busy Hwy. 246, recross the Santa Ynez River, and pass an entry to River Park. At this respite is an RV area with picnic facilities, restrooms, Kiwanas Kid's Lake and playground. This is the beginning of a 15-mile stretch (Class X, but wide shoulder) through flower-growing country.

Solvang Prelude "Threesome" (Susan Cohen Photo)

At Mission Gate Rd. is the entry to Mission La Purisima/Mission State Historical Park. Of the 21 Franciscan Missions in California, it is probably the best restored. The buildings have been carefully rebuilt, grounds planted to reflect the period, and an original aqueduct and pond system maintained. There are 12 miles of maintained hiking trails in the natural buffer zone around the mission. Past Purisima Rd. (20.9), climb two miles to a crest near Tularosa Rd. and enter Santa Rita Valley. Cycle on a couple of uphill-downhill grades past flower and Christmas tree farms and ranches. A mile past the Mail/Drum Canyon Rds. intersection is a crest with views into Buellton and the mountain ranges beyond. In 3-1/2 miles, you reach the Buellton City limit near Westwind Rd. and a return to the start point (34.1).

Up and Back Option. True lovers of the outdoors should consider an up-and-back tour on Santa Rosa Rd. This is one of the more appealing stretches in the county.

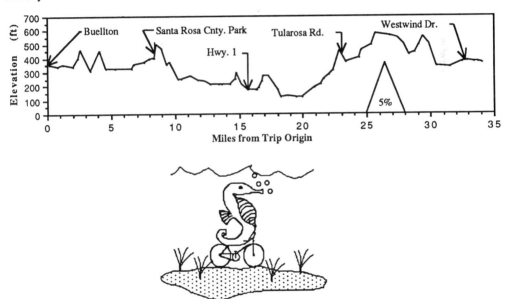

TRIP #27 - JALAMA BEACH

GENERAL LOCATION: Lompoc, Jalama Beach

LEVEL OF DIFFICULTY: One way - moderate-to-strenuous; up and back - strenuous
Distance - 18.8 miles (one-way)
Elevation gain - periodic moderate-to-steep grades

HIGHLIGHTS: This is another country biker's delight! Start from Beattie Park in Lompoc and wander through the hills above Salsipuedes Creek on State Hwy. 1 to the Jalama Rd. turnoff. The trip highlight is the 14-mile stretch along this rural road. The winding country path threads its way through ranch country with its myriad of oak-dotted hillsides and lush little valleys supported by Salsipuedes and Jalama Creeks. The basic profile is one of rolling hills with a rugged climb to Jualachichi Summit and roller-coaster workouts all the way to the beautiful Jalama Beach shores. The "moderate" rating may be understated. It applies to a one-way ride in nice, cool

111

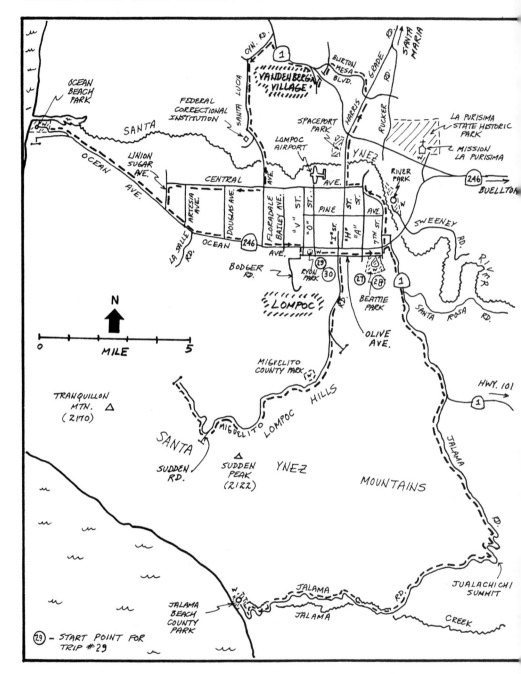

TRIP #27 - JALAMA BEACH; #28 - LOMPOC HILLS;
TRIP #29 - OCEAN BEACH COUNTY PARK; TRIP #30 - LOMPOC CITY TOUR

weather for weekend cyclists who may have to walk their bikes in some stretches, particularly the climb to the summit. The one-way tour requires an understanding friend who will provide a car shuttle.

TRAILHEAD: From U.S. Hwy. 101, exit at State Hwy. 246, drive to Lompoc and pass the Cabrillo Hwy. (Hwy. 1) intersection. Turn south in 1/4 mile at 7th St., and continue to its end at Beattie Dr. Go left and enter Beattie Park, perched on the hillside, which has restrooms, playground, and limited tree cover. From the north, follow Hwy. 1 south to Ocean Ave. (Hwy. 246) in Lompoc. Turn left (east), drive one mile to 7th St., then right and continue as above. Fill up with water as this is the last source until Jalama Beach.

TRIP DESCRIPTION: **Lompoc to Jalama Road Turnoff.** Return to Ocean Ave., go right (east) and bike 1/4 mile on the busy road to Hwy. 1. A southward turn here leaves the city behind almost immediately as cyclists head into pastoral foothills. In an uphill mile is the Santa Rosa Rd. turnoff and views into the Santa Ynez River flood plain below. Stay on Cabrillo Hwy., pedal through a narrowing canyon above the Salsipuedes Creek, and pass the gigantic diatomaceous earth strip mines (composed of ancient marine life and used in filtration as an abrasive, etc.) in the White Hills above and to the right (west). The oak-dotted hillsides surround the road as Hwy. 1 proceeds to Jalama Rd. in a valley which envelopes the creek (4.9).

Jalama Road on West Side of Jualachichi Summit

Jalama Road. Cross the bridge over Salsipuedes Creek and climb on a curving narrow road to a crest with views of the frontal rolling hills and the distant Santa Ynez Mountain Range. For the next five miles on the north side of Jualachichi Summit, bike near the creek through a succession of small valleys separated by the ever-present scrub- and oak-laden hillsides. Pedal by the Flying "A" Ranch, two miles from Hwy. 1, and begin a steady uphill that steepens after a couple more miles and gives you a clear view of the switchback route to the summit. Look for deer grazing in the hills.

The upgrade steepens and presents a one-mile, 500-foot, climb with superb over-the-shoulder views of the incoming route. In 0.3 mile beyond an apparent crest is the Jualachichi Summit (10.4) and a whole new panorama to the west and south. A

Jalama Beach

Fisherman at "Work"

winding serene downgrade drops you to valley level which leads to a narrowing access between the hills.   Oak trees become more abundant in the upper hillsides and work their way down to road level as the road crosses Jalama Creek (13.1).   Jalama Rd. now chases the creek through lush lowlands and passes the Jalama Ranch Headquarters, a large house and barn tucked into the hillside.

While cycling the next series of rolling hills, you get the first hint of ocean breezes.   Cross the creek and follow a long grade into the southern hillsides above the creek.   The first tantalizing ocean glimpses appear, along with excellent coastal views from the summit.   Enjoy the easy pedal south, cross the railroad tracks and follow the westward return, plunging down the scenic road 280 feet to Jalama Beach Park (18.8).

Jalama Beach Park.   Take a breather and enjoy this beautiful beach and park. The park has overnight camping, some tree cover, firepits, restrooms, water and a lightly-populated coastline.   A popular county surfing locale is Tarantula Point, located 1/2 mile south of the park.   Further beyond is a coast-hugging hike that can be extended to within 1/2 mile of Point Conception with the closed-to-the-public lighthouse (check tide tables and take the full tour only at low tide).   Other enjoyable activities are whale and bird watching, rock hounding, beach combing, surf fishing or just taking in the awesome beauty of this pristine area.

The Return (or Other Options).   Retrace the incoming route.   This two-way ride provides a full course for the hill-climbing fiend's appetite.   Another option is to have a friend drop you off at Jalama Rd. and Hwy. 1, then pick you up at either the beach (one-way) or Hwy. 1 (up and back).   This is the premier segment of the tour.

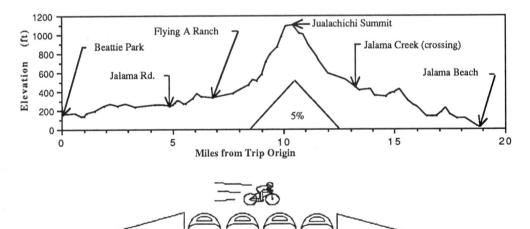

TRIP #28 - LOMPOC HILLS

GENERAL LOCATION: Lompoc

LEVEL OF DIFFICULTY: One way - moderate to strenuous; up and back - strenuous
Distance - 18.8 miles (up and back)
Elevation gain - periodic moderate-to-steep grades

BICYCLE RIDES: SANTA BARBARA AND VENTURA COUNTIES

HIGHLIGHTS: This is an elevation workout into the backcountry of Lompoc Hills. Cruise 3.4 miles to Miguelito County Park from Lompoc and follow a 4.4-mile, 1000-foot, climb to a crest at a saddle. The bicyclist gets a view of the Santa Ynez Mountains' ridgeline and the valley below, which is the ultimate destination. After plummeting into the valley, the biker must "pay the piper" on the rugged return, then enjoy a downhill coast back to Lompoc.

TRAILHEAD: From State Hwy. 1 southbound, drive to Ocean Ave. in Lompoc, turn right (west). (Hwy. 1 cuts east here.) Drive 1/2 mile, go left at "O" Street, and continue one block to the Cypress Ave. entrance to Ryon Park. This park has shade trees, grass, walking paths, restrooms, picnic benches, tennis courts and water. From Hwy. 1 northbound, drive into Lompoc to State Hwy. 246 and keep westbound 1-3/4 miles on what is now Ocean Ave. to "O" St. Go left and drive into the park.

TRIP DESCRIPTION: Lompoc to Miguelito County Park. From Ryon Park, bike south to road's end at Olive Ave., then proceed 0.4 mile to S. "I" St. Go right (south) on this street (Class II bikeway) which becomes San Miguelito Rd. Enter a small canyon, leaving the residential areas behind and pass the entrance to the Johns-Manville Plant. In the gouged-out hillsides are the gigantic diatomaceous earth mines that spread east through the White Hills to Hwy. 1. The road narrows, along with the biking shoulder, and goes one mile beyond the plant's turnoff to Miguelito County Park. This day-use park has abundant tree cover, restrooms, barbecues and hiking trails. The hiking paths are reached by crossing the walking bridges over Miguelito Creek and heading into the hills (3.4).

Miguelito Road Near the Summit

Miguelito Park to Road's End. Past the park, the road steepens, climbs into the Lompoc Hills and follows Miguelito Creek 4.4 miles and nearly 1000-feet elevation gain to a summit. On the way, the road winds among the hills and explores the lush undeveloped valleys (greenery abounded when we biked through in the spring of 1993). Sections of road are garnered with overhanging tree cover. Watch for mosquito swarms in the shaded, low-lying areas when there is standing water. The trees thin out three miles from the park, then the road continues uphill and veers right past the Sudden Rd. entry to Vandenberg Air Force Base (VAFB). Soon after a wide-road arc is the 1344-foot summit at a saddle (7.8). Views of the coastal peaks are directly west, and of a valley (several hundred feet below) to the northwest.

Think twice before tackling the next segment, as the return leg is a "lung-buster." The northbound road bombs downward and switches back to a northwest direction, entering the valley that was seen from the crest. Miguelito Rd. straightens and parallels Canada Honda Creek, becoming a very narrow road which is rough in spots. This mainly flat straightaway stays in a farming valley 1.6 miles below the summit, where the road is barricaded to civilian traffic (9.4)--this is the eastern boundary of VAFB. We encountered an unleashed dog near this terminus who eyed us very carefully, but seemed content to just watch us on our sojourn. What remains is the soul-searching climb back to the summit and a coast back to Lompoc (18.8).

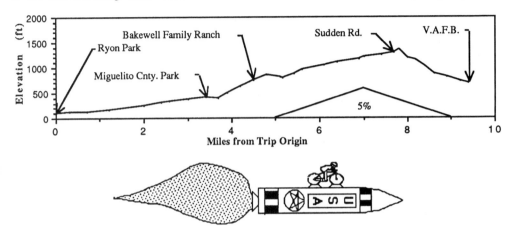

TRIP #29 - OCEAN BEACH COUNTY PARK

GENERAL LOCATION: Lompoc

LEVEL OF DIFFICULTY: Up and back - easy
                        Distance - 18.0 miles
                        Elevation gain - flat

HIGHLIGHTS: This flat ride travels from cozy Ryon Park in western Lompoc to Ocean Beach County Park at the mouth of the Santa Ynez River. Most of the tour is in the agricultural Lompoc Valley, a sight to behold during flowering season in the spring. Ocean Beach has scenic wetlands, beachside hikes and sand dunes.

TRAILHEAD: From State Hwy. 246, turn left (south) on "O" St. and head 1/2 mile west of the State Hwy. 1/"H" St. northbound junction. Drive 1/8 mile to Ryon Park. The park has shady pines, grass, picnic facilities, restrooms, playground and tennis courts. The bikeway/walkway paths in the park make for an easy family ride.

TRIP DESCRIPTION: Westbound. From the park, follow the 1.6-mile loop to the intersection of Bailey Ave. and W. Ocean Dr. at the western outskirts of Lompoc. Take a straightline, 6-1/2-mile, Class II spin on W. Ocean Dr. through a continuous mat of agricultural lands. In the spring, look for the bright colors of the flowers grown here for decoration and seeds. View the radar tracking facilities nestled on the hilltops, with a large NASA facility and an entry to Vandenberg Air Force Base (VAFB) at Arguello Blvd./13th St. Just before an upgrade, go right onto Ocean Park Rd. (8.1). This narrow road hugs the base of a small bluff, then winds across the

117

railroad tracks and beside the wetlands where the Santa Ynez River meets the sea. Enter a parking area where you find restrooms and picnic benches within Ocean Beach County Park (9.0). Plan time for a walk under the railroad trestle to the dunes off to the south (left) or cross the shallow water channel (tide dependent) to the sand spit on the park's western edge. Hikers can head south for a beachside walking tour, while joggers may test the packed sand across the water channel and head north.

"Coastal Express" at Ocean Beach

Return Trip. Retrace your steps for a total 18.0-mile tour or meander northward to Central Ave., still remaining in Lompoc Valley. A few miles and some variety is added by pursuing this option.

VAFB Tour. To gain biking entry behind the gates to portions of VAFB, check in at the Main Gate on California Blvd., west of Hwy. 1. These areas have little traffic and supply additional views of the coastal foothills that are characteristic of this region. Bikers can get a closer look at some of Vandenberg's launch pads within the base.

TRIP #30 - LOMPOC CITY TOUR

GENERAL LOCATION: Lompoc

LEVEL OF DIFFICULTY: Loop - moderate
Distance - 23.0 miles
Elevation gain - moderate grades in Vandenberg Village area

HIGHLIGHTS: This city tour starts at the southern edge of Lompoc at Ryon Park and works east and north along the Solvang-Santa Maria Century route. The circuit enters hill country in the Vandenberg Village area and returns through treed hills southward on Santa Lucia Canyon Rd. A recrossing of the Santa Ynez River leads to a six-mile-plus loop through the farmland of Lompoc Valley and returns to the city.

TRAILHEAD: From State Hwy. 1 southbound, drive to Ocean Ave. in Lompoc and turn right (west). Note that Hwy. 1 cuts east here. Drive 1/2 mile and go left at "O" Street, continuing one block to the Cypress Ave. entrance of Ryon Park. The park has trees, grass, walking paths, restrooms, picnic benches, water and tennis courts. From Hwy. 1 northbound, turn west at State Hwy. 246, and drive into Lompoc proper. Stay westbound 1-3/4 miles on what is now Ocean Ave. to "O" St., turn left and drive to the park.

TRIP DESCRIPTION: Central Lompoc. From Ryon Park, bike south to Olive Ave. and turn left (east). Cruise 2.1 miles into residential areas past Beattie Park to 7th St. At Ocean Ave., bike east and turn onto San Julian Rd. just before Ingram Park. Follow the 1993 Solvang-Santa Maria Century course (Trip #23) 8.2 miles to the turnoff from Hwy. 1 onto Santa Lucia Canyon Rd. This involves a meandering north-and-west heading through a commercial area, followed by a tour through residential zones. Head north on "H" St. (Hwy. 1), cross the Santa Ynez River and follow a steep uphill to Lompoc-Casmalia Rd. Purisima Rd. (Hwy. 1) turns west here (6.4).

Lompoc Valley From Bodger Road Overlook

119

BICYCLE RIDES: SANTA BARBARA AND VENTURA COUNTIES

Northern Periphery. The Western Spaceport Museum and Science Center and Spaceport Park facilities are reached by going left and following Hwy. 1. The reference route continues north. The road narrows to one lane in each direction, follows a testy 0.4-mile upgrade and arrives on a country-like plateau with spotty tree cover. The Purisima Hills loom directly ahead as the route turns left (west) in 1/2 mile at Burton Mesa Blvd.

A short climb on the Class II road and a modest downhill leads past Club House Rd. and into the sparkling, like-new Vandenberg Village. The marked bikeway ends after crossing Constellation Rd. and passing a shopping center. From the end of Burton Mesa Blvd. head northwest and rejoin busy Hwy. 1. At the crest of an immediate short climb on the highway is a westward view into the rolling hills of Vandenberg Air Force Base (VAFB). After 0.8 mile on a downgrade is Santa Lucia Canyon Rd.; cyclists must carefully cross over to the left lane turnoff (11.0). (Don't be in a hurry to make this lane transition as the fast traffic is not looking for bikers. An option for those who are queasy about this move is to do the trip in reverse.)

Eastside Return Segment. Bike 0.8 mile to the Lompoc Gate of VAFB and another, less threatening, "keep-your-eyes-open," junction. Cruise into rolling hills and enjoy the surrounding hill and mountain vistas with scattered quick peeks of the ocean between the trees and foliage. Pass the Federal Penitentiary ("barbed-wire city") and recross the Santa Ynez River where the road name becomes Floradale Ave. Exit the wooded Lompoc outskirts and enter the vast farmland of Lompoc Valley.

The now-flat tour follows a 6.4-mile farmland loop and reaches westward as far as Union Sugar Ave., then returns via Ocean Ave. to the Lompoc City limits (21.4). After Bailey Ave., the route is Class II and returns to residential environs. At "V" St., leave Ocean Ave. and follow a looping return to the park via Olive Ave. and S. "O" St. (23.0).

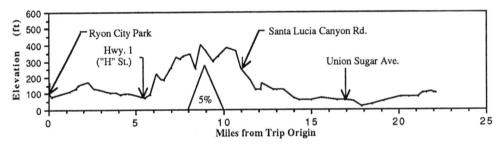

Trip Option-City Overlook. For bikers in excellent shape and looking for a reward for some grueling uphill, turn right (west) on Olive Ave. from "V" St. and then left at Bodger Rd. (past Allen Hancock College). Pump up this challenging 0.9-mile, 500-foot grade (10% average), to a vista point with panoramic views of Lompoc Valley, Burton Mesa, and the Santa Rita and Purisima Hills.

120

TRIP #31 - CASMALIA HILLS

GENERAL LOCATION: Santa Maria, Vandenberg Air Force Base (VAFB)

LEVEL OF DIFFICULTY: Loop - moderate to strenuous
Distance - 32.1 miles
Elevation gain - periodic moderate grades;
steep climb to Bishop Rd.

HIGHLIGHTS: One of our favorites, this loop provides the varied scenery that tickles most bikers.   The tour leaves expansive Waller Park in Santa Maria, crosses the western portion of Santa Maria and transits the Casmalia Hills near State Hwy. 1.   The hill segment passes nearby Casmalia, works steeply uphill to a crest near Bishop Rd. and coasts down the lightly-wooded slope of the Vandenberg Grade of Solvang Century fame.   Next is a seven-mile sojourn through peaceful, tucked-away San Antonio Valley and a visit to the periphery of the Barka Slough.   At State Hwys. 135/1, bike north through Harris and Graciosa Canyons and buzz into Orcutt via rural Graciosa Rd.   Orcutt Rd. along Hwy. 135 returns the biker to the park at the start point.

TRAILHEAD: From U.S. Hwy. 101, exit west at Betteravia Rd. and drive 1-1/4 miles to Broadway (State Hwy. 135), turn left (south) and motor 1-1/4 miles to Goodwin Rd.   A right turn leads to Waller Park.   This dense, tree-shaded park has restrooms, water, grassy hills, exercise courses, baseball fields, picnic area, barbecues, basketball courts and gazebos.   Park where it is convenient.   Northbound traffic should exit northwest at Santa Maria Wy. and drive 1-1/2 miles to Winter Rd.   At road's end, turn right (north), then left at Goodwin Rd. and continue to the park. Families can use the signed, speed-limited, park roads and paths which crisscross the park as a ride.

San Antonio Road East

The trip should be taken in the counterclockwise direction as described to follow the full route.   If taken in the opposite direction, riders are required to exit onto Hwy. 1 and thus bypass Harris Canyon Rd. and San Antonio Rd. E.   The latter isolated country road is a pure shame to miss.   The full clockwise tour is broken because of a

121

private road segment on Graciosa Rd. between the junction at Hwy. 135/Hwy. 1 (Cabrillo Hwy.) and at Harris Canyon Rd./San Antonio Rd. E. The private Garciosa Rd. segment is at the western edge of the White Hills Vineyard. Bring 2-3 quarts of water, as there are no reliable water sources outside of Santa Maria.

TRIP DESCRIPTION: To Casmalia. Exit the park, follow State Hwy. 135 south to Skyway Dr., make a hard right and follow the Class II road 1.7 miles past the Santa Maria Airport and Museum of Flight to Betteravia Rd. (also with a bike lane). Leave the land of stop lights, turn left (west) and enter the agricultural flats of Santa Maria Valley. There are scattered residences and broad fields bearing a variety of crops past the city limits. At the "Y," bear left onto Mahoney Rd. and continue to a merger with Black Rd. (5.0). Mild rolling hills take the cyclist past a residential area near Tanglewood Dr./Sandlewood Dr.

In 1.9 miles past the Black Rd. entry is the Hwy. 1 crossing. Begin a tough climb into the Casmalia Hills, pass the Aerox Rd. entry to the Aerox Mine, and enjoy over-the-shoulder views of the Santa Maria Valley. Pedal over the Southern Pacific Railroad tracks to a crest and follow a short steep downgrade into Sherman Canyon. After another uphill, the tracks disappear to the east below the Casmalia Oil Field, and you get to enjoy a modest coast into Casmalia Valley. To the right (west) is the rustic Hitching Post, Casmalia's biggest attraction; this is a place to enjoy a juicy barbecued steak. Snacks can also be purchased at the general store.

After Pt. Sal Rd. (10.6), enter the township of Casmalia, which is the former south-side entry to Pt. Sal State Beach, but has been blocked off as part of VAFB. An aerobic 1.5-mile workout on what is now Lompoc-Casmalia Rd. goes back over the railroad trestle to a Casmalia Hills crest at Bishop Rd. Just above is one of the many tracking stations within the base. This is the crest that Solvang Century riders dream about after negotiating the grueling two-mile "Vandenberg Grade" from the opposite direction. The good news is that you get to coast that challenge through wooded countryside to the flats near the Titan Gate entry and follow the winding road to a "Y" junction at San Antonio Rd. W. (15.0).

Vandenberg Grade (Solvang Century)

122

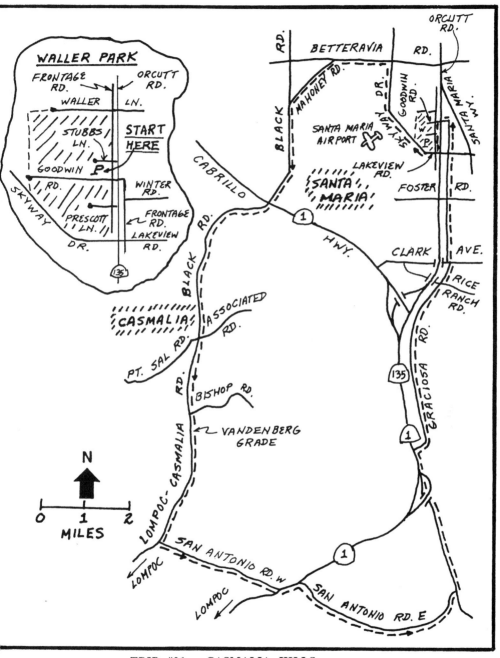

TRIP #31 - CASMALIA HILLS

San Antonio Road. Spin east into the quiet San Antonio Valley, tracking the course of San Antonio Creek on rolling terrain. Beneath the low hills, pass the Combat Arms Training Range, an out-of-place recycling center and a water plant. In

123

BICYCLE RIDES: SANTA BARBARA AND VENTURA COUNTIES

2.7 miles from Lompoc-Casmalia Rd. is the end of the western segment at Hwy. 1 (Vandenberg Rd.). A glance to the right exposes a nasty upgrade; luckily, the route plan is to turn left (north) onto the busy highway and bike on flatter terrain to the San Antonio Rd. E. junction (18.2).

A turn here places you back into the San Antonio Valley and beside the plant-filled edges of the Barka Slough. Traverse the 3.8 miles of valley on hilly terrain past the VAFB boundary and within view of several hillside vineyards. The northern road shoulder was alive with beautiful wildflowers in May 1994. The road ends at Hwy. 135 after passing a large trucking enterprise. Across the highway is Graciosa Rd., a private road which skirts the periphery of the White Hills Vineyard and parallels the upcoming highway route. Posted signs clearly indicate that visitors are not encouraged! A long lazy incline on Hwy. 135 takes you three miles through Harris Canyon, which is enclosed by the eastern edge of the Casmalia Hills and the western slopes of the Solomon Hills.

At the first junction after the Hwy. 1/Hwy. 135 fusion point (navigate carefully across the highway or take the chance of becoming "road meat" due to a nonobservant motorist) is the Graciosa Rd. turnoff (24.9). Cyclists must exit. A winding turn north takes you past the northern entry to the White Hills Vineyard (private road). Follow the frontage road north on a general downhill beside large grazing pastures and farms. Bikers pass several skeletal remnants of barns and sheds, transit Graciosa Canyon, then make a sweeping turn into the suburban southern outskirts of Orcutt.

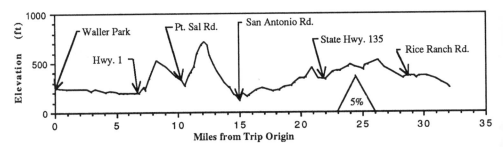

Cross Rice Ranch Rd. (28.9) and jog slightly left to join Orcutt Rd., now a Hwy. 135 frontage road. Stay on gentle rolling terrain through a residential area, pass Clark Ave. and the first gas station in a spell, then cross two tricky intersections at Foster and Lakeview Rds. (These appear to be four-way stops, but are not!) The ride is Class II beyond Clark Ave. Just after Winter Rd., the road bends left, crosses Hwy. 135 and returns to the park via Goodwin Rd. (32.1).

TRIP #32 - PURISIMA HILLS/LOS ALAMOS VALLEY

GENERAL LOCATION: Los Alamos, Mission Hills

LEVEL OF DIFFICULTY: Loop - strenuous
Distance - 34.7 miles miles
Elevation gain - steep grades to reach both Purisima Hills crests

HIGHLIGHTS: This is a must-do trip for hills and valleys gourmets and is part of the hard "50-miler" of the Nov. 1993 Solvang Prelude. A lazy cruise through the flat, see-forever Los Alamos Valley gives way to an aerobic workout while climbing the eastern slopes of the Purisima Hills. A lengthy downgrade provides many Lompoc Valley vistas while passing through the Lompoc Oil Fields and beside the La Purisima State Historic Park. A segment on State Hwy. 246 transits the Santa Rita Valley, then the circuit heads north on Drum Canyon Rd. This highlight trip portion invites a sometimes steep uphill on a remote, little-used highway into Drum Canyon. After achieving the crest, simply coast down and return to the starting point at Los Alamos County Park. (Refer to Trip #26 for tour map.)

Victorian Mansion (Los Alamos)

TRAILHEAD: From U.S. Hwy. 101, exit west at Bell St. (State Hwy. 135) in Los Alamos and drive 2/3 mile to Centennial St. Go left (south) 2/3 mile to Los Alamos County Park. The day-use park sports knarled valley oaks and other deciduous varieties. This pleasant rest stop has shade, picnic tables, barbecues, volleyball court, ball fields, horseshoe pits, ranger station, and creeks with pedestrian overcrossings. The site of the park was an old bandit hideout where many human skeletons were found in the 1850's. Much of the surrounding hillside was burned out in the Coyote Fire and was replanted by young school children.

TRIP DESCRIPTION: Los Alamos Valley. Swoop down 0.3 mile into the little burg of Los Alamos and go left on Bell St. (State Hwy. 135). A must-see is the 1880 Union

Hotel, a faithfully restored bed and breakfast, complete with a cozy bar, one-of-a-kind ping-pong and pool tables, and a statue-filled English maze among other goodies. Next door is the newly-built Victorian Mansion with custom romantic theme rooms that will rock your senses! (Yes, we have stayed here; and yes, the ambiance, plus the very personal attention from owner Dick Langdon and the staff overwhelmed us!). What follows beyond the grocery/gas/antique store and the burger stand on the town's outskirts is eight miles of flat cycling in Los Alamos Valley. The valley is stocked with agriculture, hay farms and large ranches. At the six-mile point is a San Antonio Creek crossing and, in 12.7 miles, the Harris Grade Rd. intersection (8.8).

Union Hotel (Los Alamos)

Harris Grade Road. A deceptive 1.7-mile flat spin south through farmland leads to the base of the Purisima Hills and the start of a winding 2.6-mile, 640-foot, uphill of variable steepness. Hug the contour of the scrub-dotted hills, cross several saddles and switch from one hillside to another. On the way up are excellent over-the-shoulder views of Los Alamos Valley. At the crest (12.1), a tunnel view opens down a canyon into Lompoc Valley. A curvey downhill glide leads into a solitary stand of trees and then through the Lompoc Oil Field to Rucker Rd. Veering left, the rough-in-spots straight-line country road goes into a residential area, passes Burton Mesa Blvd., and follows a short steep downhill next to the undeveloped west flank of La Purisima State Historical Park. At Purisima Rd., follow the wide-shouldered road that supports a steady traffic flow, passes the park entrance and reaches Hwy. 246 (18.6).

Highway 246. The 7.4-mile eastbound segment on this busy (but well-shouldered) highway involves a steady, mostly moderate uphill to a crest near Tularosa Rd. at the Santa Rita Valley's west-side entrance. A set of long upgrades/downgrades through farm and ranch country leads to the Mail Rd./Drum Canyon Rd. intersection.

Drum Canyon Road. This almost mystical segment is, in our minds, the trip highlight. Within 1/4 mile off the highway, the biker is effectively "in the boonies."

Proceed from a flat and wide valley into a canyon which narrows progressively during the ascent into the Purisima Hills. In 3.9 miles and roughly 400 feet above the turnoff, the road narrows to one wide lane (29.9), winds further uphill and reaches a point where cyclists see a pattern of cutouts zig-zagging above and directly ahead. This is a "wake-up call" for the upcoming no-nonsense climb to the crest.

Drum Canyon Road Near the Summit

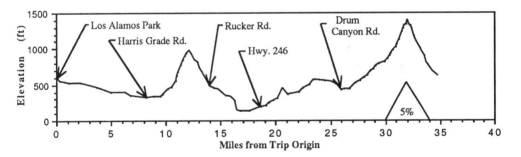

After a steep circuitous uphill with several switchbacks, enter a forest of miniature evergreens which is in sharp contrast to the barren slopes and canyon bottom characteristic of the first few miles on Drum Canyon. Cross several cattle guards, pump up more switchbacks (this is "granny-gear" time!), and achieve the ridgetop in six miles from the Hwy. 246 junction. The payback is a steep winding downhill into a pygmy forest and heart-stopping views a few hundred feet down into the adjoining canyon. The view down the canyon opens about 1/2 mile from the crest as the road hugs the hillside contour and plunges downhill. Drum Canyon Rd. reaches canyon level about two miles from the crest, then. widens and transitions to the first level stretch in a spell. Coast into a small valley filled with the knarled oaks, pass the Los Alamos Cemetery and return to Los Alamos County Park (34.7).

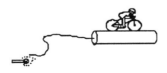

127

TRIP #33 - SOLOMON HILLS/CAT CANYON

<u>GENERAL LOCATION</u>:　Los Alamos, Sisquoc

<u>LEVEL OF DIFFICULTY</u>: Loop - moderate to strenuous
Distance - 33.7 miles
Elevation gain - moderate-to-steep grades up to the
Solomon Hills crest

<u>HIGHLIGHTS</u>:　An interesting loop through the quiet back roads of the Solomon Hills, this is a passage through California history.　The hills were named after the notorious bandito, Salomon Pico (note the spelling boo-boo), a child of wealth who chose to run a gang of robbers and ruffians in his "other life."　His targets were the stage passengers that traveled El Camino Real between Los Alamos and Santa Maria Valley.　The tour leaves sleepy Los Alamos, works its way up Palmer Rd. and visits Sisquoc, then proceeds southeast on serene and scenic Foxen Canyon Rd.　Along the way is the Fremont Foxen Memorial and the site of the Foxen Adobe.　A short workout upgrade on Alisos Canyon Rd. gives way to a relaxing meandering return on this country road.

<u>TRAILHEAD</u>:　From U.S. Hwy. 101 northbound, exit the Bell St. off ramp (State Hwy. 135) and turn right (north) once under the freeway.　Park in the city proper or drive south 1/2 mile on Centennial St. to Los Alamos County Park (see Trip #32 for park description).　For southbound drivers, exit at Bell St., follow that road to Centennial St. and go right.　Los Alamos and Sisquoc have the only sources of water.

Dominion Road with Palmer Road Below

<u>TRIP DESCRIPTION</u>: **Los Alamos to Sisquoc.**　Take Bell St. west and north 2.2 miles via Los Alamos Valley to Hwy. 101, carefully cross the divided highway and bike north on the wide shoulder.　Cycle through the pockets of hills and, in 3.2 miles from the highway entry, go east onto Palmer Rd.　Trace this sometimes rough road uphill through cattle and farm country to the Solomon Hills summit in 1.5 miles (6.9).　Veer

west and return downhill through the Cat Canyon Oil Field, which is peppered with oil pumping and storage facilities. Signs warn passersby that off-road trespassers are "entering H_2S poisonous gas areas."

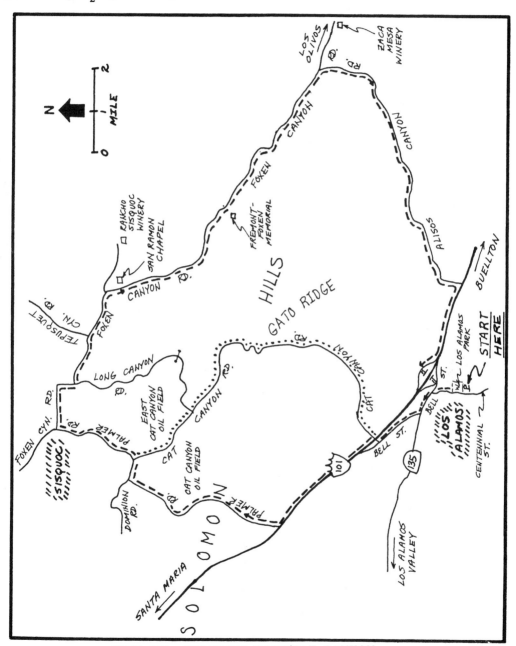

TRIP #33 - SOLOMON HILLS/CAT CANYON

At Dominion Rd. go right to stay on Palmer Rd., then steer directly into a large oil processing facility. Cat Canyon Rd. (9.8), in another 0.7 mile, is the entry to the E. Cat Canyon Oil Field. Palmer Rd. enters the north segment of Cat Canyon on a road which hugs the hills on the valley's east side and dumps into tiny Sisquoc. Turn right at Foxen Canyon Rd. (staying north leads to the "bright city lights" and a small market).

San Ramon Chapel

Foxen Canyon. Leave the town and begin a three-mile plus cruise at the southern edge of the giant Santa Maria Valley, following the contour of the foot of the Solomon Hills. After a couple of serious road jogs, the lightly-used road passes an expansive vineyard. Past Tepusquet Rd. (14.3), go sharply right and ahead into the hillside-perched San Ramon Chapel. Below and to the left is the entry to the Rancho Sisquoc Winery. The biker departs the Santa Maria Valley and barrels south into the heart of Foxen Canyon between hills populated by scattered oaks. Follow a steady

Rest Break on Foxen Canyon Road

upgrade, make a sharp turn left and pass the Fremont Foxen Memorial. This is a granite marker showing Fremont's campsite on his Foxen-guided journey to take Santa Barbara from the Spanish (which he did, without a shot being fired).

Foxen Canyon Rd. winds between the hills in farming country where there are scattered views of the San Rafael Mountains to the north. The country road holds to the contour of the lower slopes of the Solomon Hills, then makes a couple of sharp jogs that are probably the product of the property lines in the canyon bottom. Following are a couple of straight-line miles in a wider part of the canyon, which lead to Alisos Canyon Rd. (23.0).

Return to Los Alamos. A turn right and a steady one-mile climb into the beginnings of cattle country lead to the road's crest and a 5-1/2 mile gentle downhill. There are occasional rough segments on this serene little byway, where the Solomon Hills are dusted with oaks. In two miles is Rancho San Juan, which invites city dudes to try a hand at roping cattle. Follow the meandering canyon course into a wider valley, staying to the southern edge below the hills. Pedal by a lengthy row of white picket fences, which signal a passage beside the Longview Stud Ranch and Calico Farms. At nearby Hwy. 101 is an entry to the eastern edge of Los Alamos Valley (29.3). Bike north on this major thoroughfare, exit at Bell St./Hwy. 135 and return to Los Alamos County Park (33.7).

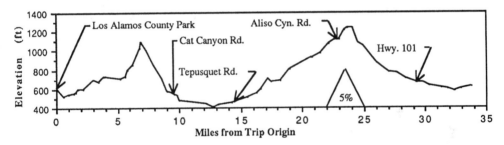

Cat Canyon Option. An interesting option is to take Cat Canyon Rd. out of Los Alamos and follow its wanderings into the hills. This route offers a challenging uphill to reach the Gato Ridge, a testier ride than Palmer Rd. This tour option adds about one mile to the trip.

TRIP #34 - LOS COCHES MOUNTAIN LOOP

GENERAL LOCATION:

LEVEL OF DIFFICULTY: Loop - strenuous
Distance - 42.3 miles
Elevation gain - steady steep climb on Tepusquet Rd.

HIGHLIGHTS: This is definitely a ride for the backcountry freak! After a light warmup on the eastern edge of Santa Maria Valley, bike through a world of

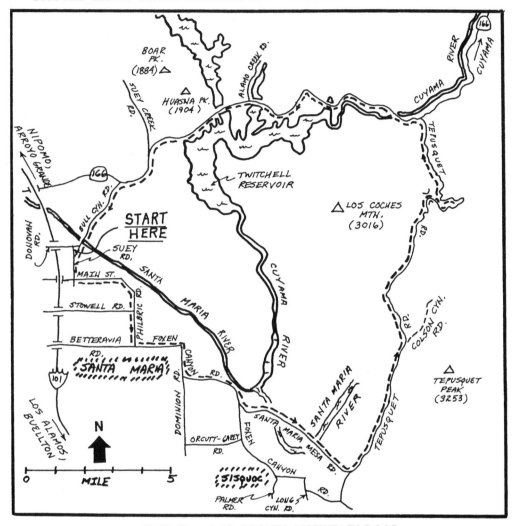

TRIP #34 - LOS COCHES MOUNTAIN LOOP

agriculture and ascend a 1500-foot challenge on Tepusquet Rd. The steady upgrade follows a lightly-used road within the successively narrowing Tepusquet Canyon. On the way, the terrain varies from very exposed to densely treed. Beyond the summit, relish a three-mile switchbacking-downhill which lets out in Buckhorn Canyon and continues to State Hwy. 166. From here is an 11.7-mile journey along the Cuyama River, which returns south along Bull Canyon Rd. After crossing the (hopefully) dry Santa Maria riverbed, return to the start point on Suey Rd.

TRAILHEAD: From U.S. Hwy. 101, exit east at Main St. (State Hwy. 166) and drive 1/2 mile to Suey Rd. Go north 3/4 mile to Suey Park just past Suey Crossing Rd., and park along Suey Rd. Check the condition of the Santa Maria River crossing before departing. If it looks threatening, plan to use the alternate route, State Hwy. 166, into Santa Maria, as described in the "Trip Option to Bull Canyon Rd." Bring 2-3 quarts of water as there are no public water sources on the tour.

132

<u>TRIP   DESCRIPTION</u>: **Santa   Maria   Valley.**   Follow a series of south-and-east tending roads 13.3 miles until the route reaches Tepusquet Rd.   To get there, skirt the Santa Maria River and bluffs to the northeast of the waterway.   Once past the Suey Rd./Main St. intersection, ply the agricultural landscape to Tepusquet Rd.   There is a stop sign at the Sisquoc River crossing (9.4) (look before entering the bed, which can flood).   Beyond are the vineyards of the Cambria Winery.   This stretch is a great warmup for what is ahead!

Tepusquet   Road.   Veer left onto that road, pass the rows of staked grapevines of the Gold Coast Vineyard and go up a narrowing canyon with a mix of scattered vineyards and open fields.   Follow meandering Tepusquet Creek, noting the loss of the center marker on this narrowing road about two miles from the canyon entry. Travel under the first of several large homes perched on the mountainsides above and pass Colson Canyon Rd. (17.7).   Next is the first of 2-1/2 miles of tree-shaded, winding steep road, and several spots where creeks wash freely across the road.

At higher elevations, the contour steepens as the road stays along Tepusquet Creek.   The asphalt ribbon hugs the mountainside to the left (west), turns sharply right with a dramatic view of a canyon dropping away below and reaches an exposed summit (23.0).   Past the crest, the deep canyon drops are on the opposite side of the road with vistas of the canyons and valleys far below.   Begin a winding switchback-laden descent through the forested mountainsides, eventually dropping over 1000 feet in three miles (average 6-1/2% grade).   At this point in Buckhorn Canyon, cyclists reach valley level and the road flattens as the canyon widens.   Pass a large farm house and, in 3/4 mile, reach Hwy. 166 (27.6).

Tepusquet Road Near the Summit

Cuyama   River.   Go west, join the high-speed traffic on Hwy. 166 and track the Cuyama River as it snakes between the mountains.   In 1.2 miles is a river crossing and, two miles further, the first straight-line stretch in awhile.   A long steady uphill leads through a section where the hills have been blown away to build the highway. The first views of the backwater of Twitchell Reservoir appear (spring of 1993) and, in one mile, there is a bridge crossing of one of the reservoir fingers.   Pass Alamo

Creek Rd. (34.2) and enjoy a view of the stately (and longest) bridge of the series that crosses over the flooded southern extremes of the Huasna Valley. Skirt the northern reservoir edge, pedal a 100-foot upgrade (the "last hoorah" in the roller-coaster series) and dive downhill past Suey Creek Rd. The first view of Santa Maria opens and an easier downhill leads to Bull Canyon Rd. (39.3).

Return Segment (Bull Canyon Road). Turn left (southwest) and follow the narrow two-lane road as it winds through the surrounding hills. In a few miles, transit the Santa Maria River plain (closed during high water) and stay on what is now Suey Crossing Rd., returning to the park (42.3).

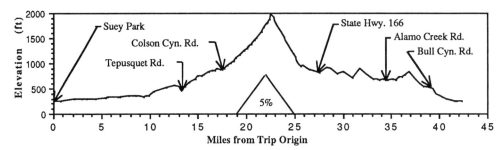

Trip Option-Bull Canyon Road. If a crossing of the Santa Maria River is not in the cards, an option is to continue beyond Bull Canyon Rd. on Hwy. 166 for three miles into Santa Maria proper. Bike onto busy Hwy. 101 southbound, exit at Broadway and go left on Donovan Rd. to road's end at Suey Park. This option adds three miles to the journey.

TRIP #35 - SANTA MARIA VALLEY

GENERAL LOCATION: Santa Maria, Orcutt

LEVEL OF DIFFICULTY: Loop - moderate
Distance - 39.8 miles
Elevation gain - moderate grades on Clark Ave.

HIGHLIGHTS: A visit to North Santa Barbara County would not be complete without a tour of this flat and expansive valley. This ride into the "land of the western barbecues" (the Elk's Rodeo #50 was held on June 3-6, 1993) features a full clockwise circuit of the valley periphery starting from Waller Park. Stoplights are restricted to Santa Maria City proper. The valley supports a multitude of crops, including corn, hay, lettuce, cauliflower, artichokes and strawberries, as well as grape vineyards.

134

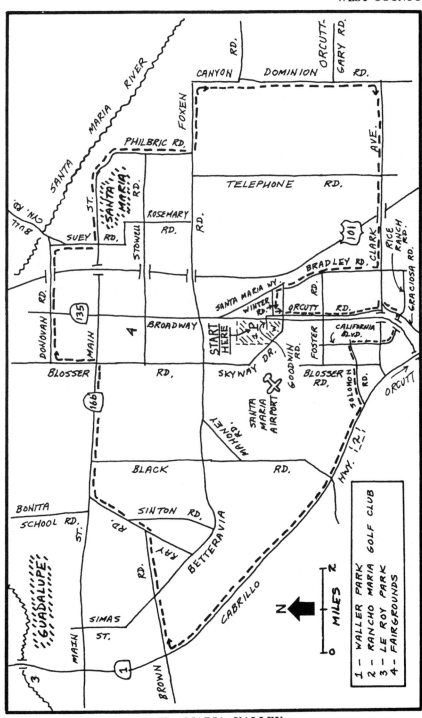

TRIP #35 - SANTA MARIA VALLEY

The trip south to Orcutt follows the Solvang Century course to Clark Ave., cuts northwest along State Hwy. 1 below the Casmalia Hills and rejoins the course beyond Black Rd. Through agricultural fields, the tour works back to Santa Maria and follows residential Donovan Rd. to the northeastern city extreme near Santa Maria. The eastside tour, which follows, returns to flat agricultural land until Dominion Rd., where small rolling hills are encountered. A testy uphill on Clark Ave. is followed by a stair-step downhill and the return to residential environs. An easy Class III return to the park follows.

TRAILHEAD: From U.S. Hwy. 101, exit west at Betteravia Rd. and drive 1-1/4 miles to Broadway (State Hwy. 135). Go left (south) for 1-1/4 miles to Goodwin Rd., then right to grand Waller Park. This park boasts grassy hills, exercise courses, baseball fields, picnic areas, barbecues, basketball courts, gazebos, restrooms, water and the adjoining Santa Maria County Club. Park where convenient. Northbound traffic should exit northwest at Santa Maria Wy. and drive 1-1/2 miles to Winter Rd. At the end of this road, turn right (north), then left at Goodwin Rd. and park. Short and safe family bike rides are possible by interlinking the crisscrossing maze of roads and pathways within the park.

Bring at least a quart of water. There are stores and eateries in the city, but no public water sources in the agricultural sections.

Cabrillo Hwy./Farm Worker

TRIP DESCRIPTION: Western Valley. Cross Hwy. 135 and follow the eastside frontage road (Orcutt Rd.) south into light commercial/residential areas. Take care when crossing the next two intersections (Lakeview and Foster Rds.) which have the appearance of being four-way stops, but are not.

The Class II frontage road heads to Rice Ranch Rd., where the course turns right (west) and passes under Hwy. 135. Follow a zig-zag route into Old Orcutt near Broadway and Clark Ave. (restaurant/bakery) and cycle over to Hwy. 1 via Solomon Rd. (Old Mill Ln. to the east) (5.3).

The seven-mile Hwy. 1 segment keeps to the base of the Casmalia Hills northwest and passes the Rancho Maria Golf Club on the Orcutt outskirts. To the east is the expansive agricultural plain of the Santa Maria Valley. Pedal a short uphill over the previously-paralleling railroad tracks (interesting valley views from this platform) to Brown Rd. (12.3). Work northeast through agricultural fields, turn onto busy State Hwy. 166 and reach the Santa Maria City limits just short of Blosser Rd. You'll find delis and several restaurants, mostly with a Mexican fare. (19.6). Turn north and pass through a suburban area on eastbound Donovan Rd. Near the Hwy. 101 overcrossing are gas stations, a coffee shop and a small shopping complex. On the east side of the highway is a mini-mart and the Santa Maria District Ranger Station. Donovan Rd. dead ends at Suey Rd. (22.8).

Eastern Valley. In a mile, the southbound residential stretch gives way to the return of "wide-open spaces." A zig-zag flat ride east and south arrives at Foxen Canyon Rd. and Dominion Rd., where bikers veer right and follow the latter road south into an elevated valley with rolling hills. A road sign, decorated with bullet holes, announces Orcutt-Gary Rd. as the small country lane stays in a mix of farm and cattle country. In 3.1 miles on Dominion Rd. is Clark Ave. (31.9).

Classic Santa Maria Valley Farm

A straight-line 1.1-mile uphill on Class II Clark Ave. leads to a crest where the eastern Santa Maria Valley first appears. Another short rise provides a view of a stair-step downgrade that follows. Past Telephone Rd., the Santa Maria suburban sprawl is clearly within view. Clark Ave. crosses Hwy. 101 and heads downhill on a marked Class II path with a short uphill before Bradley Rd. (36.0). At this point are gas stations and a small shopping complex. Now northbound on this Class II street, continue through a residential area on mild rolling hills, work northwest on Santa Maria Wy. and return to the park via Winter Rd. (39.8).

Clark Ave. Beyond Telephone Road

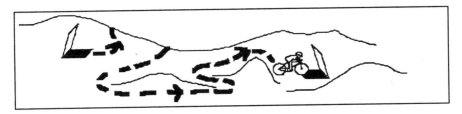

TRIP #36 - POINT SAL STATE BEACH (Mtn. Bike)

GENERAL LOCATION: Casmalia Hills, Pt. Sal State Beach

LEVEL OF DIFFICULTY: One-way strenuous; up and back - very strenuous
Distance - 27.0 miles (round trip)
Elevation gain - steep-to-sheer grades

HIGHLIGHTS: This is classified as a mountain-bike trip because of the roughly 1.7-mile stretch of washboard dirt road below the east side of Pt. Sal Ridge. This is one of the most grueling (if done up and back) and most scenically rewarding rides. The eastside trek to the crest is on a winding narrow road through Corralitos Canyon and the Casmalia Hills. From the crest area are see-forever views of both northern and southern coastlines. Past the ridge is an amazingly picturesque cannonball downhill on a narrow asphalt road with "sweaty-palm," cliff-side exposures on the upper section. Pt. Sal State Beach itself is a lightly-used coastal masterpiece.

Point Sal Road With Corralitos Ranch Below

TRAILHEAD: To reach the start point, exit west from U.S. Hwy. 101 at State Hwy. 166 in Santa Maria and drive 9-1/2 miles to Hwy. 1. Turn south and drive two miles to Brown Rd. There are two major options on this tour, both starting at Brown Rd. and State Hwy. 1: 1) bike to the beach and have a friend meet you with a car; 2) bike both directions and have a medic ready (just kidding). Don took Option 1. For either option, check your brakes before starting since there are some hang-it-out and exposed downgrades on the western side of Pt. Sal Ridge. The wide sandy beach lies below a connected series of bluffs which follow the contour of the small majestic bay. Bring 2-4 quarts of water for the test-of-stamina, round-trip, ride.

Check with the California Highway Patrol or county authorities to ensure that the road is open. Closures due to weather and other local restrictions have reportedly occurred.

138

<u>TRIP DESCRIPTION</u>: **Up to Point Sal Ridge.** The first four miles of mild-to-testy uphill are a respectable warmup for the climb to the ridge. Bike a narrowing, sometimes patchy, rough road into a mix of hillside farms and ranches in Corralitos Canyon. A cattle guard announces that this is cow country. A branch at the 3.6-mile point sends Brown Rd. left to the Corralitos Ranch, but bikers should veer right and join up with Pt. Sal Rd. Just beyond is a "Rough Road Ahead" sign. The narrowing road crosses another cattle guard, then proceeds on a very serious workout uphill with impressive Santa Maria Valley vistas framed by Corralitos Canyon behind. The road roams further up into the hills and, at 4.1 miles from the highway, returns to a steady packed-dirt washboard surface.

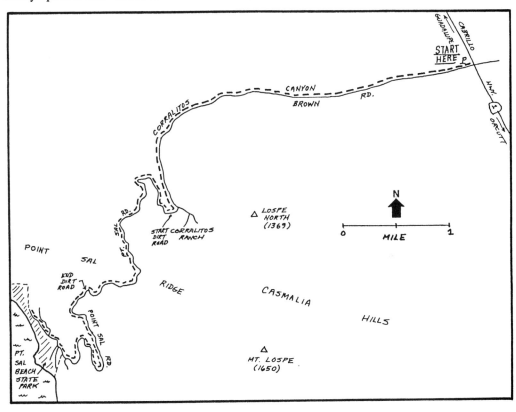

TRIP #36 - POINT SAL STATE BEACH

Corralitos Ranch looms below as the narrow path switchbacks, passes through a 20-30 yard sand patch and reaches an area with the first views of the ocean to the north. More lung-busting switchbacks lead to road sections with alternating views of Santa Maria Valley and the ocean. The grade moderates, takes a last-gasp uphill and reaches the Pt. Sal Ridge crest. A rough-road section and a "real-live" downhill follow with outstanding views of the coastal sand dunes to the north, and just beyond, a distant sight south to Vandenberg Air Force Base. A surprise (second last gasp?) uphill leads to a gate (5.8) with a "Road Not Maintained" sign, followed by a narrow, but paved, road which continues to the beach.

BICYCLE RIDES: SANTA BARBARA AND VENTURA COUNTIES

The Wild Downhill. The "Trucks Use Lower Gears" sign, which is just beyond, is an understated warning of the 2.6 miles of snaking, cannon-ball downhill which follows. The upper stretches hang cyclists out on the exposed outside curves, which offer some "interesting" drop-offs (and some beautiful coastal looks, which can only be really enjoyed by using the makeshift turnouts). A mile from the crest is an out-of-place aluminum shed where we observed a parachutist preparing for a jump. Nearer the beach, continue through some hairpin turns and move inland away from the precipitous cliffs. Several road bumps indicate earth movement in this area. In 1.7 miles from the crest is a dirt road diversion on the ocean side that leads to a fantastic coastal overlook.

Near road's end is a badly torn-up section that has to be carefully navigated. Not far beyond is a two-level parking lot which signals the end of the tour. Take time to enjoy the coastal scenery, or better yet, the beach itself. A 100-foot scramble down the steep, slightly unstable slope is required. After your break, "all" that remains is the "aerobic nightmare" ride back up to the crest and a fast runout to Hwy. 1 (27.0).

Parachutist on Point Sal Ridge

Point Sal State Beach. Few people use the beach because of the difficulties in getting there. Bathing suits are the standard, but we met a few "free spirits." We backpacked from the parking lot and found several magically scenic and secluded coves to the north (some testy rock climbing and scrambling are required if you want solitude). The overnight camping there was an unforgettable experience.

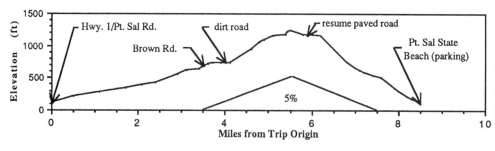

TRIP #37 - RANCHO GUADALUPE DUNES

GENERAL LOCATION: Guadalupe, Betteravia

LEVEL OF DIFFICULTY: Loop - moderate
Distance - 29.2 miles
Elevation gain - flat

HIGHLIGHTS: Two trips in one! The interesting features of the Rancho Guadalupe Dunes County Park are combined with an abbreviated tour of the western edge of the Santa Maria Valley.   The park is at the southern edge of the Guadalupe-Nipomo Dunes Preserve and offers dune walks and a visit to the Santa Maria River Estuary.   The valley ride visits the agricultural flatlands.   Thrown in for variety is the quaint little town of Guadalupe.

TRAILHEAD: From U.S. Hwy. 101, exit west on State Hwy. 166 and go 9-1/2 miles to State Hwy. 1 (Guadalupe St.).   Turn north on this road and drive one mile to 11th St.   A left turn leads to Le Roy County Park, which has old shade trees, Community Center, restrooms, grass, water, picnic tables and a children's play area.

TRIP DESCRIPTION: **Rancho Guadalupe Dunes County Park.** Cycle back into Guadalupe, admiring the quaint older architecture of this three-story limit town.   At Main St. (1.3), go west past a shopping center and bike down a sometimes-rough road that skirts the north side of an extensive agricultural area.   The dunes are immediately visible directly ahead.   In 1.4 miles from the turnoff is the gate into the dunes.   This is the southeastern edge of the Guadalupe-Nipomo Dunes Preserve; stop at the gate for a free monthly listing of the docent-lead hikes.

Pedal 2.4 miles on a winding, patchy, sand-covered road that cuts through the dunes, follows abreast of the Santa Maria River Estuary and reaches a parking area near the beach (porta-potties, no water).   Take time to enjoy a stroll along the beach, south for dune-watchers and north to the Santa Maria River outlet for bird watchers. Then jump back on your two-wheeler and return to the intersection of Hwys. 1/166 (10.8).

Guadalupe Cemetery

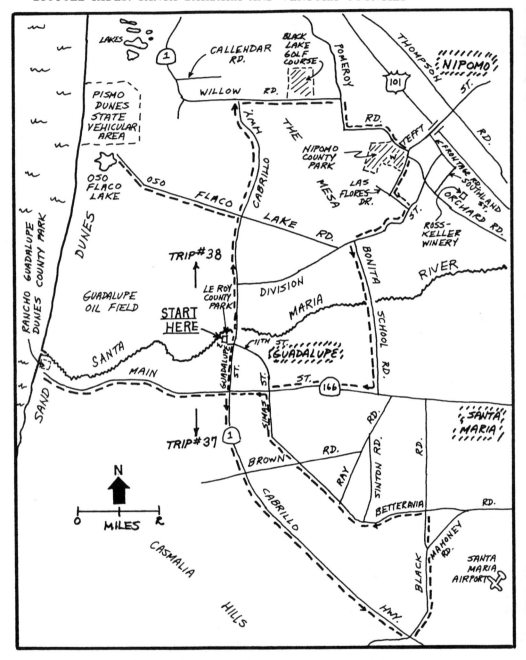

TRIP #37 - RANCHO GUADALUPE DUNES; TRIP #38 - OSO FLACO LAKE

Betteravia Loop. Cycle 8.2 miles south on Hwy. 1 along the western edge of Santa Maria Valley. Farms and open space abound to the east, while the Casmalia Hills to the west dictate the road's course. At Black Rd. the route shifts north and continues

1.9 miles past the first homes in a spell, then splits off at Mahoney Rd. (20.9). (A conscious left turn is needed to stay on Black Rd.) Pass a stand of eucalyptus trees, then bike a short downgrade--"go for it," and coast the upgrade which follows. Proceed to Betteravia Rd. and go left. The Class II road keeps west through the agricultural valley, passes the monolithic Holly Sugar Manufacturing Co. and crosses Brown Rd. Betteravia Rd. veers right in a mile and becomes Simas St. Turn west on busy Hwy. 166 and return to the Guadalupe outskirts. From the Hwy. 1 intersection, bike back through the small town and return to the park (29.2).

Santa Maria River Estuary

TRIP #38 - OSO FLACO LAKE

GENERAL LOCATION: Guadalupe, Nipomo

LEVEL OF DIFFICULTY: Loop - moderate
Distance - 27.4 miles
Elevation gain - periodic moderate grades

HIGHLIGHTS: This relatively flat ride leaves Guadalupe, crosses the Santa Maria River and visits Pismo Dunes State Vehicular Recreation Area. Allow time to explore the southern dunes and Oso Flaco Lake (by foot). The ocean visit is followed by the circuit of an out-of-place plateau above the flat agricultural valley called "The Mesa". A visit to the outskirts of Nipomo is followed by a return to the valley and a spin through Guadalupe. (See Trip #37 for tour map.)

TRAILHEAD: From U.S. Hwy. 101, exit west in Santa Maria at State Hwy. 166 and drive 9-1/2 miles to State Hwy. 1. (Guadalupe St.) Go north (right) for one mile to 11th St. (if you cross the Santa Maria River, you've gone too far). Turn left and at road's end

143

is Le Roy County Park with shade trees, Community Center, restrooms, grass, water, picnic tables and a play area.

Pismo Dunes State Vehicular Area

TRIP DESCRIPTION: To Oso Flaco Lake. Return to Hwy. 1 and pedal north on flat terrain across the Santa Maria River. Pedal 2.6 miles through farmland to Oso Flaco Lake Rd. where there are views of the coastal sand dunes to the west. The passage west on this agricultural- and sometimes sand-lined little road provides distant views of the hills. The Guadalupe Oil Fields are to the south and a nearby oil refinery to the north. At road's end is a parking lot and entry to the non-vehicular portion of the Pismo Dunes State Vehicular Recreation Area and Oso Flaco Lake (5.6).

Oso Flaco Lake Natural Area. Although part of the Pismo Dunes State Vehicular Recreation Area, it is off-limits to vehicular use. Foot trails begin at the parking lot and lead into this natural area. The Oso Flaco wetlands, creek and beach area dunes are one of the Central Coast's largest refuges for migrating shore birds and home for the least tern.

"Oso Flaco" means "lean bear" in Spanish. It was named by Gasper Portola's 1769 expedition after a grizzly bear had been shot while the group camped at the lake. (Take time out to hike the dunes as part of the tour; however, lock the bike that you must leave behind.)

On to Nipomo. After returning to Hwy. 1 (Cabrillo Hwy.), bike northward on a short steep climb to The Mesa, an out-of-place plateau with a mini-forest on its west side and a more barren landscape on its eastern extremity. (This is the largest

144

eucalyptus stand outside of Australia, and was planted for furniture use, but the wood split too easily). A passage through light rolling hills in this densely-treed area leads to a "T"-intersection and a turn east onto Willow Rd. (11.3). Bike 2.4 miles on a tree-lined road among rolling hills to road's end at Pomeroy Rd. Pass the Black Lake Golf Course with its scattered condominiums along the way. Cruise 2.4 miles through residential areas to Tefft St. on the outskirts of Nipomo. On the right is Nipomo Regional Park with grass, scattered trees, recreation fields, restrooms and water.

Return to Guadalupe. Go right on Tefft St. and glide 1.8 miles through a suburban area with scattered trees and a more rural setting. A left turn on Division St. (17.9) leads downhill where there is a wide-open view of the valley below. The street changes name to Riverside Rd. and drops to valley level, going southeast to Bonita School Rd. A beeline south takes riders through the Santa Maria River bed (flooded during storms) to Hwy. 166 (22.8). The finale is a 3.6-mile pedal through flat farmland to Hwy. 1. Continue one mile north through the City of Guadalupe to the park (27.4). Plan some time to visit the treeless, but interesting, Guadalupe Cemetery and to look over the vintage buildings within the town itself.

TRIP #39 - CUYAMA RIVER

GENERAL LOCATION: Santa Maria, New Cuyama

LEVEL OF DIFFICULTY: One way - moderate-to-strenuous
Distance - 50.4 miles
Elevation gain - moderate-to-steep grades in the
Twitchell Reservoir area

HIGHLIGHTS: Enjoy two trips in one along the winding course of the Cuyama River. No stop lights on this tour! Start in Santa Maria and explore the canyons which enclose the Twitchell Reservoir and constrain the river further eastward. The varied geology of the surrounding peaks is as interesting as the frequent glimpses into the constantly-changing face of the river plain. Near the half-way point, the terrain changes completely. The road breaks out into the broad western edge of lengthy Cuyama Valley and cuts through it below the foothills of the Sierra Madre Mountains. This is a fully Class X trip on busy highway, although the bike shoulder is adequate throughout. The one-way trip described requires a car shuttle. However, the adventure can be turned into an up-and-back century ride, with the return segment being mostly downhill.

TRAILHEAD: From U.S. Hwy. 101, exit east at Main St. (State Hwy. 166) and drive 1/2 mile to Suey Rd. Turn north and proceed 3/4 mile to Suey Park past Suey Crossing Rd. Bring 2-3 quarts of water as there are no public water sources on this trip.

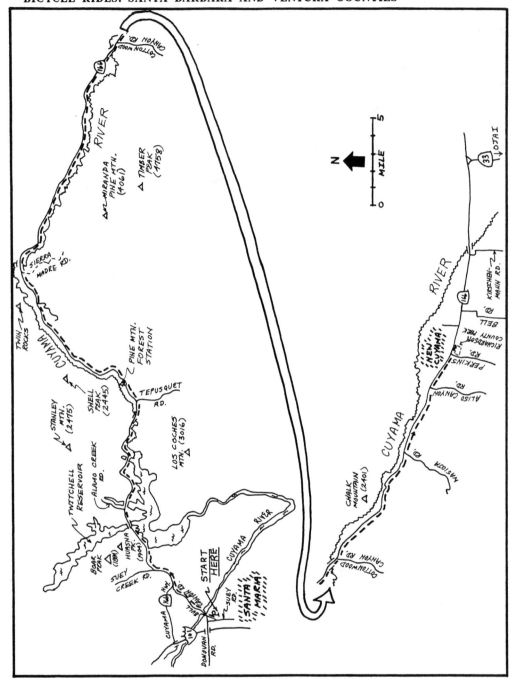

TRIP #39 - CUYAMA RIVER

TRIP DESCRIPTION: **Santa Maria to Tepusquet Road.** From the park, turn north and cross the Santa Maria River (the area floods during rains), observing the sharp mesas at the northern edge of the river. In 2.7 miles, Bull Canyon Rd. winds its way through barren hills to a dead-end at Hwy. 166, our route east. Follow the course of the Cuyama River, which works its way back and forth between Santa Barbara and San Luis Obispo Counties for the next 48 miles. A long upgrade takes you past Suey Creek Rd. to a crest in 2.4 miles. There are constant views down into the foliage near the river, which is in sharp contrast to the previous surrounding stark hills. This is a high valley surrounded by imposing peaks.

Shortly, there is the first peek at the enormous flood plain itself. The first encounter point with the Twitchell Reservoir shifts westward during rainy periods as the water level rises. Bike through the first of several sections of canyon where the road has been blasted out of the mountainsides. Cross over the Huasna River and Alamo Creek on expansive bridges and stay along the Cuyama River's north side. Beyond Alamo Creek Rd. (7.8), just before the Alamo Creek crossing, you work to a crest and roller coaster down to within 30-40 feet above river level. This is just prior to crossing the Cuyama River and reaching Tepusquet Canyon Rd. (13.8).

On to Cottonwood Canyon Road. Begin a steady, net 1000-foot, climb in 31.5 miles to reach New Cuyama. Initially, Hwy. 166 hugs the mountain contour on the river's south side, passes the Pine Mountain Ranger Station and seesaws through a narrowing canyon. The coloration of some mountains is a ribbed blend of browns and greens, a result of mixed patches of vegetation growing on the sheer mountain faces. In five miles after Tepusquet Canyon Rd., leave the narrow canyon, cross a high bridge over Clear Creek and pass below Twin Rocks and Big Rocks. These appear to be very tall rock piles built through Mother Nature's erosion process. Just past Sierra Madre Rd. (24.7) and another river crossing, bikers reach an entry to a broad plain; this is the eastern edge of the Cuyama Valley, which extends for miles to the east, and is now readily visible.

Cuyama Valley Near Cottonwood Canyon Road

Pedal on the valley's northern edge and enjoy the lush greenery of the Sierra Madre Mountains to the south and throughout the valley. Catch the shape of what looks like a mammoth flat-topped sand pile which is Chalk Mountain. Mountain views open to the distant east as you again cross the Cuyama River and reach Cottonwood Canyon Rd. (37.9).

147

BICYCLE RIDES: SANTA BARBARA AND VENTURA COUNTIES

To New Cuyama. Cycle over rolling hills and pass scattered mining operations in the badlands at the foot of the mountains to the north. Bike past Wasioja Rd. and, in four miles, Aliso Canyon Rd. which is the entry to several campgrounds on the north slopes of the Sierra Madre Mountains. Beyond are the outskirts of New Cuyama with an array of old wrecked cars along the road. This town has 1100 residents, a hamburger joint, gas station and market. At Perkins Rd., go right and bike a short distance to Richardson County Park, where your chauffeur awaits to congratulate you for completing your ride (50.4).

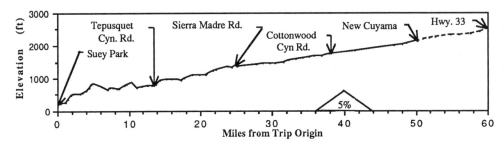

Trip Options. An easier route is to start at New Cuyama and coast back to Santa Maria. The over-achiever's choice is to ride up and back, a cool century (strenuous to very strenuous). The ride can also be continued east another ten miles to scenic State Hwy. 33.

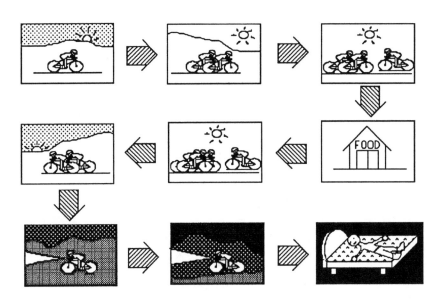

148

VENTURA COUNTY

San Buenaventura State Beach

TRIP #40 - OXNARD BIKEWAY

<u>GENERAL LOCATION</u>: Oxnard

<u>LEVEL OF DIFFICULTY</u>: Up and back - easy
Distance - 5.0 mi. (one way)
Elevation gain - essentially flat

<u>HIGHLIGHTS</u>: This short Class II trip takes a north-south slice into the City of Oxnard on quiet streets.   It is a pleasant family trip but requires crossing several stop-lighted intersections.   Highlights are Carlisle Park at the start and Community Center Park near midpoint.   An extension is to continue biking west on Bard Rd. or Pleasant Valley Rd. to Bubbling Springs Linear Park in Port Hueneme.

Community Center Park

<u>TRAILHEAD</u>: From the Ventura Fwy. (U.S. Hwy. 101) eastbound in Oxnard, go south on Oxnard Blvd. and follow State Hwy. 1. Westbounders should exit southwest at Vineyard Ave., turn south on Oxnard Blvd. and drive three miles south of Vineyard Ave. to Wooley Rd. Continue directly south on what is now Saviers Rd. (do not stay on Hwy. 1) for three miles to Hueneme Rd. Go right (west) for 0.1 mile to Courtland Ct., then turn right and continue 0.3 mile to Carlisle Park. From the L. A. area on Pacific Coast Hwy., exit at Pleasant Valley Rd., drive under the freeway for 2-1/4 miles to Saviers Rd. and turn left, then continue as above.

<u>TRIP DESCRIPTION</u>: Bike west on Clara St. and go right (north) on Class II "J" St. Parallel a fenced-in wash and pedal 0.6 mile to Bard St., which has light traffic.   This residential section is typical of the greater part of the trip.   Cruise 1.1 miles through suburbia to one of only several stop lights on the trip to Channel Islands Blvd.   (This is great for a five mile, inner-city trip!).

In another 0.4 easy-going mile, veer to the left, then pedal by W. Mark Durley Memorial Park to a stop light at Wooley Rd.   Across this street, our route mysteriously becomes Hobson Wy. and then "H" St.   In 1/4 mile, the bikeway goes through Community Center Park (recreation fields, tennis courts, restrooms, water), with the

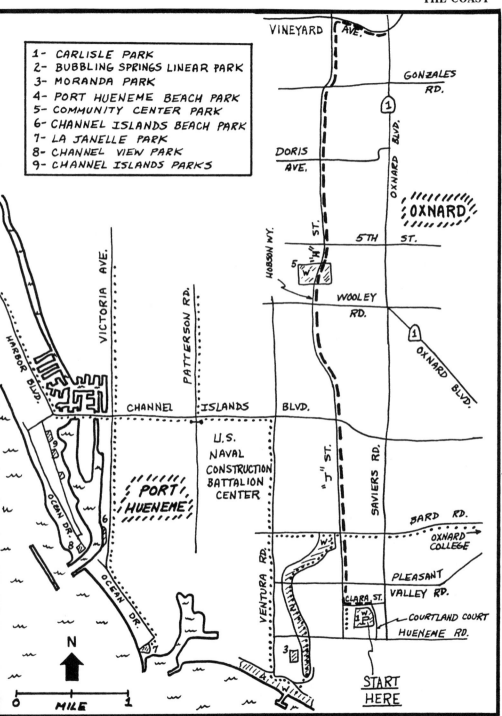

1- CARLISLE PARK
2- BUBBLING SPRINGS LINEAR PARK
3- MORANDA PARK
4- PORT HUENEME BEACH PARK
5- COMMUNITY CENTER PARK
6- CHANNEL ISLANDS BEACH PARK
7- LA JANELLE PARK
8- CHANNEL VIEW PARK
9- CHANNEL ISLANDS PARKS

VINEYARD AVE.
GONZALES RD.
OXNARD BLVD.
DORIS AVE.
OXNARD
HOBSON WY.
"H" ST.
5TH ST.
WOOLEY RD.
OXNARD BLVD.
VICTORIA AVE.
PATTERSON RD.
HARBOR BLVD.
CHANNEL ISLANDS BLVD.
U.S. NAVAL CONSTRUCTION BATTALION CENTER
"J" ST.
SAVIERS RD.
PORT HUENEME
OCEAN DR.
BARD RD.
OXNARD COLLEGE
PLEASANT VALLEY RD.
VENTURA RD.
CLARA ST.
COURTLAND COURT
HUENEME RD.
OCEAN DR.
START HERE
N
0 MILE 1

TRIP #40 - OXNARD BIKEWAY

Oxnard Civic Auditorium to the right (east) and continues through a light commercial area to Fifth St. An impressive spired church and Oxnard High School preside on opposite sides of the street (3.3). Stop and check out the small aircraft on their flight path into Ventura County Airport, which is about 1/2 mile to the west (interesting planning!).

The area returns to a more residential setting as the route passes a Buddhist Church and meets Doris Ave. Beyond is Fremont Intermediate School and Fremont Park. Another 1/2 mile brings you to the stop-lighted intersection at Gonzales Rd. and an excellent view of the foothills and mountains to the north and northwest. Bike 0.6 mile to the end of "H" St. at Vineyard Ave., where the bikeway turns right onto that Class II road. A 0.6-mile pedal on this condominium- and apartment-lined street leads to the trip's end at Oxnard Blvd. (Hwy. 1) (5.0). There is a gas station at this intersection and the large commercial Esplanade Mall 3/4 mile north (for the more ambitious or hungry). Note that Oxnard St. is a dense-traffic thoroughfare.

TRIP #41 - PLEASANT VALLEY PEDAL

GENERAL LOCATION: Camarillo, Oxnard, Point Hueneme

LEVEL OF DIFFICULTY: One way - easy; up and back - moderate
Distance - 11.3 mi. (one way)
Elevation gain - essentially flat

HIGHLIGHTS: A pleasant spin in the country, this 100% Class X ride should appeal to both casual sight-seers and serious bikers looking to get a mileage workout without a lot of traffic/lights. The wide-open and scenic segment of the trip is the ten miles between the trip's origin and State Hwy. 1. Most of this segment is on lightly-used roads with a wide-biking shoulder. Panoramas throughout include distant views of the Santa Monica Mountains to the south, Camarillo and Las Posas Hills to the north and Sulphur Mountain to the northwest.

TRAILHEAD: From the Ventura Fwy., exit at Santa Rosa/Pleasant Valley Rds. Go left at Pleasant Valley Rd., cross over the freeway, and right at the first road, Ridgeview St. Find parking within this residential area subject to posted laws. An option is to start the trip from Bubbling Springs Linear Park in Port Hueneme. Note that there is little in the way of water sources between the trip origin to beyond Hwy. 1 (9.8 miles).

TRIP   DESCRIPTION: Ventura Freeway to Camarillo Airport. Exit the residential area and turn right (south) onto the wide-bike shoulder on Pleasant Valley Rd. There are panoramic views that include the rugged northern terminus of the Santa Monica Mountains to the south; these vistas are common for the next several miles of wide-open spaces. The country road passes a stand of eucalyptus

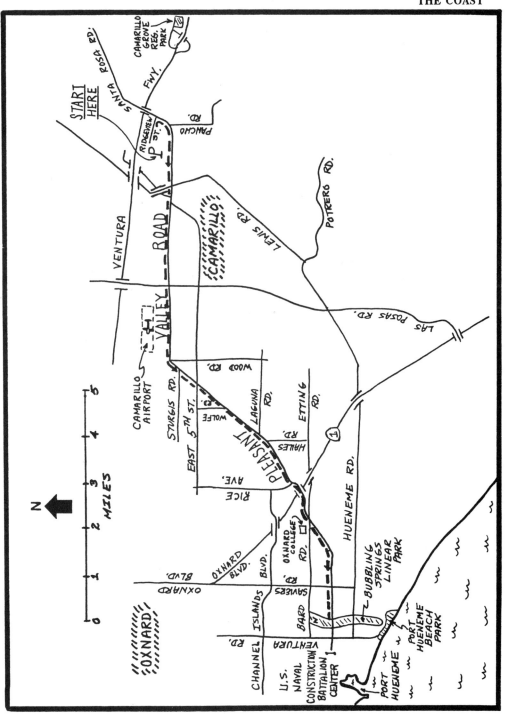

TRIP #41 - PLEASANT VALLEY PEDAL

153

trees, turns west and passes over Calleguas Creek in 1/2 mile.   Agricultural fields surround the road in this area which parallels the Ventura Fwy.

Proceed on a flat through a farming area past Lewis Rd., where there is an unobstructed view to the coast (1.4).   In 0.3 mile the road forks with Fifth St. (State Hwy. 34) and proceeds south (left); our route continues on Pleasant Valley Rd.   The bikeway narrows in 0.3 mile and goes into wide-open agricultural areas to a four-way intersection in the middle of nowhere at Las Posas Rd.   In sequence, pass Frontier High School, Eubanks St. and Freedom Park, all of which are on the southern rim of the Camarillo Airport.   The shoulder widens significantly as you return to a farming area where the road crosses Wood Rd. (4.8).

Camarillo Airport

Camarillo Airport to Highway 1.   Pleasant Valley Rd. bends southwest and, in 3/4 mile, recrosses Fifth St.   Bike over a small wash, then Wolfe Rd. and pass another eucalyptus stand while staying in wide-open farmland to Laguna Rd.   The bikeway veers slightly to the right, passes more eucalyptus trees, and continues by a trailer park and residential development.   Beyond is the intersection with Rice Rd., where you go left and follow Pleasant Valley Rd. onto the Hwy. 1 overcrossing (8.7).   Stop and enjoy the surprisingly good vista from this vantage point.

Highway 1 to Bubbling Springs Linear Park.   Once over the freeway, go left to stay on Pleasant Valley Rd. and pass a suburban area just beyond.   Pedal by Blue Gum Grove and soon meet Bard Rd., the access to Oxnard College.   Note that beyond this point, there is limited bike shoulder and traffic increases greatly in what now becomes a mixed residential/commercial area.

The route crosses Rose Ave. with the first gas station and shopping center in eons. In 1/2 mile, swing to the right, pass Cypress Rd., an older residential area, then Saviers Rd. with more stores and another gas station.   Pass "J" St. (11.3) and reach the periphery of Bubbling Springs Community Park.   Turn right and bike to the northern edge of the park for water, or in either direction for a scenic continuation.

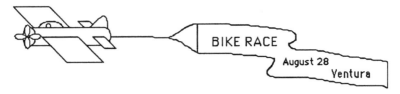

BIKE RACE

August 28
Ventura

154

TRIP #42 - PORT HUENEME BIKE ROUTE

GENERAL LOCATION: Port Hueneme

LEVEL OF DIFFICULTY: Up and back - easy
 Distance - 5.9 mi. (one way)
 Elevation gain - essentially flat

HIGHLIGHTS: A sight-seers delight, this easy-going trip is mainly on Class I/II
bikeways, with a short stint of quality Class X road along the residential Hollywood-
by-the-Sea Beach.   The flat route starts by touring four nifty parks; the path is beside
a landscaped canal.   Next comes a pedal along the edge of the U.S. Naval Construction
Battalion Center.   The finale is a tour of the scenic Hollywood-by-the-Sea Beach
which ends at the Channel Islands Harbor entrance at Channel View Park.

TRAILHEAD: From the Ventura Fwy. eastbound in Oxnard, go south on Oxnard Blvd.
and follow State Hwy. 1.   Westbound traffic should exit southwest at Vineyard Ave.,
turn south on Oxnard Blvd. and drive three miles south of Vineyard Ave. to Wooley
Rd.   Continue south on, what is now, Saviers Rd. (do not stay on Hwy. 1) 2.8 miles to
the end at Hueneme Rd.   Go right (west), travel 0.9 mile to Surfside Dr. and go left to
Ocean View Dr., and then left again.   Find beach pay parking anywhere in this area.

From the Los Angeles area on Pacific Coast Hwy., exit at Hueneme Rd.   Follow that
road 5-1/2 miles to Surfside Dr. and continue as described above.   If you miss the
turnoff and reach the end of Hueneme Rd. at Ventura Ave., follow it toward the
ocean.   It soon becomes Surfside Dr. and the fork with Ocean View Dr. is just beyond.

TRIP DESCRIPTION: **Bubbling Springs Park.**   Pedal to the end of Ocean View Dr.
and find the Class I concrete bikeway/walkway.   Take in the Port Hueneme
Beach/Pier panorama, then cross Surfside Dr. to a bridge over the canal.   There was a
small wedding ceremony at the bridge when he biked through.   Cycle along the
scenic and landscaped canal while observing the ducks and oncoming bikers, as well
as folks relaxing on the park benches.   In 0.2 mile, pedal by Moranda Park which is
across the canal.   Pass the "Bubbling Springs Recreational Greenbelt" sign which
signals that bikers are within the one-mile plus Bubbling Springs Linear Park.

The Class I path crosses Hueneme Rd. and passes through a shaded area, stays
along the canal and does a little jig-jog near Joyce Dr. (the path is clearly marked).
In 0.2 mile, cross over the canal and reach Pleasant Valley Rd. veering right to rejoin
the canal.   Across the creek is a long shaded park which gives way to larger
Bubbling Springs Community Park (recreation fields, barbecues, picnic facilities,
restrooms, water) near the north end, which stops at Bard Rd. (1.4).

U.S. Naval Construction Battalion Center.   Head left (west) onto this Class II
bikeway and ride 0.3 mile into a residential area to Ventura Rd.   Go right and proceed
on this pleasant and treed Class II stretch past the guarded entry to the Construction
Battalion Center; the Seabee Museum is inside the entrance at Sunkist St./Cutting Rd.
(2.2).   Continue alongside this facility for 1/2 mile and go left (west) at Channel
Islands Blvd.

Stay on the Class II path and bike along this highway which has a picturesque
center median complete with trees and canal.   Pass a shopping center, Patterson Rd.,
another shopping center, and a four-story skeletal building which serves as a Seabee
practice site.   Pass yet another shopping center which stretches west to Victoria Ave.
(4.0).

155

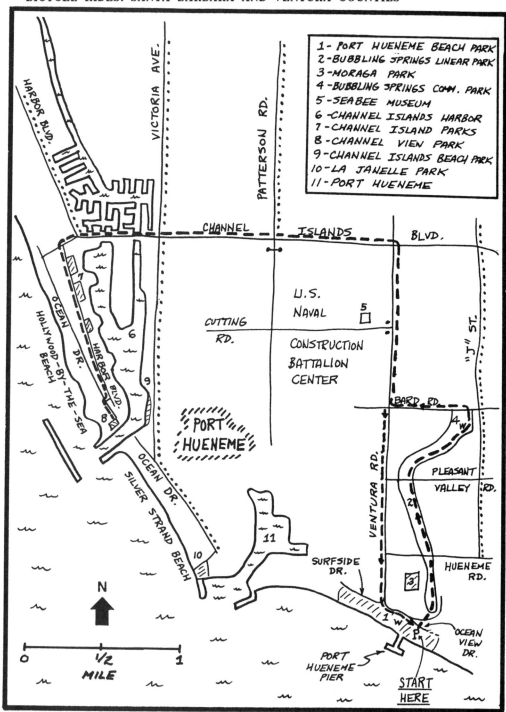

LEGEND:
1- PORT HUENEME BEACH PARK
2- BUBBLING SPRINGS LINEAR PARK
3- MORAGA PARK
4- BUBBLING SPRINGS COMM. PARK
5- SEABEE MUSEUM
6- CHANNEL ISLANDS HARBOR
7- CHANNEL ISLAND PARKS
8- CHANNEL VIEW PARK
9- CHANNEL ISLANDS BEACH PARK
10- LA JANELLE PARK
11- PORT HUENEME

TRIP #42 - PORT HUENEME BIKE ROUTE

Bubbling Springs Linear Park

Channel Islands Harbor/Hollywood Beach. The complexion of the trip changes as the road passes the northern fingers of the Channel Islands Harbor Marina, continues past the Peninsula St. turnoff and proceeds onto a bridge over the main channel. There is a great view from the bridge--close up is the harbor with its handsome homes and boats, while in a distance are the local mountains and the sea. Pass over the bridge to the junction with Harbor Blvd. A diversion right (north) leads to a 5-1/2 mile Class II scenic ride that parallels the beach and provides a wide range of natural scenery. However, the outlined route turns south on Harbor Blvd.

Follow Class X Harbor Blvd. into a pleasant seaside community, passing each of three separated portions of the small Channel Island Parks (5.2). A diversion on any street right leads to exceptional Hollywood-by-the-Sea Beach. Side trips to the inner side of the peninsula provide a view of the Channel Islands Harbor, Channel Islands Landing and U.S. Coast Guard Station. Bike 0.7 mile on the strand to the path's end at Channel View Park, a great vantage point for observing the comings and goings at the harbor entrance.

Return Trip. Retrace the route to Ventura Rd. On this side of the street, bikers can use the wide sidewalk as posted. For variety, the recommended route is to continue south on Class X Ventura Rd. beyond Bard Rd. The tour stays on a treed street, passes the Bard Memorial, Pleasant Valley Rd. and Port Hueneme Civic Center. Next on the agenda is a fast-foot outlet (a favorite place for the local Seabees, who raced by us on their one-speed, government-issue, bikes), Hueneme Rd., Surfside Dr. and a beach snack stand (5.9).

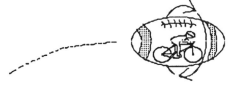

TRIP #43 - VENTURA-PORT HUENEME STRAIGHTAWAY

GENERAL LOCATION: Ventura, Oxnard, Port Hueneme

LEVEL OF DIFFICULTY: One way - moderate; up and back - moderate
Distance - 10.4 miles (one way)
Elevation gain - steady, moderate to steep upgrades
in foothills; essentially flat south
of Telegraph Rd.

HIGHLIGHTS: This is a beeline trip from the foothills to the sea on Class II Victoria Ave. The scenic variety on this short trip is mind boggling! The circuit starts in the hills at secluded Arroyo Verde Park, cruises through the Ventura City periphery, visits the wide-open spaces east of Oxnard, and winds up at the Silver Strand Beach, where there are incredible beaches, parks and the Channel Islands Harbor Marina. The full up-and-back ride is a credible workout because there are some steep upgrades in the northern-most section.

TRAILHEAD: From the Ventura Fwy., exit at Victoria Ave. and drive north 2.2 miles to Foothill Rd. Go left (west) for 0.7 mile to Day Rd., then turn right into Arroyo Verde Park (modest entrance fee with restrooms, water, barbecues, picnic facilities, hiking trails). From the Los Angeles area, follow State Hwy. 1 to the Ventura Fwy. (road sign says "Ventura" direction). In 2.0 miles, exit at Victoria Ave. and continue as above. From the Santa Paula Fwy., exit north on Victoria Ave. and drive one mile north to Foothill Rd. Continue as described above. There are scattered commercial water sources, but little in the way of public sources on this trip.

The trip can be done in reverse, starting from the Silver Strand area. This option makes more sense if an "up-and-back" trip is planned, since it puts the hardest part of the trip (the foothills) in the middle of the tour.

Free Spirit at Arroyo Verde Park

TRIP DESCRIPTION: **City of Ventura.** Exit the park and pedal down Class II Day Rd. on a moderate downhill that becomes steep. Turn left (east) at Telegraph Rd. and

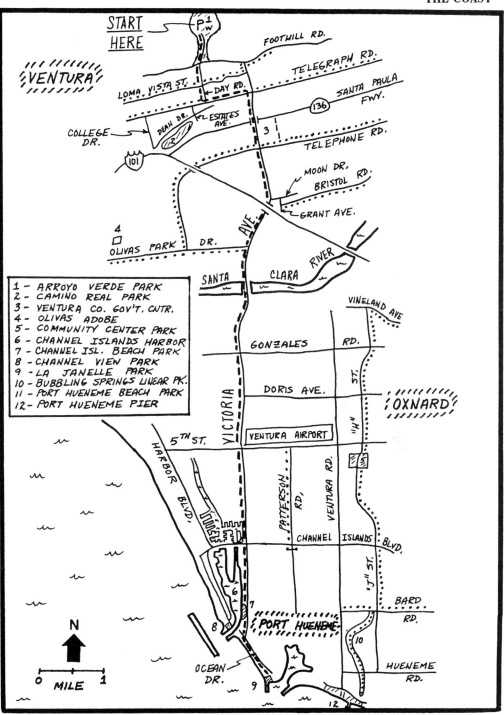

START HERE

VENTURA

FOOTHILL RD.

TELEGRAPH RD.

LOMA VISTA ST. — DAY RD.

SANTA PAULA FWY.

136

COLLEGE DR.

DEAN DR. — ESTATES AVE.

TELEPHONE RD.

3

101

MOON DR.
BRISTOL RD.

GRANT AVE.

4
OLIVAS PARK DR.

AVE.

SANTA CLARA RIVER

VINELAND AVE.

1 – ARROYO VERDE PARK
2 – CAMINO REAL PARK
3 – VENTURA CO. GOV'T. CNTR.
4 – OLIVAS ADOBE
5 – COMMUNITY CENTER PARK
6 – CHANNEL ISLANDS HARBOR
7 – CHANNEL ISL. BEACH PARK
8 – CHANNEL VIEW PARK
9 – LA JANELLE PARK
10 – BUBBLING SPRINGS LINEAR PK.
11 – PORT HUENEME BEACH PARK
12 – PORT HUENEME PIER

GONZALES RD.

DORIS AVE.

OXNARD

VICTORIA

VENTURA AIRPORT

"H" ST.

5TH ST.

HARBOR BLVD.

PATTERSON RD.

VENTURA RD.

CHANNEL ISLANDS BLVD.

"J" ST.

BARD RD.

6

7

8

PORT HUENEME

10

OCEAN DR.

9

HUENEME RD.

12

N

0   MILE   1

TRIP #43 - VENTURA - PORT HUENEME STRAIGHTAWAY

cruise through a treed, country-like, residential area. This Class II road follows some minor curves and has a mild upgrade prior to Victoria Ave. Go right (south) on the Class II route and enjoy a clear view west to the coast.

Follow a short steep downhill and, in 0.2 mile, cross Telegraph Rd. (gas station). Bike past Buena High School and cross over the Santa Paula Fwy. Another short downhill leads into a light commercial area past Telephone Rd.; the structures and impressive grounds of the Ventura County Government Center are at this intersection (2.1). Cruise through a mix of residential/commercial areas, passing Ralston St. and an area near Walker St. with a gas station and a group of eateries. Then follow a passage under the Ventura Fwy. (2.8).

Long-distance Biker's Favorite Fruit (Victoria Ave.)

Wide-Open Spaces. On the south side of the freeway, the route passes Valentine Rd. and starts an uphill to a bridge over the Southern Pacific railroad tracks; there is an exceptional view of the nearby cities from this raised platform. Cruise into an agricultural area past Olivas Park Dr. and pedal by some "fragrant" horse pastures. Victoria Ave. crosses a bridge over the Santa Clara River where cyclists are treated to another panoramic view. (4.1).

Continue on the flat past a eucalyptus grove, Gonzales Rd. and an area that is filled with acres of hothouses. Beyond is the Victoria Tree Farm (Christmas trees), Ventura County Airport, Fifth St., and Wooley Rd. (7.2). There are many newer housing developments here. The bike lane striping is very light here, but what counts is that the bike shoulder is wide. In 1/2 mile, the trek passes a gas station at Hemlock St.

Port Hueneme/Silver Strand. In a short distance is Channel Islands Blvd., where the northern end of the Channel Islands Harbor Marina is visible to the left (west). In succession, pass the Channel Islands Landing and Yacht Club, Jack's Landing, along with the U.S. Coast Guard Station and Harbor Administration Bldg. There is a mini-beach within Channel Islands Beach Park, which is a local favorite

(9.2), and a nice site for a overlook of the harbor with views out to the Channel Islands.

Ocean Drive at Channel Island Harbor Entrance

Beyond Island View Ave., veer left where the route becomes Class X Ocean Dr. (light traffic and reasonable bike room). Pass beside the Silver Strand beachfront community (read that as "Sardineville"). To the right are successive street accesses to the Silver Strand County Beach; this is a wide, pristine beach with a great view to the Channel Islands. Continue for roughly one mile until the road ends near a point at the entry to La Janelle Park (follow the dirt road to the west) (10.4). At this terminus is a tiny rustic tavern which is a local favorite brew stop.

TRIP #44 - VENTURA BIKEWAY SYSTEM

<u>GENERAL LOCATION</u>: Ventura

<u>LEVEL OF DIFFICULTY</u>: Loop - moderate
Distance - 16.6 mi. (loop)
Elevation gain - periodic moderate grades in foothills;
essentially flat below Telegraph Blvd.

<u>HIGHLIGHTS</u>: This mostly Class II "looper" provides a taste for the variety within the Ventura Bikeway System. Throughout the trip, the rider sees many bikepath spurs off the described route. Start in the Ventura Harbor area, visit the western portion of the City of Ventura, including the agricultural outskirts near Saticoy, and

161

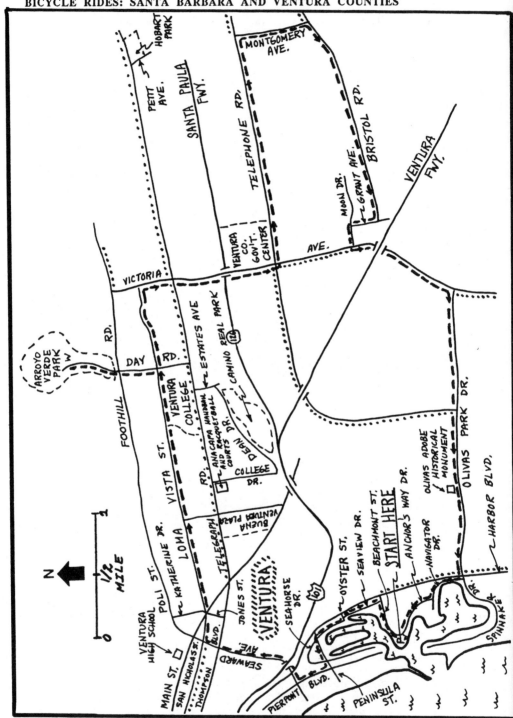

TRIP #44 - VENTURA BIKEWAY SYSTEM

traverse the wide-open spaces west of Oxnard on the return leg. The permutations and combinations of routes within the system are large; bikers are encouraged to explore other options besides the route explained.

TRAILHEAD: From the Ventura Fwy., exit at Victoria Ave., go left (west) and pass under the freeway, continuing 3/4 mile to Olivas Park Dr. Drive 2-1/2 miles to Harbor Blvd., cross this street which is now called Spinnaker Dr., and go to Navigator Dr. Turn right, travel 1/3 mile to Anchors Way Dr., then turn right again, driving 1/2 mile to the parking area near the boat ramp. Do not park in the areas reserved for cars with boat trailers. There are public and commercial water sources scattered along the bike route.

TRIP DESCRIPTION: **Ventura Harbor.** From the parking area, turn left on Anchors Way Dr. and pedal through the suburban area. The street name becomes Beachmont St. and meets Seaview Ave. just short of returning to Harbor Blvd. Go left (north) and pass a mini-beach (read that as a "sliver of sand"), and continue to road's end at Oyster St. Turn left, then look for the nearby turn to the right on Seahorse Ave. Skirt the residential marina at the northernmost end of the harbor. Pedal 0.2 mile to Peninsula St., turn left and then right in 0.3 mile at Pierpont Blvd. Beeline north through more beachfront environs 0.2 mile to Seaward Ave. (gas station, restaurant).

Ventura City, West. Go right (away from the coast) and follow the busy Class II road across the Southern Pacific tracks. Pass busy Thompson Blvd. in 0.4 mile and continue to quieter San Nicholas St. (2.5). Turn right and follow San Nicholas St. through the residential/light-commercial area 0.3 mile to S. Katherine Dr. Jog north, cross busy Main St. and continue to Loma Vista St.

The Foothills. Start a moderate uphill in 1/2 mile and pass the grounds of the Ventura County General Hospital. The grade crests in 0.3 mile above N. Mills Rd. Stay in the residential area and pass N. Ashwood Ave. after a short downgrade. Appearing at this point are the large open fields enclosing Ventura College, followed by several campus entries. At Day Rd., the Class II route turns left and follows a steep 0.1 mile upgrade; this levels somewhat and continues to a crest at Foothill Rd. (5.1).

Continue across this road to Arroyo Verde Park, an interesting and grassy space nestled within the hillsides (restrooms, water, shade, playground, barbecues). Return to Day Rd. and Loma Vista St., going left (east) on the latter street. Bike through the treed rural/residential setting on several uphill curves and turn right at Victoria Ave., where there is a view to the coast. Bike a steep 0.1 mile downhill which levels somewhat for 0.2 mile before reaching Telegraph Rd. (gas station). Pass Buena High School and cross over the Santa Paula Fwy. Follow a short downhill into a light-commercial area to Telephone Rd., with the grand structures and impressive grounds of Ventura County Government Center (7.6).

The Western Segment. Turn left at Telephone Rd. where the path is on the sidewalk (per bike signs). The bikeway returns to the street shortly. Follow an easy upgrade through a commercial/industrial zone, pass Johnson Dr. and head into a more wide-open industrial space. Pedal by an open agricultural area in 1/2 mile and enjoy the far-reaching hill and mountain views. After Kimball Rd., with a gas station (9.0), continue through citrus orchards and meet Montgomery Ave. in 1/2 mile.

Go right (south) and cruise 0.6 mile on this palm-treed, lightly-used rural road on a downgrade to Bristol Rd. This Class II street (with narrow shoulder) continues through agricultural fields with views to the south/southwest, where the taller city

View from Channel Islands National Park
Observation Tower (Spinnaker Dr.)

buildings are seen. Ride through more citrus groves past the Saticoy Lemon Association building, Johnson Dr. and return to a suburban area, then coast on a downhill past a gas station and convenience store to the end of Bristol Rd. Turn right onto Class X Grant Ave., bike an uphill to Moon Dr., turn left and pedal to Victoria Ave. (12.3).

The Wide-Open Return Segment. Turn left (south) and pedal to the nearby Ventura Fwy. Prior to this at Walker St. are a gas station and, on the other side of Victoria Ave., a group of eateries. On the south side of the freeway, pass Valentine Rd. and begin an upgrade to a bridge over the Southern Pacific tracks; there is an exceptional view of the nearby cities from here. Ride through farming areas to Olivas Park Dr. (13.2).

Turn right (west) and continue into open farmland past a eucalyptus stand, then begin an upgrade which goes through more citrus groves. Pass the Telephone Rd. terminus, Olivas Park Golf Course, Olivas Adobe Historical Site, and bike in open spaces to Harbor Blvd. Cross Harbor Blvd. to what is now Spinnaker Dr., go right at Navigator Dr., right again in 0.3 mile at Anchor's Way Dr., then bike 0.5 mile to the parking area (16.6).

164

TRIP #45 ▫ VENTURA HARBOR TOUR

<u>GENERAL LOCATION</u>: Ventura

<u>LEVEL OF DIFFICULTY</u>: Loop - easy
                                Distance - 17.0 miles (loop)
                                Elevation gain - essentially flat

<u>HIGHLIGHTS</u>: This jim-dandy tour visits the full periphery of the Ventura Harbor on an excellent Class II bikeway.   Highlights are visits to both the southern and northern points of the main channel outlet.   The south side boasts of scenic Channel Islands National Park and Marina Cove Play Area, while the northside provides Marina Park and the North Jetty.   As if this wasn't enough to boggle the senses, the route is extended to include a Class I tour north to the Ventura Pier and Ventura Promenade.

<u>TRAILHEAD</u>: From the Ventura Fwy., exit at Victoria Ave., go left (west) and pass under the freeway, then drive 3/4 mile to Olivas Park Dr.   Travel 2-1/2 miles to Harbor Blvd., cross this street now called Spinnaker Dr., and head for Navigator Dr. Turn right, drive 1/3 mile to Anchors Way Dr. and turn right in 1/2 mile to the parking area near the boat ramp, with restrooms and water.   Do not park in areas reserved for cars with boat trailers.   There are public/commercial water sources scattered along the route.

San Buenaventura State Beach

<u>TRIP   DESCRIPTION</u>: **South Ventura Harbor and Channel Islands National Park.**   After enjoying the harbor view, bike to Anchors Way Dr. and go right (south).   Pass Schooner Dr. and pedal to the end at Navigator Dr.   Head right 0.2 mile and check out the harbor dredges docked at road's end.   Backtrack along Navigator Dr. and head toward the harbor to a small walkway/bikeway on the harbor's edge. Pass a shopping center with a U.S. Post Office and follow the Class I path as it turns right (south).

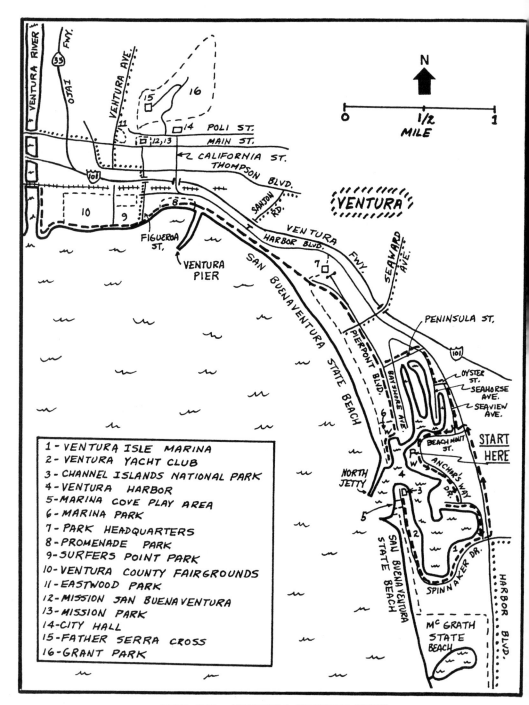

1 - VENTURA ISLE MARINA
2 - VENTURA YACHT CLUB
3 - CHANNEL ISLANDS NATIONAL PARK
4 - VENTURA HARBOR
5 - MARINA COVE PLAY AREA
6 - MARINA PARK
7 - PARK HEADQUARTERS
8 - PROMENADE PARK
9 - SURFERS POINT PARK
10 - VENTURA COUNTY FAIRGROUNDS
11 - EASTWOOD PARK
12 - MISSION SAN BUENAVENTURA
13 - MISSION PARK
14 - CITY HALL
15 - FATHER SERRA CROSS
16 - GRANT PARK

TRIP #45 - VENTURA HARBOR TOUR

Bike to Navigator Dr. which ends at Spinnaker Dr. Bear right onto a Class II road that winds by the Ventura Harbor Village (with a market) on the harbor side and sand dunes on the ocean side. Hike up the dunes anywhere in the next mile to enjoy San Buenaventura State Beach and views of the Channel Islands. The road wanders by the Bay Queen Harbor Cruises entry, Ventura Yacht Club and a deli (2.1).

Beyond is the Channel Islands National Park with a 360-degree lookout perch atop the park's building. Views of the ocean, beaches, Channel Islands, Ventura Harbor and the distant mountains are great! After a few revs on the return route, pass the Marina Cove Play Area (a little nook sheltered by the breakwater and home for sunbathers, swimmers, windsurfers and jetty explorers).

North Ventura Harbor and Marina Park. Return to the intersection of Spinnaker and Navigator Drs. and follow the former street to Harbor Blvd. Cruise north on the treed Class II path to Beachmont St. and turn left (west) (4.4). Bike through a residential area and then right in 0.1 mile at Seaview Ave. The bikeway skirts the marina edge by following a zig-zag route: 0.3 mile on Seaview Ave., left on Oyster St. for 0.1 mile, right on Seahorse Ave. for 0.2, mile and left on Peninsula St. for 0.3 mile to its terminus at Pierpont Blvd. (5.5).

Go left and pedal into a beachside residential area 0.3 mile to Marina Park. Bike through this popular park, staying to the harbor side, where there is a super view of the entire harbor. Ride toward the ocean and pass the small sailing ship that has "run aground" in the park's sand. Beyond is the route out to the North Jetty; there may be a limited stretch which is buried in sand. At the jetty's end is a magnificent view of the coastline (also views of wondrous "natural" objects on the nearby San Buenaventura State Beach) (6.3).

Beach Bikeway Near Ventura Pier

Ventura Pier and Ventura Promenade. Backtrack to Peninsula St. and pedal north on Pierpont Blvd. to Seaward Ave. (gas station and restaurant to the right). Cycle on Pierpont Blvd. 0.3 mile as it crosses San Pedro St. and enters a park area within the San Buenaventura State Beach complex. The route transitions from Class II road to Class I bikepath and veers toward the beach. Follow the path down a palm-treed section; there is a parking entry and shaded picnic area (water) nearby. Beyond is a segment with sand dunes piled high on the ocean side. Take some time to enjoy the panoramic view from the top of the dunes (8.1).

Transition to an open area with the Ventura Pier seen ahead, as well as a view to Port Hueneme. Bike on a small bridge over a wash, pass another parking lot and stay on the Class I path under the Ventura Pier. The path heads toward the Ventura Fwy., loops back toward the ocean and passes the landmark Holiday Inn. The crowded mall-like bikeway/walkway here is known as the Ventura Promenade. The path cruises by several shops, a restaurant (get a seat near the big picture window), a rocky clamming area and a hotel swimming pool on the promenade itself. The promenade ends after crossing the road access to the beachfront parking at Figueroa St. (9.4).

Trip Terminus. The Class I bikepath returns to the beach, passes Surfer's Point Park and the Ventura County Fairgrounds. Soon it veers north along the Ventura River, passes under the Ventura Fwy. and reaches the end point at Main St. (11.0).

Return Trip. Backtrack to Seaview Ave. and Beachmont St. At the intersection, go right toward the ocean on Beachmont St., follow the curving road as it becomes Anchors Way Dr. and return to the start point in another 1/2 mile (17.0).

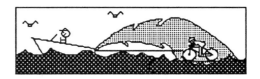

TRIP #46 - VENTURA TO OJAI

GENERAL LOCATION: Ventura, Ojai

LEVEL OF DIFFICULTY: **Ventura Avenue Tour:**   Up and back - easy
                          Distance - 3.5 miles (one way)
                          Elevation gain - essentially flat

                          Ventura to Ojai: Loop - moderate
                          Distance - 24.5 miles (loop)
                          Elevation gain - periodic moderate grades

HIGHLIGHTS: The Class II Ventura Ave. tour explores the western edges of Ventura on the highway leading to Ojai. The bikeway offers scenic views of the hillsides both north and west, as well as a tour through the historic part of town. The key features of the trip are its access to such interesting sites as the Ortega Adobe, City Hall, San Buenaventura Mission, and Ventura County Historical Museum.

The Ventura to Ojai loop is a fun country spin. Varied scenery includes small forests, open countryside, river bottomland, rolling hills, farmland and quaint towns. Most of the tour is on less-traveled Class X roads, but there is a busier part in the Mira Monte area. Trip options are to take a "gut-buster" ride up Casitas Vista Rd. to an overlook of Lake Casitas, or bike to an easy, 8.5-mile, Class I spur trip on the Ojai Valley Trail.

TRAILHEAD: From the Ventura Fwy., exit at California St., turn north and proceed 0.2 mile to Santa Clara St. Go right (east) and drive one block past Chestnut St. to free parking along the road, next to Plaza Park. There are water sources at the park along the route.

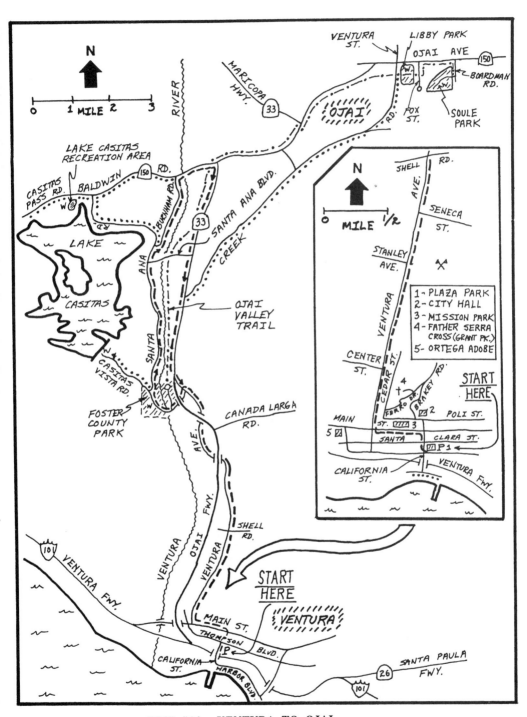

TRIP #46 - VENTURA TO OJAI

BICYCLE RIDES: SANTA BARBARA AND VENTURA COUNTIES

TRIP DESCRIPTION: Inner City. Bike west on Santa Clara St. past Plaza Park (shade, restrooms, water, picnic facilities) and pedal 0.2 mile to California St. Turn right (north) and enter the historic section of town by going left at Main St. There are several diversions at this point. Just north on California St., at the Poli St. intersection, is the elegant City Hall, with its classic Spanish design (adorned in front with a statue of Father Junipero Serra). For insanely mad bikers, divert west 0.1 mile from City Hall on Poli St. and bike up very steep and winding Brakey Rd. to Grant Park--the 360-degree views from here are awesome!! This is the site of the Padre Serra Cross.

Meanwhile, back to the reference route. Stay on Main St. past the entrance to Mission Park and Mission San Buenaventura at Figueroa Plaza. Main St. has a multitude of older, classic commercial buildings. Pass Valdez Alley and the entrance to Eastwood Park, followed by the Ventura Ave. intersection (0.8).

Ventura Avenue Above Main Street. Cycle north on a narrow bike shoulder (on what locals call "The Avenue") into a commercial/ residential area that widens later on a clearly-marked Class II bikepath. Long-distance views of the hills are straight ahead, with close-up looks of the hills below Grant Park to the right (east), which improve over the next mile.

San Buenaventura City Hall

Bike through this older part of town past Center St.; the population density wanes and keeps dropping after leaving the city proper (1.3). In 0.9 mile is Stanley Ave. with a gravel operation at road's end. Ride through a more rural area amid orchards to Seneca St. (2.6). Reach an area near Dakota Dr. in 0.4 mile that overlooks the Ojai Fwy. Though the sign notes the end of the bikepath, the striped wide shoulder continues 0.9 mile on the valley floor beside the freeway. There are scattered industrial plants, homes and a row of small hills to the left (west). In 3.5 miles from the trip's origin near Shell Rd., the bike shoulder disappears. This is the turnaround point for the Ventura Ave. tour.

North to Santa Ana Road. Continued pedaling returns you to a residential area. Pass a small market near Holt St. and return to open country and citrus groves. Pedal under the Ojai Fwy. and enjoy the lush northern end of the valley. Pass under the freeway again and, in 1/2 mile, reach Casitas Vista Rd. Head left (west), pass under the freeway a third time, and cross a bridge over the Ventura River. The next tree-lined 0.4 mile leads to Santa Ana Rd. and the northern edge of wooded Foster Park (restrooms, water, barbecue facilities, overnight camping) (6.7).

Note that there is a 4.2-mile, round-trip, diversion to an impressive Lake Casistas overlook that can be taken by staying on Casitas Vista Rd. The trip to the overlook is on a tree-lined, winding rural road. Besides the grand vista, there are restrooms, water and a reasonable chance to see dozens of hawks perched atop the dam levee. The bad news is the trip to the overlook is one steady and tough uphill with a very steep 1/2-mile grade before reaching this scenic spot.

Grant Park/Father Serra Cross

Santa Ana Road to Highway 150. For this reference ride, go right (north) on Santa Ana Rd. and bike on narrow, lightly-used, Class X road into the wooded countryside. In a mile, a hillside provides a perch for viewing the Ventura River drainage and surrounding hills. Past is a moderate uphill where the road goes east and follows a steep downhill with a clear view into the river bottomland. Return north and pass through farmland, reaching Santa Ana Blvd. and a market. Burnham Rd. is reached in 0.1 mile. Go right through a rural community past Riverside Rd., then return to open country and a modest uphill. Just beyond is Baldwin Rd. (State Hwy. 150) (11.9). (A more scenic, but more difficult, option is to continue north on Santa Ana Rd. Refer to Trip #62.)

Highway 150 and the Return Segment. Turn right (east) and cross the Ventura River, passing into the southern reaches of Meiners Oaks. Then turn right on State Hwy. 33. (An option is to bike a mile further on Baldwin Rd. to the Ojai City limits.) Bike on busy Class X road or use the parallel Class I Ojai Valley Trail (it ends in 5.4 miles at Foster Park, as described below). Pass a commercial area with several fast-food outlets and a liquor store, and follow along a tree-lined road through Mira Monte.

Pedal into a less-developed area with views of the Ventura River bottomland. Enter the City of Oak View, coast downhill through the commercial part of town, passing Oak View Ave. (15.4) and then Larimer Ave. Enjoy a somewhat steep and winding downhill into a canyon, pass Creek Rd. and bike a flat at river level. Cycle into pleasant Casitas Springs and enjoy the shade of the overhanging trees. Pass a market, tackle a short uphill, then proceed downhill into a treed canyon area and

171

Ojai Valley Trail

pass Casitas Vista Rd. Return by backtracking along Ventura Ave. (24.5).

Trip Option- Ojai Valley Trail. From the north edge of Foster Park is a great Class I, 8.5-mile, side excursion sandwiched between State Hwy. 33 and the Ventura River. Segments of the trail have scenic views of the river drainage and the Santa Ynez Mountains beyond. The northbound ride is mainly uphill with a few hundred feet elevation gain, primarily occuring in the Foster Park-Baldwin Rd. area. The Class I trail ends at Fox St. in Ojai. However, the trip can be extended by biking a two-mile flat route through Ojai on wide-shouldered Ojai Ave. (Hwy. 150). The destination is Soule Park, which has shade, restrooms, picnic facilities, recreation fields and the ever-present tennis courts.

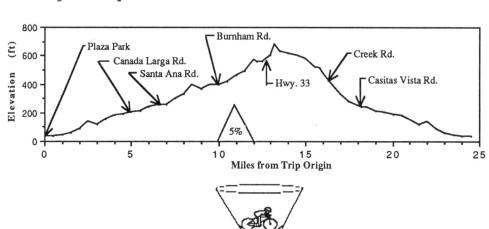

TRIP #47 ᵒ VENTURA TO SANTA BARBARA

GENERAL LOCATION: Ventura, Carpinteria, Santa Barbara

LEVEL OF DIFFICULTY: One way - moderate; loop - strenuous
Distance - 63.1 (loop)
Elevation gain - periodic moderate grades

HIGHLIGHTS: This mainly Class II trip is a scenic delight! Most of the tour follows the Pacific Coast Bicentennial Bike Route. Leave the Surfer's Point Park area, cruise into Emma Wood State Beach County Beach on the Class I coastal trail, ride the old Rincon Hwy., then join Hwy. 101 and zig-zag on a variety of frontage roads to Santa Barbara. The vistas are superb and as varied as the mix of bikeways. A highlight is the scenic and restful Chase Palm Park near the trip's end. A warning--the on-freeway portion is dangerous, especially for inexperienced or non-attentive bikers!!

TRAILHEAD: From the Ventura Fwy., exit at California St., drive south toward the ocean to road's end and go right at Harbor Blvd. Motor 0.2 mile to Figueroa St. and turn left to the parking lot of Surfer's Point Park. Bring a filled water bottle or two, since there are long and exposed sections of bikeway. Gas stations in the Montecito-Santa Barbara area seemed less than excited about directing bikers to water sources.

TRIP DESCRIPTION: **Ventura to Faria County Park.** Follow the Class I beachfront bikepath right (west) past the Ventura County Fairgrounds. In 0.4 mile, meet the Ventura River, turn north, pass under Hwy. 101 (Ventura Fwy.) and meet Main St. in 0.1 mile. Bear left (west) and proceed over a bridge that crosses the river. At this point, there are views into the inland hills and, just beyond, glimpses out to the Channel Islands. Bike along the tree-lined street as it goes under the freeway and meets the southern entry of Emma Wood State Beach County Park (1.6) (restrooms, water, overnight campsites).

Surfer's Point Park

Pedal the Class I brush-surrounded path as it hugs the coast above the railroad tracks and below the freeway, where there are inspiring ocean views. In one mile, pass a small recreational vehicle camping area and fuse with the Old Coast Hwy. along the beach. Bike this Class II path along the coast to Emma Wood State Beach County Park. There are portable restrooms along the sea wall here

(3.7). (It must be exciting to be in one of these "throne rooms" when the waves are breaking!) The view north takes in Solimar Beach and Pitas Point, with distant views northwest to the mountains.

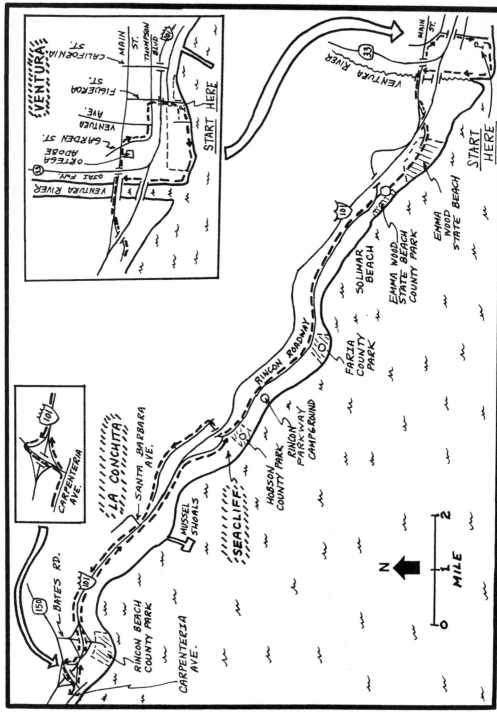

TRIP #47 - VENTURA TO SANTA BARBARA (Southern Segment)

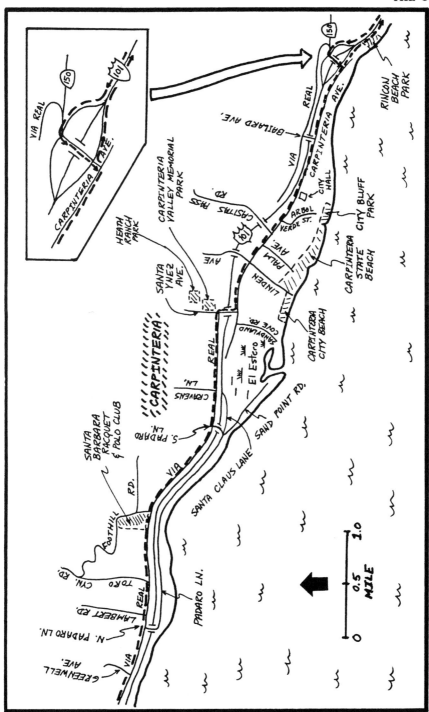

TRIP #47 - VENTURA TO SANTA BARBARA (Middle Segment)

TRIP #47 - VENTURA TO SANTA BARBARA (Northern Segment)

Follow the straightaway road past the residential area at Solimar Beach. The road curves west, passes a surfer's cove and a beach entry, then cruises by Pitas Point with its row of beach-hugging homes (6.9). Pass one more beach entry and, in 1/2 mile, reach the turn-off to Faria County Park.

Faria County Park to Highway 150 Turnoff. The road becomes the Rincon Rdwy. along this flat beachside stretch of bumper-to-bumper recreational vehicles where more porta-potties dot the landscape. There are great views along the coastline as you pedal by Hobson County Park (9.4), the homes of Sea Cliff, and the coastal oil rigs--"eight little rigs all in a row." A short distance beyond is the spot where a bug flew into Don's ear (a long story)!

Pedal to Rincon Beach Park Dr., go under the freeway, turn left (north) at a "T"-intersection and pass a fire station and an area with oil drilling equipment. Bike to road's end and follow a small bikepath along the Ventura Fwy., which fuses with the freeway in 0.2 mile (11.6). (There is a wide striped shoulder in this and all other freeway biking on this trip. Do not stray outside the marked area!) Back to the south are two piers in the Punta Gorda area.

Cruise by one of our favorite hotels, the Cliff House (with an inviting swimming pool and gorgeous sunsets), and enjoy the view north to the Santa Ynez Mountains. Beyond is a direct access road to Santa Barbara Ave. and La Conchita (gas station). Pedal another two miles, with the cars whipping by, to the Bates Rd. exit. Follow the roller-coaster off-ramp to the on-ramp on the north side of Bates Rd. (bikers must exit). In 0.8 mile, exit at the State Hwy. 150 off-ramp, pump a testy uphill to that road and turn left (west) (15.2). Cruise 0.2 mile to the frontage road above the beach. Left (south) is a workout upgrade to a vista point, to the right is the reference route.

View From the Cliff House

Highway 150 Turnoff to Lookout Park (Summerland). Follow little-used Carpinteria Ave. past Bailard Ave. There is a spectacular overlook at the western terminus of this road. Bike on the marked Class II downhill runout past the

BICYCLE RIDES: SANTA BARBARA AND VENTURA COUNTIES

Carpinteria City Hall. Cruise through the commercial city center past Arbol Verde St., Casitas Pass Rd. and Palm Ave. (entry to Carpinteria beaches) (17.7). The road then passes a quaint little market across the road from a stately Spanish-styled hotel.

Soon after is Santa Ynez Ave., where you go right and use the pedestrian/biker walkway to cross over Hwy. 101 (as noted on the signpost). Once over the bridge, head left at Via Real and cross a smaller bridge over Santa Monica Creek. (Do not turn right into the Class I path that follows the creek.) Stay on the frontage road past Santa Monica Rd. (last gas station for a spell), pass another market in 0.3 mile, and bike into a wide-open agricultural area with several scattered nurseries. Via Real passes a lovely hedgerow which opens to reveal the fields of the Santa Barbara Polo and Racquet Club (21.2).

Head into a treed, rural suburban area, pass Ocean View Ave., continue through citrus groves and start a moderate uphill near Lambert Rd. The upgrade peaks shortly and bikers are greeted with the first views of Santa Barbara. Pass Greenwell Ave., the Summerland Market, Nugget Saloon and Grill (outdoor dining under umbrellas), rustic Stocky's Seaside Restaurant and reach Evans St. (23.7). A diversion at this point is to travel under the freeway (south) to reach Lookout Park, a rest spot with a coastal overlook. Another possibility for cyclists seeking a greater challenge is to continue north up and over Ortega Hill Rd. However, our route keeps west along the frontage road to the freeway on-ramp.

"Contemplation" at Chase Palm Park

Lookout Park (Summerland) to Santa Barbara. Bike onto the freeway and pump up a short testy upgrade. In 1/2 mile, exit as required at Sheffield Dr. Go right to stay north of the freeway and find N. Jameson Ln. Turn left and follow this frontage road on a nice downhill runout past Hixon Rd., San Ysidro Rd. and Olive Mill Rd. Cross the latter road and follow what is now Country Village Rd. alongside a gas station and the Spanish-styled Montecito Inn. Pedal through this treed, stylish and low-key commercial area and pass a shopping center. Beyond is Hot Springs Rd. and another gas station (26.9).

Cruise to Country Village Rd. in 0.1 mile, turn left and follow the road under the dual freeway overpasses. Cross Los Patos Wy. and bike alongside the beautiful hill-surrounded lagoon and Andree Clark Bird Refuge. Stay on the pleasant 1/2-mile cruise along the lagoon and cross Ninos Dr., at the site of the elegant Santa Barbara Sheraton Hotel. Cruise 0.3 mile to Milpas St. and cross over to East Beach along the palm-tree lined Chase Palm Park (water, restrooms) and enjoy the harbor views. Within the next 1/2 mile are a collection of shaded, scenic rest spots. In 0.9 mile, cross the bridge over a small lagoon and pass the lengthy Stearn's Wharf, car traffic and all (30.6). Pedal through a parking lot and pass the Breakwater Restaurant.

Cruise through another parking lot that leads to a Class I path and pass the Sea Cove Cafe, complete with an umbrella-lined veranda. Bike past yet another parking area to Loma Alta Dr. In 0.2 mile is a pretty palm-treed beach area with views of the bluffs to the north and east. The bikepath ends at this turnaround point (31.8).

The Return Trip. Head back to the north end of the lagoon at Los Patos Wy. and turn right (east). Follow the Class II path beside the Santa Barbara Cemetery. Make a sharp right turn where the road becomes Channel Dr. Pedal uphill to a super-scenic coastal overlook as the road goes downhill along the coast and passes the lovely grounds of the Biltmore Hotel (36.5). Curve left and, in 0.3 mile, cross the freeway to N. Jameson Ln.

Follow this frontage road 0.4 mile to San Ysidro Rd., cross back over the freeway and cruise another 0.3 mile to the entrance. Bike onto Hwy. 101 and, in 0.8 mile, face a testy 0.3-mile uphill to a crest with unobstructed Channel Islands views. Cruise 0.2 mile to the next off-ramp (Evans St.) and exit, passing next to Lookout Park. Retrace the incoming route to Hwy. 150 and reenter the southbound freeway. Exit at Sea Cliff Dr. (Rincon Beach Park Dr.) and go right (south) onto the coastal road. Continue retracing the incoming route, going right onto the little Class I path where the old highway curves inland (59.8).

Return to the bridge over the Ventura River. As an option to the outgoing ride, stay east on Class II Main St. Once across the bridge, bike below the freeway, pass the Ortega Adobe and a shopping center and go right at Garden St. Follow the Class II road as it curves left and meets Ventura Ave. In 0.2 mile, on what is now Thompson Blvd., turn right at Figueroa St. and go under the freeway to the trip's origin (63.1).

Scenic Option. On either outbound or inbound segments, divert to Padaro Ln., a frontage road south of Hwy. 101. Santa Claus Ln., with a unique set of stores, is just west of S. Padaro Ln. and there is a particularly nice residential greenbelt here.

Biking   Worldwide

BICYCLE RIDES: SANTA BARBARA AND VENTURA COUNTIES

TRIPS #48A-48C - PACIFIC COAST HIGHWAY

The entire tour described follows the Pacific Coast Bicentennial Bike Route. The early part traverses Hueneme Rd. from Bubbling Springs Linear Park to Navalair Rd., a distance of 4.9 miles. The remainder hugs the coastline and follows Pacific Coast Hwy. (PCH) to an outlet in Santa Monica. The total 44.3-mile trip, which is mapped below, is a strenuous one-way shot and a very strenuous up-and-back trip.

Trip #48A, the easiest segment, is on wide, striped road shoulder. (Class II bike route, but not marked with bike signs.) On this portion, bikers visit the agricultural Ventura County countryside, Pt. Mugu and Sycamore Cove. Trip #48B is on a comparable road and is the most naturally scenic; it is also one mean roller-coaster ride! This tour visits Leo Carillo Beach, Pt. Dume and Malibu. Trip #48C is mostly flat, but on a conjested roadway with limited bike shoulder over long stretches. There are, however, many coastal views, plus the bonus of touring through Malibu, Topanga Beach and Santa Monica.

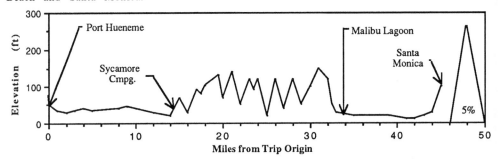

TRIP #48A - PCH: PORT HUENEME TO SYCAMORE COVE

GENERAL LOCATION: Port Hueneme, Point Mugu, Sycamore Cove

LEVEL OF DIFFICULTY: One way - moderate; up and back - moderate
Distance - 13.7 miles (one way)
Elevation gain - periodic moderate grades

HIGHLIGHTS: The northern segment along PCH starts at Port Hueneme Beach Park and cruises Hueneme Rd. through open farmland, passes along the Pacific Missile Test Center, meets Pt. Mugu and follows along the scenic coast to its end at Sycamore Cove Campground. Tour through a mix of scenic areas on a variety of road classes; the trip highlight is the scenic coastal section from Pt. Mugu to Sycamore Cove Campground, which is primarily Class II or on a marked road with a wide shoulder.

TRAILHEAD: From the Ventura Fwy. eastbound in Oxnard, travel south on Oxnard Blvd. and follow State Hwy. 1. Westbound traffic should exit southwest at Vineyard Ave. and go south on Oxnard Blvd. for three miles to Wooley Rd. Stay south on what is now Saviers Rd. (do not stay on Hwy. 1) 2.8 miles to its end at Hueneme Rd. Turn right (west) and drive 0.7 mile to Surfside Dr., bear left to Ocean View Dr. and then left again. Find pay beach parking anywhere in this area.

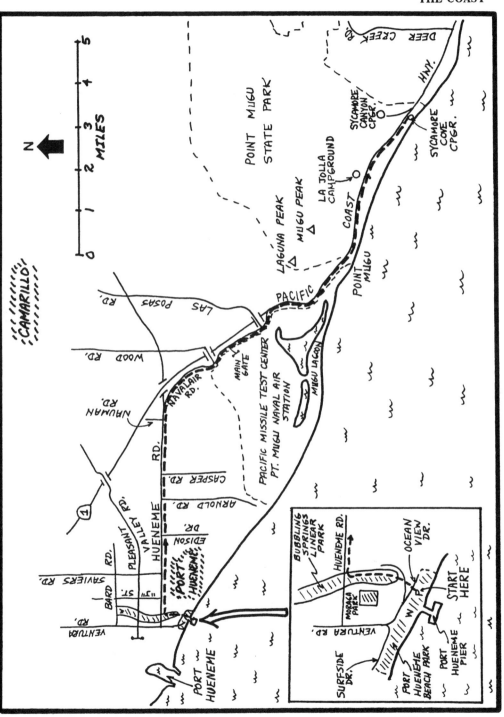

TRIP #48A - PCH: PORT HUENEME TO SYCAMORE COVE

BICYCLE RIDES: SANTA BARBARA AND VENTURA COUNTIES

From the Los Angeles area on PCH, exit at Hueneme Rd., drive 5-1/2 miles to Surfside Dr. and continue as described above. (If you reach the Hueneme Rd. terminus at Ventura Ave., follow that road toward the ocean; it becomes Surfside Dr. at the fork with Ocean View Dr.)

Water sources are scattered at the parks along the way, although the first segment is limited to public water only at the beginning and end.

TRIP DESCRIPTION: **Port Hueneme.** Bike to the end of Ocean View Dr. and link up with the Class I concrete bikeway/walkway. Follow this path through Bubbling Springs Linear Park along the landscaped canal. The first major intersection is Hueneme Rd. with great views of the mountains to the east from this area. Go right (east) on this Class X road into a mixed residential/light-commercial area past Saviers Rd. and Edison Dr. (1.8), then pedal into an open farming area. Enjoy the expansive views here as the narrowing bike shoulder will demand more attention later.

Bike on a country road through a farming area to where the road signs indicate off-ramps to both Navalair Rd. and the Hwy. 1 Fwy. (4.9). Go right on Navalair Rd. just west of the freeway and stay on the Class II route that parallels this highway. Pass Wood Rd., the Pt. Mugu missile model display, Pacific Missile Test Center/Pt. Mugu Naval Air Station main gate (6.6), and cycle on a narrowing road. The curving road, which is fenced on both sides, reaches its end at Las Posas Rd. Enter the freeway on-ramp (southbound) and bike a few hundred yards to where the freeway ends. Welcome to Pacific Coast Hwy.!

Beach at Point Mugu

Point Mugu to Sycamore Cove Campground. Pass over Calleguas Creek, which lets out at the Mugu Lagoon. Cross under electronic tower-bedecked Mugu Peak (8.6), proceed on a moderate uphill and meet a scenic point overlooking the marshlands of the lagoon. There is a striped shoulder here that continues through most of the remaining trip.

Pass a rifle range (10.2), a gravel turnout area, and continue into a blasted-out area of hillside that is Pt. Mugu itself. Once up to and through these portals, great ocean/mountain views open up to the south. Meander along the land-side cliffs about 20 feet above the ocean, passing several scenic locations on the beach. Shortly, pass the beach at the La Jolla Canyon outlet. At this point are rock-strewn La Jolla Canyon Beach and La Jolla Canyon Campground (water) (12.2).

Continue along the beach and pass a giant sand dune that nature has built up along the hillside (kids go nuts here!). Start a steady uphill that reaches a summit in 0.6 mile. Pass Sycamore Grove Campground in 0.2 mile and a thin sandy beach (13.7) with water, restroom and ranger station. This is a relaxing rest stop before returning to Port Hueneme or continuing south.

TRIP #48B - PCH: SYCAMORE COVE TO MALIBU LAGOON

GENERAL LOCATION: Sycamore Cove, Leo Carillo Beach, Pt. Dume, Malibu

LEVEL OF DIFFICULTY: One way - moderate to strenuous;
up and back - strenuous
Distance - 20.1 miles (one way)
Elevation gain - continuous moderate-to-steep grades

HIGHLIGHTS: This is the roller-coaster portion of PCH, rich in hills and breathtaking scenery. Leave Sycamore Cove and pass near Leo Carillo State and Zuma County Beaches, Point Dume and Malibu, ending at Malibu Lagoon State Beach. The hills are many and varied in challenge, with the entire workout on a wide-striped bike shoulder. A round-trip provides, what appears to the eye, to be two distinct trips. Why did God make hills? Knowledgeable bikers explain, "So bikers can stand up and pump, thereby awaking their backsides!"

TRAILHEAD. From the Ventura Fwy. eastbound in Oxnard, go south on Oxnard Blvd. and follow State Hwy. 1. Westbound traffic should exit southwest at Vineyard Ave. and turn south on Oxnard Blvd. Follow Hwy. 1 to the ocean for three miles past Pt. Mugu to the Sycamore Cove Campground. From the Ventura Fwy. in the San Fernando Valley, exit south at Westlake Blvd., which becomes Decker Rd. (State Hwy. 23), and motor to the coast. Turn right (west) and proceed 12 miles to the campground. Comply with all parking signs. There are several scattered, but reliable, water stops on this challenging trip.

TRIP DESCRIPTION: **Sycamore Cove to Leo Carillo State Beach.** Leave the Sycamore Cove Campground and begin a steep uphill that passes around a land point in 1/2 mile (great way to start a trip!). The road has a wide striped shoulder that continues for the remainder of the trip. Bike a milder upgrade with exceptional views of the ocean and land points south. Follow the sea cliffs on the inland side past a coastal access, with parking and a wading beach.

The route runs east about 20-30 feet above the beach, follows a 0.1-mile moderate uphill and meets another coastal access at Deer Creek Rd., an area with more

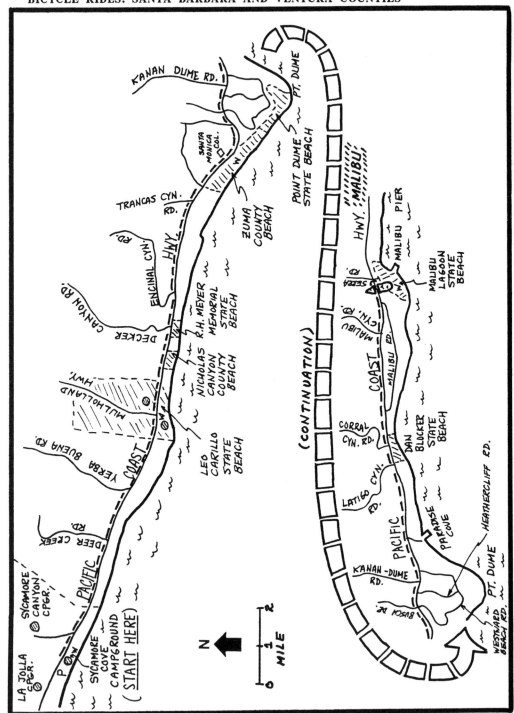

KANAN DUME RD.

PT. DUME

SANTA MONICA COL.

TRANCAS CYN. RD.

POINT DUME STATE BEACH

HWY. MALIBU

ZUMA COUNTY BEACH

MALIBU PIER

HWY.

ENCINAL CYN. RD.

DECKER CANYON RD.

R.H. MEYER MEMORIAL STATE BEACH

MALIBU LAGOON STATE BEACH

SERRA RD.

NICHOLAS CANYON COUNTY BEACH

MULHOLLAND HWY.

MALIBU CYN. RD.

COAST

(CONTINUATION)

LEO CARILLO STATE BEACH

YERBA BUENA RD.

MALIBU RD.

CORRAL CYN. RD.

DAN BLOCKER STATE BEACH

LATIGO CYN. RD.

DEER CREEK RD.

HEATHERCLIFF RD.

PARADISE COVE

PACIFIC

SYCAMORE CANYON CPGR.

KANAN-DUME RD.

PT. DUME

COAST

BUSCH DR.

WESTWARD BEACH RD.

LA JOLLA CPGR.

PACIFIC

SYCAMORE COVE CAMPGROUND
(START HERE)

N

2

1
MILE

0

excellent views down the coast. Cruise a medium upgrade cresting in 0.3 mile and pass yet another coastal access. Pedal through the rolling hills and arrive at Yerba Buena Rd. in 0.4 mile. Beyond is a long upgrade which passes Tonga St. in a lightly-populated area (3.6). In 0.4 mile, reach a crest about 100-200 feet above the ocean, with superior views southward along the coastline (notice how bike book authors rarely look back!?). Cross the L.A. County Line, as the road flattens for a stretch, then begin a steep downhill that returns to sea level at Leo Carillo State Beach (restrooms, water).

Leo Carillo State Beach to Trancas Beach. Pass Mulholland Hwy. in 0.2 mile, start a steep 1/2-mile upgrade before leveling off, and pass Nicholas Canyon County Beach. Cruise by the Malibu Ride and Country Club, start a steep downhill and stare directly into another testy upgrade. Reach Decker Canyon Rd. before starting this uphill. Beyond the crest is a pocket of expensive beach homes, a turnoff to La Piedra State Beach (7.8) and, in 0.2 mile, Encinal Canyon Rd. and a surrounding area of rolling hills.

Pass within view of a monolithic estate on the ocean side, cruise by the El Matador State Beach turnoff and begin a steep downhill. There are more spine-tingling coastal views on PCH as you continue to follow the teeter-totter up again, pass more scattered hillside homes and head back downhill. Follow an overdue long and flat stretch, passing Trancas Canyon Rd. and the Trancas Beach turnoff (gas station) (10.4).

Malibu Lagoon

Trancas Beach to Paradise Cove. Pass the local marina, Malibu Yacht Club, Trancas Creek and Morningside Dr. (turnoff to Santa Monica College). Next is an entry to wide and sandy Zuma County Beach (restrooms, water), which also provides access to out-of-the-way Pt. Dume State Beach. Pass Westward Beach Rd. and cycle a long workout uphill to the Corral Beach turnoff (gas station). This heart-throbbing grade crests near Heathercliff Rd. (gas station); Pt. Dume and Dume Cove are

accessible here.   Head back downhill past Kanan-Dume Rd. to Paradise Cove Rd.
Paradise Cove and Pier are accessible from this road (14.0).

Paradise Cove to Malibu Lagoon.   Too much downhill can spoil a person!   The
road stair steps back uphill, reaching a crest with a view of distant Santa Monica.
Pass Geoffrey's Restaurant (bring your Rolls!), and free-wheel downhill and start a
steep uphill at Escondido Rd.   Next, roller-coaster a steep downgrade past Latigo
Canyon Rd. to a flat at Corral Canyon Rd. (gas station).   Pass the entrance to the
Malibu Beach RV Park and begin a long steep upgrade.   From the summit, the view
back to the north is breath-taking! (17.8).

Pass John Tyler Dr. and the large, grassy frontal grounds of the Pepperdine
College hillside campus.   Head uphill and level at Malibu Canyon Rd. (18.9).   Proceed
downhill into a residential area past Webb Hwy. (gas station), Malibu Country Mart
and Cross Creek Rd.   Nearby is Serra Rd., the Malibu Lagoon State Beach and the ride's
terminus (20.1).   Before returning or heading onward, tour the beach, Malibu Lagoon
and don't forget to visit the Malibu Lagoon Museum.

Helmet   No Helmet

TRIP #48C - PCH: MALIBU LAGOON TO
SANTA MONICA

GENERAL LOCATION: Malibu, Topanga Beach, Santa Monica

LEVEL OF DIFFICULTY: One way - moderate; up and back - moderate
                                     Distance - 10.5 miles (one-way)
                                     Elevation gain - periodic moderate grades

HIGHLIGHTS: Another excellent scenic stretch of PCH, this busy portion of the
Pacific Coast Bicentennial Bike Route is short on bike room, but long on fantastic
views, landmarks and sight-seeing attractions.   Don't bike this if you are nervous
about sharing the road with speedy traffic.   The mostly flat route starts at cozy Malibu
Lagoon State Beach and passes near such points of interest as Las Flores Beach, Big
Rock, Topanga State Beach, Will Rogers State Beach, J. Paul Getty Museum, Santa
Monica State Beach and Palisades Park.   There are also numerous exploratory
adventures that can be taken from this 10.5 mile Class X tour.

TRAILHEAD: From the Ventura/Oxnard area, there are two basic choices.   One
scenic option is to exit the Ventura Fwy. in Oxnard on State Hwy. 1 south to the ocean.
Drive 23 miles to Malibu Lagoon State Beach (about one mile past Malibu Canyon Rd.).
The second option for both Ventura County and San Fernando Valley residents is to
exit the Ventura Fwy. (U.S. Hwy. 101) south at Las Virgenes Rd. (becomes Malibu
Canyon Rd.) and proceed nine miles to the coast.   Turn left (east) and drive one mile
to Malibu Lagoon State Beach.   Park in the Serra Rd. lot (pay parking) or on PCH.

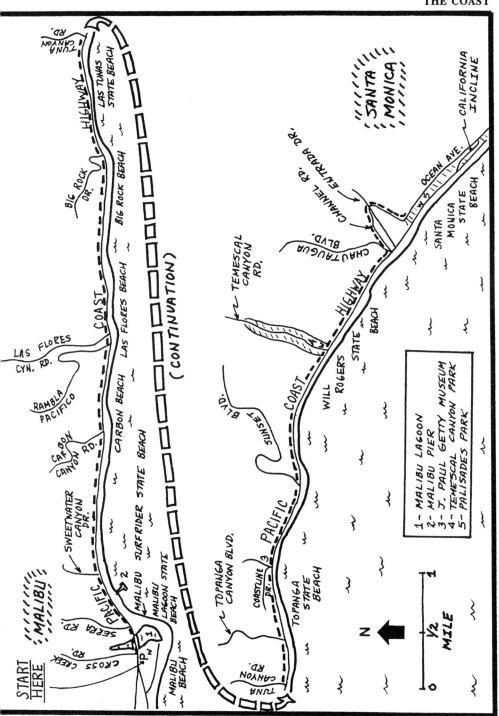

TRIP #48C - MALIBU LAGOON TO SANTA MONICA

BICYCLE RIDES: SANTA BARBARA AND VENTURA COUNTIES

Bring a filled water bottle. There are a few public water sources and scattered commercial sources. Bring a second bottle if you want to squirt water at non-yielding drivers (just kidding!).

TRIP DESCRIPTION: **Malibu Lagoon State Beach to Topanga State Beach.**
Leave the beach, go right (east) on PCH and pass the ocean-side tide pools and land-side Malibu Lagoon. Beyond is the Malibu Lagoon Museum and Malibu Pier. Go by the Malibu Inn in 0.3 mile and enter an extended area with limited bike shoulder and heavy traffic. Pedal by the La Salsa Tacos El Carbon Restaurant with a giant Mexican caricature on the roof). Cruise through a residential area with stop signs at every intersection (quite a change from the two prior segments). Pass Carbon Canyon Rd. and a lovely mixed hillside/seaside residential site. Down the road is Rambla Pacifico (gas station) and a commercial area. Pass Las Flores Canyon Rd. on still-narrow bikeway and the waterfront Moonshadows Bar and Restaurant, one of our personal favorites (3.9).

Pier View Cafe & Cantina

In 0.3 mile, the highway passes below homes built to the edge of the palisades, crosses Big Rock Rd. (periodic slides here), and continues on the winding path along the coast. In less than 1/2 mile, near another slide area, is one super view of the Santa Monica area coastline. The coastal tour continues past Topanga Canyon Blvd. and Topanga State Beach (5.9).

Topanga Canyon State Beach to Santa Monica. PCH rounds a bend where you are treated to another quality view of Santa Monica and the bay, then pass the Chart House Restaurant (another favorite) in an area with many residences upon the imposing coastal palisades. Follow a moderate uphill to Coastline Rd. and the entrance to the J. Paul Getty Museum (6.7).

188

In 0.6 mile of seaside riding, pass Gladstones 4 Fish at Sunset Blvd. (gas station) and enter another one-mile long slide area. Nearby is the northern portion of the Will Rogers State Beach (bikepath, restrooms, water) and Temescal Canyon Rd. To the north is shady and inviting Temescal Canyon Park (water, picnic facilities). The Santa Monica skyscrapers are seen in 1/2 mile with a breath-taking long-distance, view across the bay to the Palos Verdes Peninsula. The biker is completely at the mercy of the car traffic in this busy area, as there is almost no shoulder. Use extreme caution!

Down the home stretch, PCH goes under the north end of Palisades Park (path entry from Chautauqua Blvd. and Corona Del Mar) and reaches Santa Monica State Beach. This is a nice rest stop before turning around and heading back. With just a little more pain and adventurism, you can turn inland at Chautauqua Blvd., make an immediate right onto Channel Rd. and follow that street 0.3 mile on a moderate upgrade to Entrada Dr. Bike a steeper uphill to Ocean Ave., make a hairpin turn and another very-steep uphill 0.3 mile to Santa Monica's magnificant Palisades Park (restrooms, water, shade and superb scenic ocean views) (10.5).

TRIP #49 - COASTAL "CENTURY"

GENERAL LOCATION: Ventura, Port Hueneme, Pt. Mugu, Pt. Dume, Malibu

LEVEL OF DIFFICULTY: Up and back - very strenuous
Distance - 48.9 miles (one way)
Elevation gain - periodic moderate to steep grades (PCH south of Sycamore Grove Campground)

HIGHLIGHTS: This fantastic coastal trip becomes a "century" ride when taken as an up-and-back trek, provided that the biker takes at least one short diversionary trip. Suggestions for fun diversions arc Ventura Harbor and Channel Islands National Park, McGrath State Beach, Channel Islands Harbor, Pt. Dume and Malibu. The coastal scenery is excellent and a short inland countryside segment is added. The route is primarily Class II/III with wide biking shoulder.

TRAILHEAD: From the Ventura Fwy. (State Hwy. 101), exit at California St., go south towards the ocean and turn right at road's end at Harbor Blvd. Drive 0.2 mile to Figueroa St. and head left to the parking lot at the beach. Bring 2-3 filled water bottles. Century riders are not prone to make many water stops.

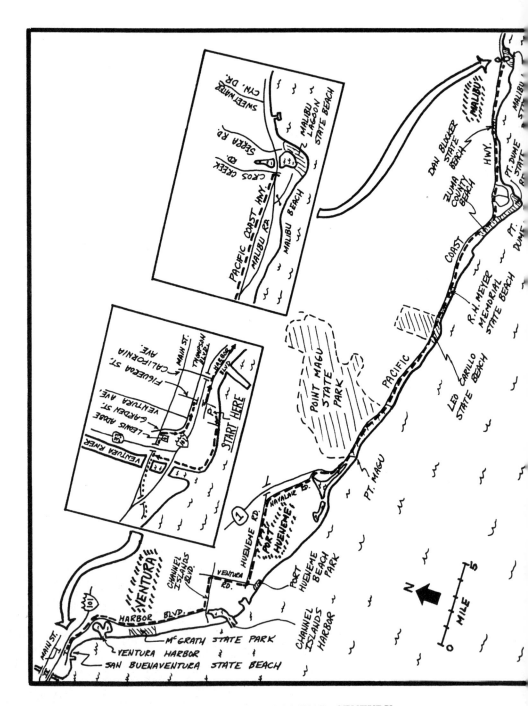

TRIP #49 - COASTAL CENTURY

TRIP DESCRIPTION: **Warmup Loop.** From the parking lot, pedal west on the Class I bikepath along the beach; the path curves north beside the Ventura River and reaches Main St. Turn right and follow Class II Main St. past the Ortega Adobe. Turn right at Garden St. and follow this road as it curves left and meets Ventura Ave. Bike another 0.2 mile on what is now Thompson Blvd., head right again at Figueroa St. and cycle under the freeway to Harbor Blvd. (1.8). See the insert of the Trip #47 (Southern Segment) map for this warmup loop.

Ventura to Port Hueneme. Turn left at Harbor Blvd., bike south past Seaward Ave., Spinnaker Dr./Olivas Park Dr. (5.6), McGrath State Beach, Gonzales Rd., W. Fifth St. and head left at Channel Islands Blvd. (11.0). This part is on a flat Class II path with scenic variety, both inland and coastal. See the maps for Trips #42 and #45 for additional details.

Follow Channel Islands Blvd. to Ventura Rd., turn right (south) (13.0) and bike 1.9 miles to Hueneme Rd. This segment is covered in the Trip #42 map. Bear left to Bubbling Springs Linear Park (15.1). Follow the map information on Trip #48A **(Port Hueneme to Sycamore Cove)** (add 13.7 miles) and Trip #48B **(Sycamore Cove to Malibu Lagoon)** (add 20.1 miles). The total one-way trip length is 48.9 miles, making the up-and-back a "cool century" if a short diversion trip is taken.

TRIP #50 - AGOURA HILLS LOOP

GENERAL LOCATION: Agoura Hills, Thousand Oaks

LEVEL OF DIFFICULTY: Loop - moderate
Distance - 8.7 miles (loop)
Elevation gain - periodic moderate grades

HIGHLIGHTS: This pleasant loop goes by several parks up to the base of Conejo Ridge, cruises through some scenic "outback," coasts down Lindero Canyon Rd. and returns through the heart of the City of Agoura Hills. The route has little traffic and is mainly on Class II bikeway; the Class X portion has a wide bike shoulder. This path can be combined with the North Ranch Loop (Trip #53) to add a myriad of options.

TRAILHEAD: From the Ventura Fwy., exit north at Kanan Rd. Drive 3/4 mile to Thousand Oaks Blvd., turn right and head 1/3 mile to Argos St. Go right again to reach Chumash Park (grass, some shade, restrooms, water, playgrounds, recreation fields).

TRIP DESCRIPTION: **Kanan Road.** Cruise 0.4 mile back to the intersection of Thousand Oaks Blvd. and Kanan Rd. Bear right (north) on Kanan Rd. and head uphill on a Class II path (cars are parked within the painted strip). Pass a shopping

191

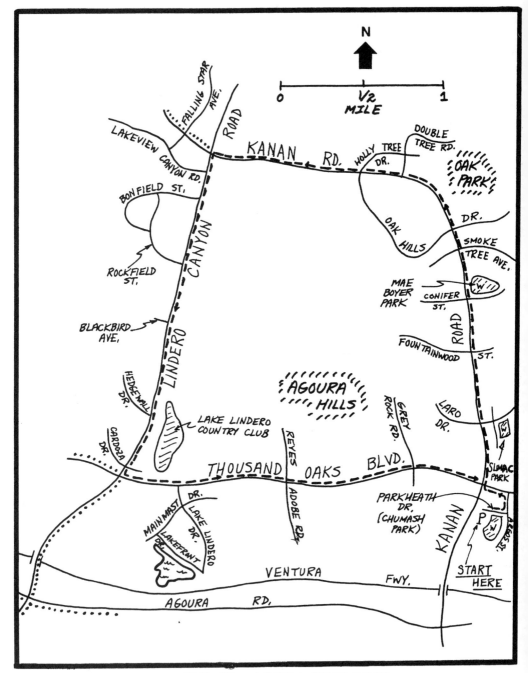

TRIP #50 - AGOURA HILLS LOOP

center to the left and cycle to a crest near Laro Dr. To the right is Sumac Park with restrooms, water, picnic area, barbecues and some shade. Cruise into this residential area taking in the views of the hills directly ahead. The path is free of cars here. Pedal an easy uphill to Fountainwood St., reach a flat and stay on a moderate grade that peaks near Conifer St. (1.6). On the right is Mae Boyer Park (locked restrooms, water, tennis courts, playground, some shade). That's it for parks, folks--it's "tough-it-out" time from here!

Bikepath Along Medea Creek

Start uphill again through this suburban area to reach the top of a grade in 0.3 mile. A few spins of the pedal take you to Smoke Tree Ave. and an upgrade into a thinning residential area. Near Oak Hills Dr, the road levels and begins to swing left. The curving road passes Oak Park High School going west; the hills to the north below the Conejo Ridge are sparsely developed. Head downhill to a flat near Holly Tree Dr. where the marked bikepath ends (the shoulder remains wide). Next is a moderately-steep upgrade which reaches a crest in a small flat area, rounds a bend and greets the biker with a view into a small valley with scattered homes. A short moderate-to-steep uphill follows. Continue through this residential area and meet Lindero Canyon Rd. (4.1).

Lindero Canyon Road. Go left (south) and stay on the Class X, wide-shouldered road to Lakeview Canyon Rd. Head between a set of small hills to Rockfield St. and climb a mild uphill with an easy downgrade where the road flattens and reaches Hedgewall Dr. The path transitions to Class II in a high-density residential area on a tree-lined street, then returns to Thousand Oaks Blvd. (gas station) (6.2).

Thousand Oaks Boulevard. Turn left (east) on the Class II path on a busier road proceeding into Agoura Hills. Peek at the Santa Monica Mountains to the south and follow a downhill past a shopping mall on rolling hills past Lake Lindero Rd. (6.5); Lake Lindero is 1/2 mile to the south. Pass through another high-density residential area beyond Reyes Adobe Ave. and, in 0.3-mile, pedal a moderate uphill to a crest with views of the hills to the east. Coast downhill to Grey Rock Rd. with hillside homes sprinkled on both sides. Stay on the roller-coaster ride until the road flattens near Kanan Rd., pass this junction to Argos St. and return to Chumash Park (8.7).

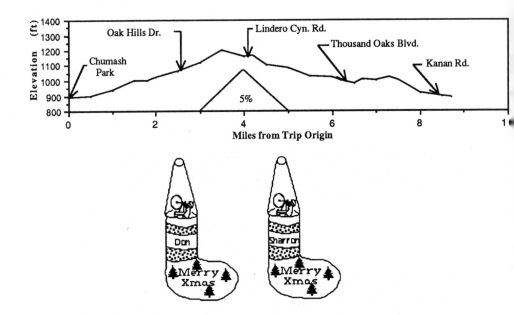

TRIP #51 - WESTLAKE VILLAGE TOUR

GENERAL LOCATION: Westlake Village

LEVEL OF DIFFICULTY: Loop - easy
Distance - 9.2 miles (loop)
Elevation gain - periodic moderate grades

HIGHLIGHTS: This easy-going Class I/II trip is centered around Westlake Lake. The tour begins in a cleverly-planned neighborhood, travels across the Ventura Fwy. into the Woodland Hills business and shopping area, then proceeds along the southern edge of lovely Westlake Lake. The return segment transits areas with a few light-rolling hills. There are several marked diversion routes throughout the Westlake Village locale.

TRAILHEAD: From the Ventura Fwy., exit northbound on Westlake Blvd. and drive 1/2 mile to Cascade Ave., the next left turn exit beyond Thousand Oaks Blvd. Go left (west) and head down Cascade Ave. to the end across from a school and Russell Park.

TRIP DESCRIPTION: Southbound-Westlake Lake. Leave the cul-de-sac and go left on Cascade Ave. 0.4 mile to North Westlake Blvd. Head right (south) on the Class II bikepath across Thousand Oaks Blvd. Stop and enjoy the many vistas into the surrounding hills and Santa Monica Mountains to the south. Cross the Ventura Fwy. in 1/4 mile and enter the Woodland Hills business and shopping area. The locale changes into residential and remains so up to a left turn at Trifuno Canyon Rd. (2.1). (There is a mixed Class II/Class X diversion up to Lakes Eleanor or Sherwood by staying on S. Westlake Blvd.)

Pedal another 0.4 mile on an unmarked road with a wide shoulder (this entire section rides like a Class II bikeway) to a bridge with a view of picturesque Westlake

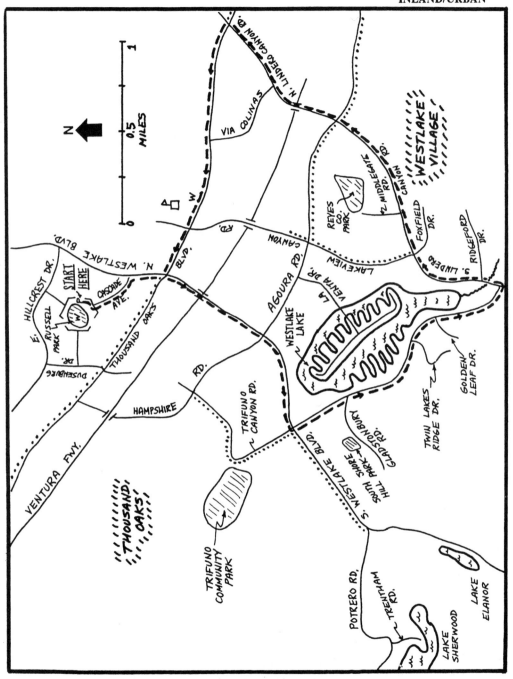

TRIP #51 - WESTLAKE VILLAGE TOUR

Lake. This is a popular "high-altitude" duck feeding spot. Bike past Gladstonbury Rd., taking periodic peeks down the lanes to the lake and reach Golden Leaf Dr. (3.5). This is the open end of the lake with views of the center island, small boats and a tree-covered rest area.   In 0.2 mile, pass "tennis-court city" and make a sharp left on S. Lindero Canyon Rd.

Westlake Lake

Northbound-Open Country.   Bike over a bridge that crosses Trifuno Canyon Creek and pass Ridgeford Dr. (or turn on that street for a challenging Class X uphill). Pedal 0.1 mile to the top of a knoll where there are views of the lake's south end.   At Lakeview Canyon Dr., the marked Class II path resumes.   You can divert left to reach the island at the lake's center.   However, the designated route cruises 0.9 mile to Agoura Rd., where the bikeway is on a tree-lined road and bordered by walls of the surrounding suburban tracts.   In 0.2 mile beyond Agoura Rd., cross back over the freeway and bike a moderate upgrade to reach Via Colinas and the open fields of the Valley Oaks Memorial Park Cemetery.   The uphill continues to Thousand Oaks Blvd. where there is a small shopping center (6.6).

Westbound-Rolling Hills.   Head west on the Class II bikeway and cycle 0.3 mile uphill.   Now the roller coaster begins!   Free-wheel downhill to Via Colinas and pedal uphill 0.3 mile while enjoying views south to the Santa Monica Mountains.   After a 0.2-mile downhill, the road narrows and the path shifts to the sidewalk as posted (Class I).   Pass below the Westlake High School baseball fields in 0.2 mile (drinking fountain near the middle) and continue to Lakeview Canyon Rd.   In 0.3 mile, the sidewalk route intersects N. Westlake Blvd.   Go right (north), proceed to Cascade Ave. and return to the start point (9.2).

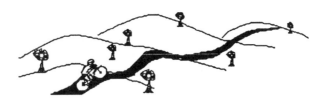

196

TRIP #52 - THOUSAND OAKS BIKEWAY SYSTEM

GENERAL LOCATION: Thousand Oaks

LEVEL OF DIFFICULTY: Loop - moderate
Distance - 18.3 miles (loop)
Elevation gain - periodic moderate-to-steep upgrades
(steep upgrade above Pederson Rd.)

HIGHLIGHTS: This mixed Class II/III loop is particularly enjoyable for the variety of biking settings that it provides. In order from the start is an enjoyable commercial area tour, a long workout upgrade into a rural residential area, a "hang-it-out" downhill to a well-landscaped country club, and a long flat return segment. The scenery is enchanting, particularly from the summit near McCrea Rd. There are also several interesting diversionary trips off the main loop.

TRAILHEAD: From the Ventura Fwy., exit northbound on Westlake Blvd. and drive 1/2 mile to Cascade Ave., which is the next left turn exit past Thousand Oaks Blvd. Go left (west) and proceed down Cascade Ave. to its terminus across from a school and next to Russell Park. Bring a filled water bottle or two for the Erbes Rd. segment, especially on hot days. There are strategically-placed watering spots at the start and midpoint.

TRIP DESCRIPTION: The counterclockwise loop has a steady upgrade on Erbes Rd. on the beginning (eastern) half of the loop--the return is a breeze! In the reverse direction, there is a very long and steep upgrade near the mid-point on Erbes Rd. from Olsen Rd. to McCrea Rd., again with an easy return leg. The Thousand Oaks portion is interesting, but has heavy traffic; an option is to skip this segment and start at one of the parks on Erbes Rd.

Thousand Oaks Boulevard. Leave the cul-de-sac, go left on Cascade Ave., and bike 0.4 mile to N. Westlake Blvd. Head right (south), follow the Class II path to Thousand Oaks Blvd., then go right (west). Caltrans notes this as Class III bikeway, but there is very limited biking room; you can use the sidewalk for about 1/4 mile. Cruise past a shopping center, Dusenburg Dr. and Conejo School Rd. (2.3) in a high traffic area. The area sports a variety of interesting commercial businesses. The Ventura Fwy., paralleling Thousand Oaks Blvd., is visible in the hills to the left (south). Pedal 1/2 mile and turn right (north) on Erbes Rd.

Erbes Road-Up, Up and Away. At the entry to narrow Class III Erbes Rd., start a steady uphill into a lightly-treed area. The road widens and continues uphill past set-back Estella Park to Hillcrest Dr. (Don't let the name fool you!) The ride remains in a rural setting, passing country-style homes before reaching the top of a grade (3.8). In 0.3 mile, bear left (west) on La Granada Dr. and stay to the right as the Class III road name becomes Janss Rd. At El Monte Rd. go right and bike a short grade to the summit; take in the views of Conejo Creek Park (the northern section has a large grassy area with horse and walking trails). Follow a short and steep downgrade, cruise a flat stretch through a quiet residential area and return to Erbes Rd. (5.7).

Turn left on the Class II roadway and follow a moderate uphill which levels off in 0.3 mile, pass Avd. De Los Arboles (shopping center) and continue to Pederson Rd. Little Oakbrook Neighborhood Park is on the southwest corner. Bike an easy 0.3 mile and reach a 1/4-mile steep uphill that tops out near Sunset Hills Blvd. and Sunset Hills Park (a cozy park nestled under the hills with a water fountain). Pedal up a short upgrade to the trip's high point at McCrea Rd. and enjoy the panoramic view.

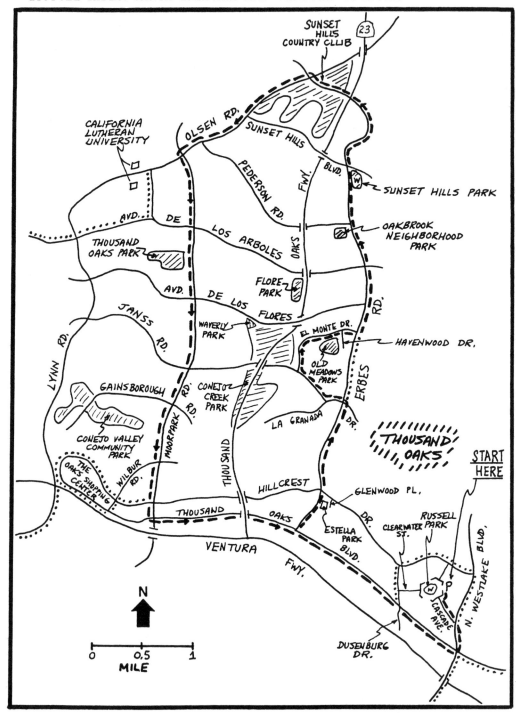

TRIP #52 - THOUSAND OAKS BIKEWAY SYSTEM

The Valley Floor. Erbes Rd. winds steeply downhill, looses several hundred feet in 3/4 mile before leveling out and passing under the Moorpark Fwy. (State Hwy. 23). Travel through the naturally-scenic Sunset Hills Country Club and reach Olsen Rd. (9.0). Head left (west) on Class II bikeway, proceed on a long upgrade, reach a crest at Sunset Hills Blvd. and work downhill for 0.8 mile through open countryside to Moorpark Rd.

Erbes Road Below Sunset Hills Boulevard

Moorpark Road. Turn left (south) at the gas station and bike on the mostly flat Class II route into a residential neighborhood. There are a few small rolling rises, but no major grades for the remainder of the trip. Cross Avd. De Los Arboles, the edge of Thousand Oaks Community Park, and reach Avd. De Los Flores (12.0). In 1/2 mile, pass a shopping center before reaching Janss Rd. In 1/4-mile is Gainsborough Rd., where a diversion right leads to Conejo Valley Community Park and the California Botanical Gardens. Stay on Moorpark Rd. and pedal up a 1/4-mile grade and pass the Janss Mall (14.0). Next is the Hillcrest Dr. turnoff to the Oaks Shopping Center. (There is a nice Class I diversion loop here.) In 0.2 mile, reach an area where the road narrows considerably and, in 0.1 mile, turns left (east) onto Thousand Oaks Blvd.

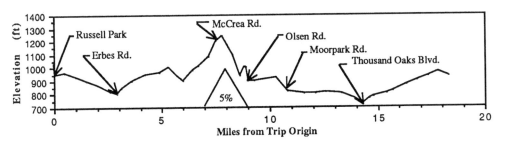

The Return Leg. Bike east on busy Thousand Oaks Blvd. through a dense commercial neighborhood. The Class III path crosses back under the Moorpark Fwy., passes Rancho Rd./Encino Vista Dr. and returns to Erbes Rd. The remaining tour follows the incoming path back to N. Moorpark Rd. and Cascade Ave. to the starting point (18.3). A return option is to turn left at Dusenburg Dr., right at Clearwater St., continue to the street's end, and cross to Russell Park.

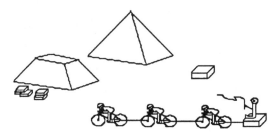

TRIP #53 - NORTH RANCH LOOP

GENERAL LOCATION: Thousand Oaks, Westlake Village

LEVEL OF DIFFICULTY: Loop - moderate
Distance - 10.9 miles (loop)
Elevation gain - periodic moderate upgrades

HIGHLIGHTS: This is a grand rural loop on lightly-traveled roads. The majority of the route is on a Class II path or Class X road with a wide shoulder. The tour highlights include a visit to the classy North Ranch residential area, a long mild runout on Lindero Canyon Rd. (paid for with prior uphill pumping), and a ride by the northern periphery of Westlake Village. This path can be linked with the Agoura Hills Loop (Trip #50) and the Westlake Village Tour (Trip #51), sufficient to keep a biker going all day.

TRAILHEAD: From the Ventura Fwy., exit northbound on Westlake Blvd. and continue 1/2 mile to Cascade Ave., which is the next left turn beyond Thousand Oaks Blvd. Go left (west) and proceed down Cascade Ave. to its terminus next to Russell Park. Bring a filled water bottle; nearly the entire segment north of Thousand Oaks Blvd. is waterless.

TRIP DESCRIPTION: Westlake Boulevard. Leave the parking area and bike up Cascade Ave. to Westlake Blvd., turn left (north) and pedal the mild downgrade on a road that has a tree-lined center median. Stay on the marked Class II path, pass a residential pocket and Hillcrest Dr., then bike through less-developed territory bordered by hills. Pedal on a light downgrade past Skelton Canyon Dr. and meet Deepwood Dr. Pump up a 0.3-mile grade, enjoy a short downgrade with a canyon view, pass Valley Spring Dr. and begin another uphill. The bike lane ends (the wide shoulder continues) on an uphill in an area with a view of North Ranch. A short pedal brings you to Kanan Rd. (2.4).

Kanan Road. Turn right (east) and bike on the Class X road with a wide bike shoulder. The street skirts the northern perimeter of North Ranch with the rolling hills of the Conejo Ridge on the opposite (north) side of Kanan Rd. In 0.2 mile, cycle a short upgrade which levels near Rayburn St. Next is a 1/2-mile upgrade beside the North Ranch Golf Course that "gets serious" about 0.2 mile before reaching a crest

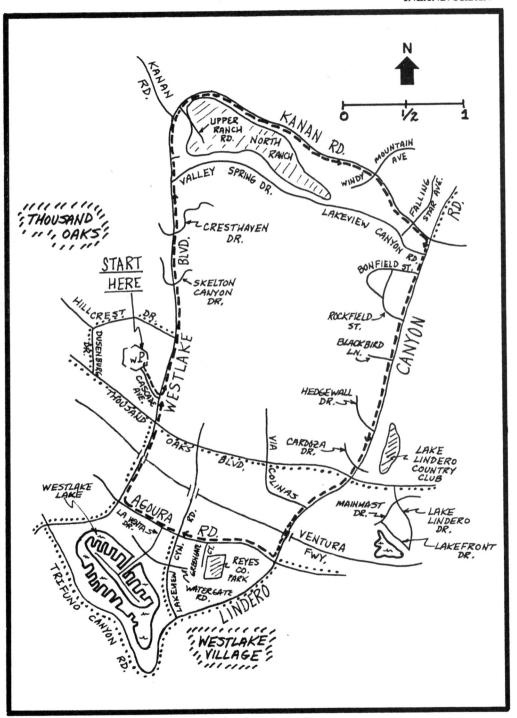

TRIP #53 - NORTH RANCH LOOP

(3.5). Cruise to the end of the golf course, pass Windy Mountain Ave., and follow the downhill past South Rim St. There are homes on both sides of the road and an occasional hawk soaring above for bird watchers. The route levels near Falling Star Ave. (4.7) and, in 0.2 mile, continues to the junction at Lindero Canyon Rd.

Lindero Canyon Road. Turn right (south) and cruise on the Class X, wide-shouldered road past Lakeview Canyon Rd. Pass between a set of small hills, transit Rockfield St. and follow a light upgrade. Another downhill ensues, then Lindero Canyon Rd. flattens and reaches Hedgewall Dr. The path transitions to Class II, goes through a suburban area on a tree-lined street and reaches Thousand Oaks Blvd. (gas station). Pass a shopping center and coast downhill past the Valley Oaks Memorial Park Cemetery. Cruise a moderate downhill across Via Colinas (7.6) and reach the Ventura Fwy. in 0.3 mile. Cycle another 0.3 mile and arrive at Agoura Rd.

Kanan Road Above North Ranch

Closing the Loop. Go right on Class II Agoura Rd. and bike alongside the Westlake Village Golf Club (right) and the northern periphery of a Westlake Village residential area. In 0.3 mile, cross Lakeview Canyon Rd. and bike along the southern edge of Westlake Plaza. At the end of the shopping center, turn right (north) at Westlake Blvd. and pedal uphill on Class II road over the Ventura Fwy.

Cruise 0.3 mile to Thousand Oaks Blvd., pedaling another 0.2 mile to Cascade Ave. Go left (west) and return to Russell Park (10.9).

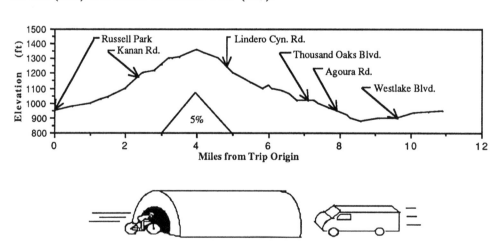

TRIP #54 · SIMI VALLEY BIKEWAY SYSTEM

GENERAL LOCATION: Simi Valley

LEVEL OF DIFFICULTY: Loop - moderate
Distance - 22.1 miles
Elevation gain - essentially flat

HIGHLIGHTS: There is no lack of marked bikepaths or bikers in Simi Valley. Our route passes from one edge of town to the other. Bikepaths are interwoven throughout the city, with a Class I route along the Arroyo Simi. Several excellent parks are scattered along the route. The views of the foothills and mountains are everywhere. If the city cruise becomes too tame, try the gut-buster trip up Santa Susana Pass.

TRAILHEAD: From the Simi Valley-San Fernando Fwy. (State Hwy. 118), exit south at Kuehner Dr. and travel 1-1/4 miles until the road becomes Santa Susana Pass Rd. Make a hard left at Katherine Rd. and park at nearby Santa Susana Park.

There are many sources of water in commercial establishments along the ride. Note that Simi Valley uses a smaller version of the bike-route sign found in L.A. County. Also, small "No Parking" signs are sometimes used as a base for "Bike Route" stickers. In addition, the Class II bikepath markings are light in places.

Strathern Park (Side Trip)

TRIP   DESCRIPTION: Los Angeles Avenue. Exit the park and go left on Santa Susana Pass Rd./Kuehner Dr., pedaling past South Rd. and Katherine Rd. There are views in all directions of the rugged surrounding hills. Go left on Los Angeles Ave. (1.0) and stare directly ahead to the eight-plus mile stretch of straight-line

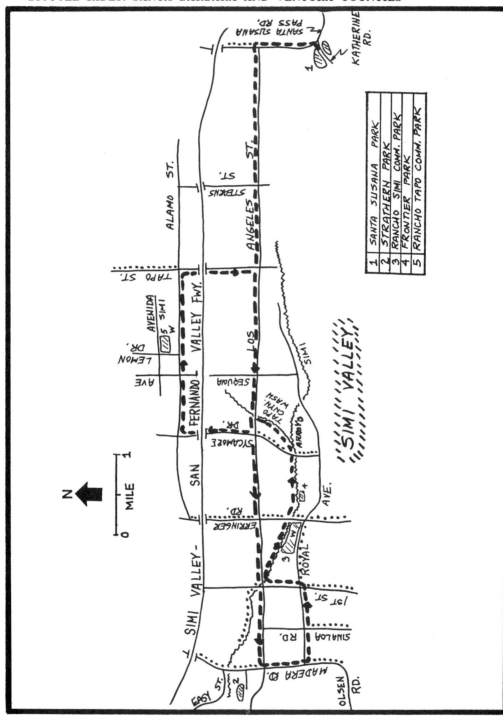

]TRIP #54 - SIMI VALLEY BIKEWAY SYSTEM

roadway/bikepath. Cruise down the marked bikeway into a suburban area past Yosemite Ave. and Stearns St., both with shopping centers. Cycle near the Santa Susana Business Center where the road narrows. In 1/2 mile, pass through a scattered commercial development, cross Tapo St. and beeline to Sequoia St. and another shopping center (5.1). Cross the Tapo Canyon Wash, Sycamore Dr. and soon reach Erringer Dr. in a high-density section of town. Los Angeles Ave. passes a three-story "skyscraper" in 1/2 mile. (Five stories was our building watcher's best on this tour.) Bike to First St., cross the Arroyo Simi, and reach the end of the line at Madera Rd. at the edge of town (8.9).

Arroyo Simi. Turn left (south) past the Posade Royale commercial center with its eye-catching Spanish architecture. Pedal 0.5 mile to Royal Ave., go left, then left again at First St. to the pedestrian/bikepath entrance to the Arroyo Simi. Head west on the Class I path along the arroyo, with homes on both sides of the waterway. In 0.6 mile, pass horse pens and reach Erringer Rd. (12.7). To the right (south) is the Rancho Simi Community Park, which has restrooms, water, recreation fields, picnic areas, pedestrian paths and even a small lake.

Stoney Point

The bikepath is interrupted here, continuing on the opposite side of Erringer Rd. (a similar street crossing is at Sycamore Dr.). Across the arroyo in 0.3 mile is Frontier Park with its elevated children's wood fort. The path goes through a large cactus patch and reaches Sycamore Dr. The arroyo splits and the bikepath follows the Tapo Canyon Wash northeast. Beyond is a kid's bike motorcross area and the trail's end at Los Angeles Ave. (14.1).

Alamo Street. Go left and return to Sycamore Dr. Bear right (north) 1/2 mile on this busy road, and pass under the Simi Valley-San Fernando Valley Fwy. to Alamo St. Turn right and enjoy the views of the Santa Susana Mountains to the north and east. Ride into a pleasant suburban area past Sequoia Ave. and alongside a eucalyptus grove, reaching a shopping center at Tapo Canyon Rd. (16.9). The width of the bike shoulder varies from very wide to non-existing over this stretch. Bike to Tapo St. and yet another shopping center.

Return Leg. Cycle back under the freeway 1.0 mile and reach Los Angeles Ave. Turn left (east) and retrace the bikepath to its origin at Santa Susana Park (22.1).

Trip Option-Santa Susana Pass. A connector to the San Fernando Valley involves a 4.3-mile trek over Santa Susana Pass to Topanga Blvd. From Simi Valley, there is a 2.0-mile, 500-foot, climb to the pass and a more strenuous 700-foot ascent in about the same distance if you bike an up-and-back trip to the San Fernando Valley. The road is winding, but the traffic is light. Some segments have very little biking shoulder. This is more than compensated by the grand views on both sides of the pass, with an exceptional turnout view on the east side 1-1/2-miles from the summit. Stoney Point in Chatsworth is a grand place for both sightseers and hikers to visit.

TRIP #55 ▫ ROCKY PEAK (Mountain Bike)

GENERAL LOCATION: Santa Susana Pass, Simi Valley

LEVEL OF DIFFICULTY: Loop - Strenuous
Distance - 11.4 miles (loop)
Elevation gain - continuous steep grades to Rocky Peak
and Santa Susana Pass

HIGHLIGHTS: The 2.5-mile Rocky Peak Trail is a neat mountain bike trip providing excellent vistas from the trailhead to the ridgeline below Rocky Peak. The trail is surrounded by interesting and varied rock formations. A mile extension along the scenic ridgeline puts the biker at the Chumash Trail junction. This 2.4-mile serpentine, single-track downhill is very steep, in poor condition in some areas and has other sections with steep drops along the narrow trail. Riders could arrange for a car shuttle at trail's end at Chumash Park, or bike 5.4 more miles into Simi Valley and up Santa Paula Pass Rd. to complete the loop.

TRAILHEAD: From the Simi Valley area, take Santa Susana Pass Rd. two miles from the Kuehner Dr./Katherine Rd. intersection and go left (north) on the bridge over the Simi Valley Fwy. (State Hwy 118). The road dead ends in a parking area at the signed entrance to Rocky Peak Park. From L. A. County, follow the Simi Valley Fwy. west to the Santa Susana Pass summit and exit at the next off-ramp. Dead ahead is the parking area. The Santa Susana Pass was used by Chumash Indian hunting and trading parties for centuries as a preferred route from Simi Valley to the inland mountain areas.

Bring one or two quarts of water on hot days. The first available water source is in Simi Valley.

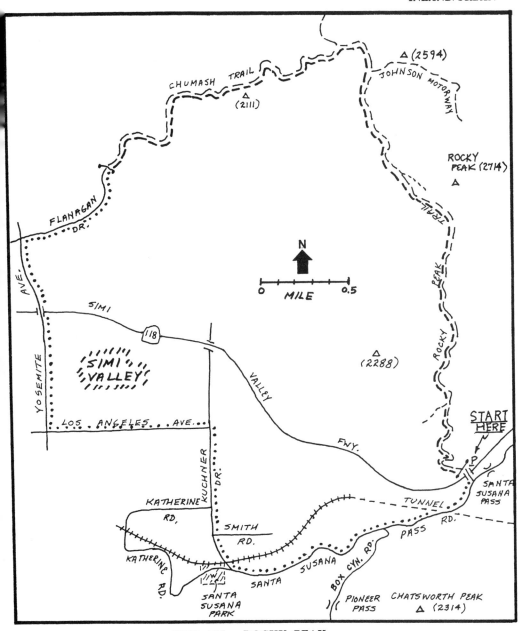

TRIP #55 - ROCKY PEAK

TRIP DESCRIPTION: **Rocky Peak Trailhead to Chumash Park.** Wheel your bike around the barrier and climb steeply uphill on the rocky, rutted fire road that is shared by hikers, bikers and equestrians. This workout, winding uphill provides mixed views of Simi Valley and the crusty peaks of Big Mountain to the west and has spectacular rock formations scattered about the trail. The rugged climb is shared by passages along several rock-strewn plateaus on either side of the road. In two miles

207

BICYCLE RIDES: SANTA BARBARA AND VENTURA COUNTIES

Rocky Peak Trail

of steady uphill, reach a lengthy plateau from where the steep, switchbacked final push on the western flank of Rocky Peak comes into view. This very steep 1/2-mile transit takes you to the top of a ridge. On the right is an unsigned, 1/2-mile, single-track trail leading to Rocky Peak, with 360-degree vistas (on a clear day) of Anacapa Island, Simi Valley, the Santa Monica Mountains and San Fernando Valley.

Keep north along the ridge, where more beautiful views await. About one ridgeline-mile after the Rocky Peak summit trail junction, and after passing the Johnson Motorway (fire road) junction, is the signed **Chumash Trail** to the left (3.5). Route options are: 1) return to the Rocky Peak trailhead; 2) stay north along the ridgeline for two miles to the park boundary (we understand that there is a large, inspiring oak savanna there); or 3) take the 2.4-mile Chumash Trail south and west down to Chumash Park. The reference route follows the latter option. A word of warning--this trail has some extremely steep parts with dramatic drop-offs and should only be attempted by patient and experienced riders. Conditions of the trail are best explained by noting that the existing, narrow-foot trail was "hacked out" after only several days. Highlights of this winding 1150-foot (average 9% grade) downhill are a mostly flat 0.6-mile ride past a forest of massive "rock piles," and a 0.8-mile downhill, which includes a traverse 150-feet above an unnamed canyon. Climb to a saddle and follow a super-steep, 400-foot drop in less than 1/2 mile. The undeveloped grassy knolls of Chumash Park are seen on the last and flatter 0.2 mile of the trail (6.0).

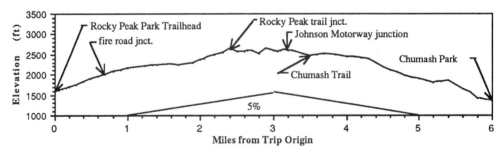

Rocky Peak Loop Option. If you did not arrange a car shuttle, close the loop by cycling on the asphalt roadways into Simi Valley and up Santa Susana Pass Rd. The 5.4-mile segment involves a fast downhill on Flanagan Dr., a more shallow downgrade on Yosemite Ave. and a flat cruise east on Los Angeles St., the trip's lowest point. Simi Valley proper has many eateries, service stations and markets. Follow a wide curve right (south) on Kuehner Dr. on Class II bikeway and pass Katherine Rd., the entrance to Santa Susana Park (restrooms, water, picnic tables) just beyond the

Lone Rider with Rocky Peak Backdrop

railroad tracks (9.5). Swing east and pedal by picturesque Hideout Willies and several other interesting, venerable establishments.

The road narrows to two lanes and begins some serious uphill on what is now Santa Susana Pass Rd. The winding road ascends past Box Canyon Rd. and works its way near to, and at the elevation of, the Simi Valley Fwy. There is a train tunnel in the canyon between the freeway and Santa Susana Pass Rd. Locals say the sound of trains leaving the tunnel and entering Simi Valley is downright eerie. In 1.5 miles from Hideout Willies is the freeway overpass which returns you to the trailhead (11.4).

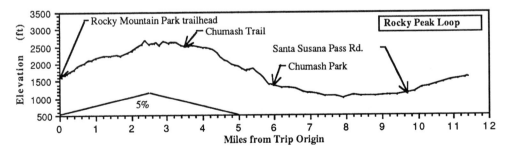

TRIP #56 - VENTURA VALLEYS LOOP

GENERAL LOCATION: Simi Valley-Moorpark-Fillmore-Santa Paula-Camarillo

LEVEL OF DIFFICULTY: Loop - strenuous
Distance - 65.0 miles
Elevation gain - periodic moderate-to-steep grades; single
steady grade to Grimes Canyon Rd. summit

HIGHLIGHTS: **You want valleys? We got valleys!** This is not a trip to be taken lightly because of the distance, one severe upgrade (State Hwy. 23 north of Moorpark), and an area of wild, exposed switchback downhills (Hwy. 23 entry into Grimes Canyon). Other than this, there are some pleasant flats to bike (Little Simi Valley, Santa Clara River Basin, Pleasant Valley, Santa Rosa Valley, Tierra Rejada Valley). The scenery is quite varied, as is the quality of the developed, picturesque and rural areas on the mainly Class X roadways. (We helped modify this route, which was used by the American Heart Association for the 77-mile, 4th Annual Great American Tour de Heart ride in June, 1994.) For the less ambitious, there is also a 29.8-mile mini loop which uses a portion of the route.

The tour should be taken in the direction written, unless the biker is in exceptional condition. The southbound climb out of Grime's Canyon covers over 600 feet elevation gain in 1-1/2 miles (average 7-3/4% grade).

Los Angeles Ave. at Santa Clara River

TRAILHEAD: From the Simi Valley-San Fernando Valley Fwy. (State Hwy. 118), exit south at Madera Rd., drive about 3/4 mile to Strathern Pl. and go right. Park along the road outside Strathern Historical Park. From the Ventura Fwy. (U.S. Hwy. 101), exit north onto the Moorpark Fwy. (Hwy. 23), head north nine miles (the road becomes the Conejo Creek Fwy.) and turn at Tierra Rejada Rd. Drive west 3-1/2 miles

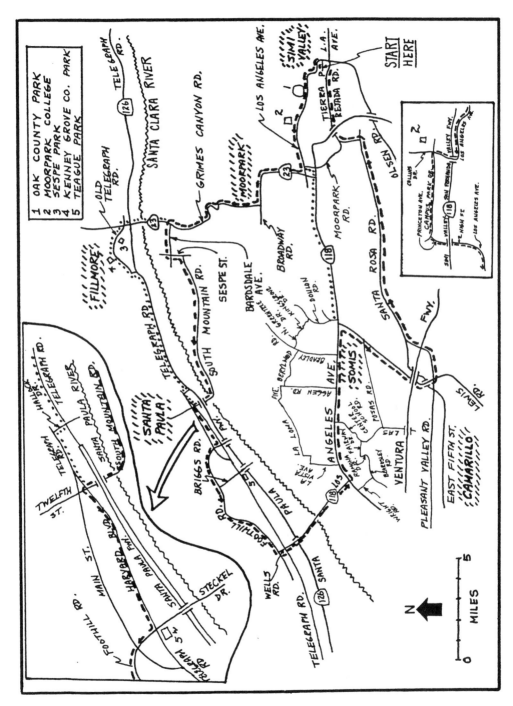

TRIP #56 - VENTURA VALLEYS LOOP

to Madera Rd., go left (north) for 1/4 mile to Strathern Pl. Turn left into the parking area.

Bring a large water supply (at least two full bottles). There are long distances without water sources and several long and exposed stretches. A bike maintenance check, particularly the brakes, is recommended before starting this trip.

TRIP DESCRIPTION: **Little Simi Valley.** Leave the park and go left (north) on Madera Rd. Bike 0.7 mile to Easy St. (this name is a definite "set-up") and turn left, pedaling in an area with rolling hills. The street, now named Los Angeles Ave., crosses a treed area with a cactus patch, Oak County Park, a residential area in the foothills, and passes over the Simi Valley-San Fernando Valley Fwy. (3.4). To the north is the entrance to Moorpark College.

The road becomes Collins Ave. Bike north and turn left (west) at Campus Park Dr. Bear left at Princeton Ave, go back under the freeway, and follow a street which changes name to Los Angeles Ave., then High St. Pass a gravel extraction operation, reaching Moorpark Rd. and the shaded entry into the City of Moorpark. Cycle on High St. into this quaint metropolis to the westward Moorpark Rd. junction (6.1). This is a major decision point. Turn left (south) and bike to Los Angeles Ave. for the 29.8-mile mini-loop (Los Angeles Ave. to State Hwy. 34 south) or turn right on Hwy. 23 for the full valley tour. The latter route follows Hwy. 23 for 8.8 miles, almost into Fillmore.

The Canyon Roads (Way up - and Way Down!). Pedal a moderate uphill on what is now Walnut Canyon Rd. This becomes a workout climb before reaching a flat, and then proceeds on a series of stair steps where Hwy. 23 veers sharply left (west) and the street becomes Broadway Rd. To the east is a horse corral with beautiful animals. Follow this country road amid citrus groves and scattered homes on the hilly course to a point where Hwy. 23 makes a sharp turn north and becomes Grimes Canyon Rd. (9.4).

Puff uphill past a "fragrant" chicken farm and bike onto what becomes a steep, snaking upgrade for the next mile to Oak Ridge summit. The following 1-1/2 miles provide a steep and winding downgrade with several exposed outside curves. The views of the canyon are stunning and the downhill exhilarating! The "I Love Mary" and other carvings on the roadside sandstone provide some visual entertainment. Drop into Grimes Canyon, pass a mining operation (12.8), and begin to level out alongside citrus orchards which are peppered with oil pumping rigs (where else but in Southern California!).

Santa Clara River Basin (Bardsdale to Santa Paula). Cycle through the flat valley into little Bardsdale to where the road reaches Bardsdale Ave. (left)/Bellevue Ave. (right). A right turn provides an 11.3-mile ride north into Fillmore and heads west on Hwy. 126 to the junction of South Mountain Rd. in Santa Paula. (This is the best option if a mid-trip break is needed. Stop at Kenny Grove County Park off Old Telegraph Rd. on N. Oak Ave. This large shaded park has all the necessary amenities for picnicking or overnight camping.) Our reference route turns left instead and heads west 1-1/2 miles through citrus groves to Sespe St. Go left, heading back toward the mountains, then right again in 0.4 mile at South Mountain Rd. (16.8).

The ride along South Mountain Rd. is on a lightly-used, two-lane road passing a continuous line of citrus trees. This serene stretch is rural biking at its best! Head generally west (wear sunglasses for afternoon rides) into modest rolling hills and pass Balcomb Canyon Rd. (19.2). Stop here and take in the views of the Santa Paula

Ridge and more distant ranges. The winding road butts up against the foothills, passes through rolling hills and follows a long segment with lush Santa Clara River bottomland vistas. Follow the river course to an area where the aircraft landing approach into Santa Paula Airport becomes visible. In 1/2 mile, follow a sharp turn north, cross the Santa Clara River, bike under the Santa Paula Fwy. (State Hwy. 126) and reach Harvard Ave. in Santa Paula. Go left (west) and pedal 1-1/2 miles into the city to Teague Park on Steckle Dr. (shade, water, recreation fields and playground) (25.6). Another 1/2 mile of cycling brings you to Peck Rd.

Los Angeles Ave. in Santa Rosa Valley

Santa Paula to Saticoy. This is another decision point. One way to proceed would be to pedal 5.2 miles on Harvard Blvd. (name changes to Telegraph Rd. past Peck Rd.) along the mostly straight, flat, and moderately-used route by citrus orchards and countryside to Wells Rd. However, our quieter and scenic route turns right (north), proceeds 0.7 mile to Foothill Rd. and then turns left. Though short of biking shoulder in some areas, the traffic is light and the setting is rural. Most of the ride is on rolling hills through a string of citrus orchards with the foothills to the right (north). In a mile, an extended stretch with exceptional views into the Santa Clara River basin opens up. Past Aliso Canyon Rd. is a 1/2-mile workout grade. The tallest buildings in the Camarillo area, Santa Monica Mountains and Pt. Mugu can be seen from the crest. Cross these streets in sequence: Briggs Rd., Cummings Rd., Wheeler Canyon Rd., Aliso Canyon Rd. and Wells Rd. (33.2).

Saticoy to Somis. Head left (southeast) and enjoy a restful downgrade. Pass Telegraph Rd. (gas station), and bike over the Santa Paula Fwy. into the small City of Saticoy. Follow Hwy. 118 into Somis as it jogs left, then right, and makes a three-mile straight-line route over the Santa Clara River to road's end. Turn left on Los Angeles Ave. and ride between rolling hills filled with more orchards. The road straightens past Mesa Union High School, transits a small agricultural valley past Center School Rd. (40.1) and reaches Somis Rd. (Hwy. 34) in 2.9 miles.

Pleasant and Santa Rosa Valleys. Bear right (south) and cruise into the small farming town of Somis with the eastern edge of Camarillo Heights to the west. Veer right (44.9) as the road flattens (becoming Lewis Rd. in the Las Posas Rd. area) and pass Adolfo Rd.   Bike under the Ventura Fwy., pass an early California Spanish structure and pedal to Pleasant Valley Rd. (48.8).

This picturesque stretch of country road passes beside a long stand of eucalyptus trees, crosses a wash and veers northeast near Pancho Rd.   Recross the freeway (the name becomes Santa Rosa Rd.) and follow the rolling hills past Woodcreek Rd., Santa Rosa Plaza at Oak Canyon Rd. and enter the "big open spaces" within Santa Rosa Valley.   This is mainly agricultural country with peaceful roads that seem to go on forever.   The serenity is jogged only by passage of little cross roads such as Hill Canyon Rd., Las Posas Rd. and finally the junction point at Moorpark Rd. (59.2).

Tierra Rejada Valley.   Go left (north) and bike the steep upgrade to a flat. From here are views of the valley and a glimpse of the Moorpark-Conejo Creek Fwy. in the distance.   Cycle on Moorpark Rd. as it veers left (north) at Read Rd.   In one mile, turn right (east) at Tierra Rejada Rd. and continue the journey through the farming valley.   Go under the freeway, head uphill for 1/4 mile and through a mix of flats and uphills to the summit in 1.7 miles   A view of Simi Valley and the "home stretch" is seen here.   Turn left at Madera Rd. in 1.2 miles and return to Strathern Historical Park (65.0).

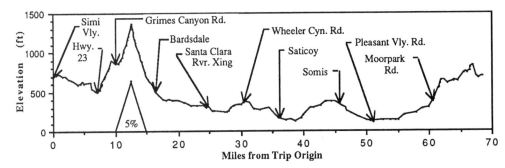

Trip Option-The Shortcut.   As noted above, a shorter (but still scenic) route is to continue west from the Moorpark Rd. junction (6.1) to Hwy. 34.   Follow the reference trip's description at the 43.0 beyond this point.

Trip Option-Camarillo Heights/Somis Hills.   There are interesting side excursions in the hilly areas both north and south of Los Angeles St. in the Camarillo Heights/Somis area.   The serene northern tour is through countryside hills.   (See the "Crazy Eight" Loop, Trip #59, in the section titled Somis Loop.)   Bring along a street map as it is easy to lose direction; there are few straight-through roads in these areas.

TRIP #57 - POTRERO ROAD COUNTRYSIDE TOUR

GENERAL LOCATION: Hidden Valley, Potrero Valley

LEVEL OF DIFFICULTY: **Basic Route:**   One way - moderate;
Up and back- moderate to strenuous
Distance - 11.3 miles (one way)
Elevation gain - periodic moderate-
to-steep grades

The Full Enchilada: One way - moderate;
Up and back - very strenuous
Distance - 16.5 miles (one way)
Elevation gain - same as above with very
steep grades on return

HIGHLIGHTS: One of our favorite rural routes, this ten-mile-plus gem cruises the periphery of Lake Sherwood and through some of the most pleasant and relaxing valley-ranch land that we have biked.   There are many miles of green grass, white fences, scattered farms and homes, and a whole bunch of quiet.   The route is mainly Class X with reasonable bike shoulder and little traffic past the lake. There is a very challenging downhill into Camarillo that has been added as an option for adventurous and experienced bikers.   Triathletes in training tell us that the return upgrade is great for building "thunder thighs."

TRAILHEAD: From the Ventura Fwy. (State Hwy. 101), exit at Westlake Blvd., turn left and pass under the freeway.   Travel 3/4 mile to Evenstar Ave. (1/4 mile past Hampshire Rd./Agoura Rd.) and go right.   Follow Evenstar Ave. around the bend to Evenstar Park (recreation fields, playground, water fountain, scattered shade trees). The ten-mile stretch between the trip origin and Reino Rd. is exposed and waterless, so plan accordingly.

Lake Sherwood

215

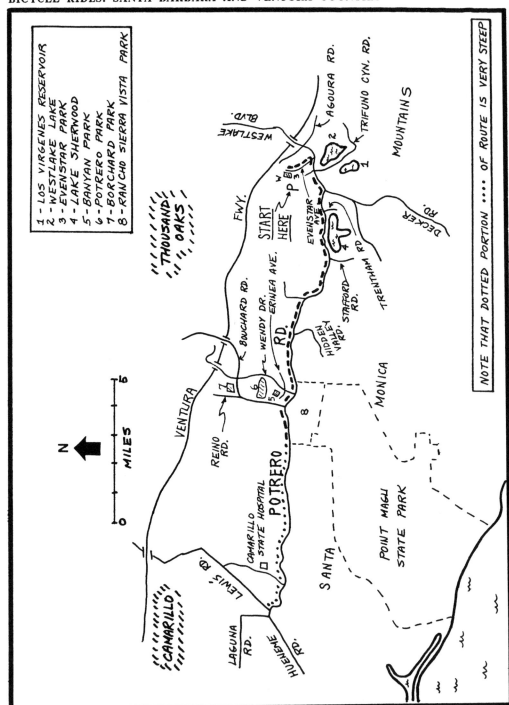

Map Legend:
1 - LOS VIRGENES RESERVOIR
2 - WESTLAKE LAKE
3 - EVENSTAR PARK
4 - LAKE SHERWOOD
5 - BANYAN PARK
6 - POTRERO PARK
7 - BORCHARD PARK
8 - RANCHO SIERRA VISTA PARK

THOUSAND OAKS

NOTE THAT DOTTED PORTION •••• OF ROUTE IS VERY STEEP

START HERE

N

MILES

0 5

TRIP #57 - POTRERO ROAD COUNTRYSIDE TOUR

TRIP DESCRIPTION: Lake Sherwood. Return to Westlake Blvd. and turn right (southwest). Begin an upgrade on the tree-lined, Class II, residential road which passes Trifuno Canyon Rd. and reaches Potrero Rd. in 0.8 mile. Turn right onto the Class II road, pass the community center (with a swimming pool you may think about later), and follow a moderate upgrade to a point where the road narrows (2.0). The marked bikepath ends as the road crosses Potrero Valley Creek and begins a progressively steeper winding uphill.

Portreo Rd. passes above horse stables and reaches the first vantage point into beautiful, blue, tree-lined, Lake Sherwood. The road remains above and parallels the lake on a steady winding uphill. After a mile of tough workout, reach a crest and follow a steep winding downhill into a little farm-filled valley. The now flat route passes the northeast lake edge and a fire station (3.2).

Potrero Valley

The Hidden Valley Countryside. The surroundings change to "instant countryside" as Potrero Rd. continues into a pristine, flat valley with only green fields, white fences, and scattered estates and ranches. The tree-lined road (this must be heaven!) takes a sharp course change to the right (north), heads for the hills and returns to its westerly course in 0.8 mile through more of this lovely ranchland. Following is a workout grade which moderates before reaching a residential pocket and Hidden Valley Rd. (7.3).

Potrero Valley. Beyond is another steep and winding grade which passes White Stallion Rd., crests and proceeds steeply downhill through hilly, wide-open countryside. Bike through rolling hills to Wendy Dr. (9.2); just north and west on Erinlea Ave. is Banyan Park (water and shade). To the south is the Rancho Sierra

Vista (Satwiwa) Park, which has hiking and mountain bike trails. (See Trip #58 - Sycamore Canyon for a description of the trails.)

Cruise downhill past a residential area to Reino Rd., jig-jog left and uphill on Potrero Rd., enjoying the views of Boney Mountain to the left (southeast). Stair step past Pinehill Ave. and begin a steep uphill around a curve, which gives way to a steeper straightaway that looks ten-miles long (well, kind of long). Puff a mile on this grade to a crest where one of life's important decisions awaits (11.3).

The Downgrade. Beyond are two very steep downgrades that run out five miles later at Lewis Rd. in Camarillo. The road is narrow and precipitous, particularly in the switchback zones, and a biker is almost guaranteed to have car traffic on his tail. (The uphill in the reverse direction is tough and the traffic probably impatient.) We chose to revisit this area early on a Sunday morning when there was little traffic.

Just past the crest, begin a steep winding descent for about one mile before reaching a compact valley floor. Another (less-steep) 3/4-mile winding downhill is followed by a passage through some rolling grades into a small canyon. In 2-1/2 miles from the initial crest, a 3/4-mile downgrade lets out in flat agricultural land, winds near the Camarillo floor, passes Round Mountain and reaches Lewis Rd. in 1-1/2 miles (16.5).

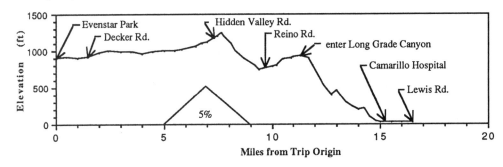

TRIP #58 - SYCAMORE CANYON (Mountain Bike)

<u>GENERAL LOCATION</u>:   Point Mugu State Park

<u>LEVEL OF DIFFICULTY</u>: Loop - strenuous (including Overlook Trail)
                                 (easy to moderate otherwise)
                   Distance - 16.7 miles
                   Elevation gain - steep-to-sheer grades on Overlook Trail
                                 (steady moderate upgrade otherwise)

HIGHLIGHTS: Any off-roader will enjoy this super-scenic network of paths highlighted by the popular Big Sycamore Canyon and Overlook Trails. Leave the Sycamore Canyon Campground and proceed on a mild uphill in a sylvan setting to the Wood Canyon Trail. Continue a modest climb into lush forest cover to the trail's end at Ranch Center. There are over a dozen spirited, but non-difficult, creek crossings along the way. A short steep upgrade and refreshing 2.1-mile runout on paved Ranch Center Rd. brings bikers to the northern end of the Big Sycamore Canyon Trail, where a spin under overhanging tree cover and through a lovely tree-dotted meadow returns you to the Wood Canyon Trail junction. Less experienced cyclists should retrace the incoming route, staying south on Big Sycamore Canyon Trail.

A serious and rewarding challenge awaits the cyclist who retraces the Wood Canyon Trail westward and tackles the quick-and-dirty "Hell Hill" segment of Overlook Trail. This is a little-used, sheer and exposed upgrade which goes to the Overlook Trail summit from the "backside." From the summit is a sinuous downhill with a variety of scenic exposures, including views of La Jolla Canyon, Sycamore Canyon and the coastal shoreline. Alternates to the "Hell Hill" ascent are to use the Wood Canyon Vista Trail entry or to follow the most popular approach, which is an up-and-back ride on the Overlook Trail from its southernmost entry.

EDITOR'S NOTE: The trip as described was taken before November 1993, when a devastating fire burned most of this area. In August 1994, the entire area was bursting with new vegetation. All hiking/biking trails are open and available to those wishing to explore this great outdoor arena.

TRAILHEAD: South Entrance. On State Hwy. 1, drive four miles east of Pt. Mugu or 25 miles west of the Malibu Civic Center to the Sycamore Canyon Campground entrance. Use the camping area parking or hike/bike parking as appropriate (a fee is required and the park is strict on parking rules). Alternatives are to park on either side of Hwy. 1 for a fee or to use the free Caltrans parking lot outside the park west of the Caltrans Big Sycamore Maintenance Station. Observe and respect all parking signs.

Creek Crossing in Wood Canyon

BICYCLE RIDES: SANTA BARBARA AND VENTURA COUNTIES

North Entrance. On Potrero Rd. in Newbury Park, turn south at Pinehill St., which is 1/4 mile west of Reino Rd. Park at Rancho Sierra Vista or the Satwiwa Cultural Center (restrooms, picnic facilities, ranger, station), that gives out information about Native American Indians and National Park lands.

Bring a couple quarts of water if you tackle the waterless Overlook Trail. In contrast, there are water spigots sprinkled throughout the lower canyon areas.

Point Mugu State Park. This 15,000-acre park has several miles of scenic coastline, and a huge backcountry with lush canyons, chaparral-filled highlands and many scattered peaks. Its name comes from the Chumash Indian word MUWU, meaning "beach." The Indians lived here for 6000 years before the arrival of the explorer Cabrillo and were one of the most culturally-advanced tribes in California.

<u>TRIP DESCRIPTION</u>: **Lower Big Sycamore Canyon Trail.** From the south entrance hike/bike area, return to the camp entrance and follow the main road north to its end, where a car barrier guards a small bridge over Sycamore Creek. Once on the east side of the creek, follow the graded-dirt path north on Sycamore Canyon Trail, passing hikers, walkers, runners and returning bikers. After 1/2 mile on a modest grade in a wide canyon with sycamores and oaks, you come to the Overlook Trail turnoff; it cuts back almost parallel to this path and is easy to miss, even with the trail marker present. Views west into the hillsides show the lower switchbacks of the scenic "sky-bound" trail.

Pass one of the many water spigots scattered throughout the park. At 0.8 mile is the first of over a dozen shallow creek crossings. (There was typically 6-8 inches of water, and a few deeper, when we passed through in July 1993.) The secret is to bike down to the creek, pick a route between the rocks, dive in and pedal hard past the midway point to master the climb up the bank on the opposite side. The increasingly shaded route passes several hiking trail junctions (no bikes!), a picnic area (2.2) and the easy-to-miss, single track, Wood Canyon Vista Trail junction--more later.

"Togetherness" on Upper Big Sycamore Canyon Trail

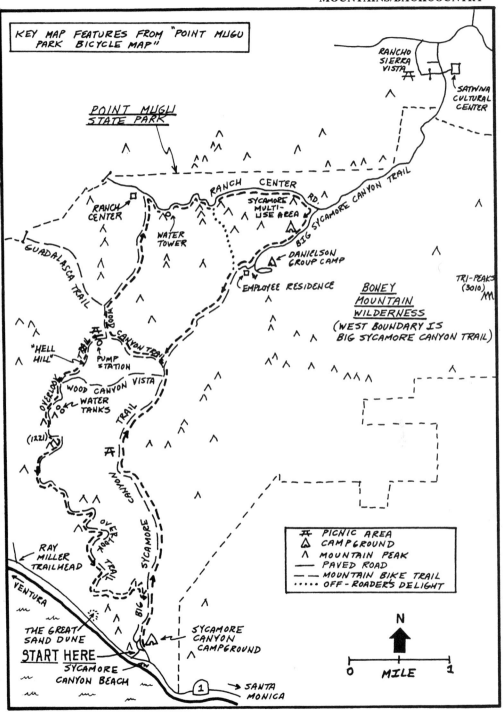

KEY MAP FEATURES FROM "POINT MUGU PARK BICYCLE MAP"

POINT MUGU STATE PARK

RANCH CENTER RD.

RANCH CENTER

SYCAMORE MULTI-USE AREA

BIG SYCAMORE CANYON TRAIL

WATER TOWER

GUADALASCA TRAIL

DANIELSON GROUP CAMP

EMPLOYEE RESIDENCE

TRI-PEAKS (3010)

BONEY MOUNTAIN WILDERNESS
(WEST BOUNDARY IS BIG SYCAMORE CANYON TRAIL)

"HELL HILL"

PUMP STATION

WOOD CANYON TRAIL

OVERLOOK TRAIL

WOOD CANYON VISTA

WATER TANKS

(1221)

BIG SYCAMORE CANYON TRAIL

OVERLOOK TRAIL

PICNIC AREA
CAMPGROUND
MOUNTAIN PEAK
PAVED ROAD
MOUNTAIN BIKE TRAIL
OFF-ROADER'S DELIGHT

RAY MILLER TRAILHEAD

VENTURA

THE GREAT SAND DUNE

START HERE

SYCAMORE CANYON BEACH

SYCAMORE CANYON CAMPGROUND

SYCAMORE CANYON

N

1 → SANTA MONICA

0   MILE   1

RANCHO SIERRA VISTA

SATWIWA CULTURAL CENTER

TRIP #58 - SYCAMORE CANYON

221

Wood Canyon Trail. Reach a fork (3.0) with the Sycamore Canyon Trail/Backbone Trail to the right and our destination to the left on the Wood Canyon Trail. In 0.7 mile of winding mild uphill in shaded canyon is the Deer Creek Junction, another picnic area and the northern terminus of the Overlook Trail to the left-- more later. Go right (north) 1.3 miles on a narrowing trail under overhanging trees with lengthy segments of filtered sunlight. Several more creek crossings bring the cyclist to a more exposed area where the canyon widens and into Ranch Center, a small park employee community (5.3).

Ranch Center Road. The next 2.5 miles east on this asphalt ribbon parallels the northern park boundary. First is a no-nonsense, exposed 1/2 mile, 200-foot, climb to a water tower. Beyond is an unnamed, but bikeable, dirt trail that is a short-cut to the Upper Sycamore Canyon Trail. There are distant views of the Boney Mountain Ridge to the west of this junction. Stay on the paved road and follow a refreshing traverse of the hillsides and "let it out" with a nifty downhill that leads to a "T"-intersection at another paved road. To the left (north) is Rancho Sierra Vista/Satwiwa Cultural Center, two miles and a 500-foot climb away.

Upper Big Sycamore Canyon Trail. A turn right leads back to shaded road with scattered sycamore trees and into a large meandering meadow. Follow the road to its end near an employee residence or follow the paralleling dirt trail on the meadow's western edge. In either case, maintain a southern direction and bike past the dirt trail junction which is signed "To Ranch Center Road." (This is the outlet of the shortcut trail from the water tower previously mentioned.) Follow the steady downhill back to the Wood Canyon Trail Junction (10.5).

Calling Home from Lower Big Sycamore Canyon (Susan Cohen Photo)

Overlook Trail. Non-seasoned bikers should stay on Big Sycamore Canyon Trail and return to the starting point (13.5 total trail miles). Riders looking for a challenge (and who have extra water handy) could go west and repeat the short ride to Deer Creek Junction. In contrast to the prior visit, follow the marked Overlook Trail on an immediate steep grade which climbs above Wood Canyon and begins a slow turn to the south. What follows is an exposed sheer uphill which is so steep that it is difficult to get restarted uphill once you have stopped. Don half-rode, half-walked this hillside traverse, seeking whatever shade was available at periodic rest stops. The view back down into the canyon and beyond are superb, making the hard work more bearable.

A mile of this aerobic challenge leads to the La Jolla Valley Trail junction (hiking only) with views across the valley below and the Laguna Mountain Radar Facility at Pt. Mugu. The grade eases and the Overlook Trail meets the outlet of the Wood Canyon Vista Trail--more later. After an uphill 1/2-mile trek, which includes passing a pair of water towers and several saddle crossings, a summit is reached with a great 180-degree panorama of Sycamore Canyon and the Boney Mountain Ridge to the west (12.7). Don met three CORBA (Concerned Off-road Bicyclist Association) riders who explained that he had just negotiated "Hell Hill," a path seldom used anymore. The best route is the single-track Wood Canyon Vista Trail, twice as long, but designed for saner people!

The reward for the uphill effort is a scenic ride across the ridgeline with a nice downhill and a final short upgrade to a second crest. Next is a dandy 3.3-mile, 1100-foot, meandering descent back to the Big Sycamore Canyon Trail. (The most popular route is to use this ascent segment from the campground and return the same way.) The first ocean view is beyond, and the trail winds through a series of hills in a manner that provides many vistas into La Jolla and Sycamore Canyons. In 1.2 miles from the second crest is the Backbone Trail entry, which leads south and west down to the Ray Miller Trailhead. In the intervening stretch are scattered shale patches and at least one deep trail rut, which occupied nearly the entire trail--keep your speed in check on the descent.

The path goes by an unnamed trailhead outlet and follows a wide set of sweeps on yet another long hillside traverse which provides views into the campground at the Ray Miller Trailhead. The dirt track turns south, crosses a saddle and works downward off this massive hillside to a point that parallels a hiker's scenic trail. More ocean views appear as the trail works east on a sloping meadow, then reaches a series of steep switchbacks which drop you back into Big Sycamore Canyon. Once back on the main trail, go right (south) and return 1/2 mile to the trip start point (16.7).

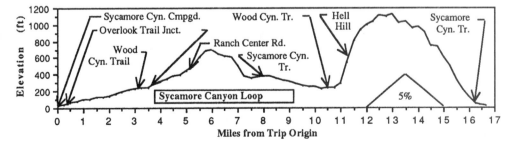

Trip Option. Biking Sycamore Canyon Trail by itself is a treat. The "cheater" option is to start from Rancho Sierra Vista and have a friend pick you up at Sycamore

Canyon Campground (it will take your "SAG wagon" longer to get there than you, since this is a lengthy automobile drive). Another easy option is to bike from the campground uphill as far as you want to go, then coast back to the start point.

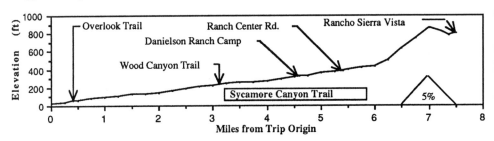

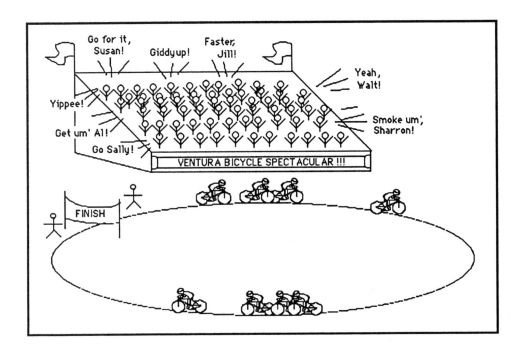

TRIP #59 - "CRAZY EIGHT" LOOP

GENERAL LOCATION: Fillmore, Santa Paula, Balcomb Canyon, Somis, Bardsdale

LEVEL OF DIFFICULTY: Fillmore Loop plus Somis Loop - strenuous
Distance - 74.8 miles
Elevation gain - sheer grade in Balcolm Canyon

HIGHLIGHTS: There are two separate trips which, for the strong of heart and leg, can be linked in the form of a "crazy eight." The motivation for the full trip is a scenic and "tough-as-nails" uphill through Balcolm Canyon and an exciting return.

224

The trips are labeled "Fillmore Loop" for the 34.9-mile circuit along the Santa Clara River that begins in Fillmore, and the 30.7-mile "Somis Loop" for the ride in the Las Posas Hills that starts in Somis. The Fillmore Loop is a mostly flat ride that plies both north and south banks of the Santa Clara River, while the Somis Loop primarily wanders through the citrus-covered Las Posas Hills on rolling terrain. For lovers of the solitude of isolated countryside, the latter loop offers a true delight in the hills.

TRAILHEAD: Fillmore Loop. From U.S. Hwy. 101, drive inland on State Hwy. 126 to the outskirts of Fillmore and turn left onto Sycamore Rd. Drive 2-3/4 miles and in 1/2 mile past 7th St., head right into Kenney Grove Park. This tree-shaded park has complete facilities for picnicking, as well as overnight camping. From Interstate Hwy. 5., drive west on State Hwy. 126 past the center of Fillmore and make a hard right on Old Telegraph Rd. Drive 1/2 mile to 7th St., turn left, then right at Oak Ave., and continue 1/2 mile to the park's entrance. Water can be obtained at commercial establishments along Hwy. 126. The southern Somis Loop portion is waterless.

Somis Loop. One of many options is to park in Somis, which is 1/2 mile off State Hwy. 118. We do not recommend parking off one of the isolated country roads.

Bradley Road

TRIP DESCRIPTION: Fillmore Loop. From the park, return to Oak Ave. and work over to the Old Telegraph Rd. intersection with Hwy. 126 (where the name changes from Ventura St. to Telegraph Rd.). Follow this busy road on wide bike shoulder on the northern valley edge. Track the Santa Clara River and transit to an area filled with citrus groves. Full 360-degree valley and mountain views are the rule. In 6.2 miles of mostly flat biking is Orcutt Rd., a passage over Juan Creek, and a turn right (north) at Hallock Dr., where bikers must exit. Next, pedal through the City of Santa Paula, go south on 12th St. under Hwy. 126 onto S. Mountain Rd. (8.2), and cross the Santa Clara River.

The city falls behind as you follow the winding contour of the foot of South Mountain on the south side of the river. View the Santa Paula Ridge to the north and cycle beside citrus orchards on a narrow rural road in rolling hills. In 4.3 miles from the river crossing is Balcolm Canyon Rd. and the option to do the "Crazy Eight"

225

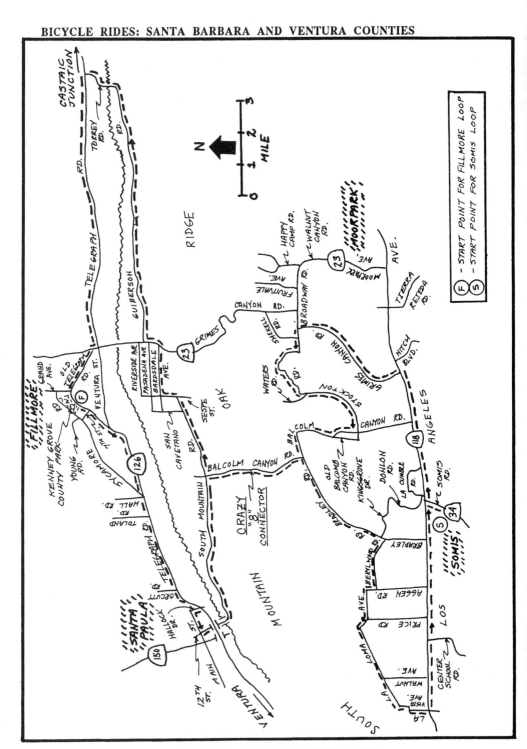

TRIP #59 - "CRAZY EIGHT" LOOP

loop (12.5). This loop continues through citrus groves to homey little Bardsdale and follows a patchwork route to Guiberson Rd. A seven-mile beeline in "citrusville" gives way to a sharp turn northward at Torrey Rd. This road recrosses the Santa Clara River at near-river level (subject to flooding) and returns to Hwy. 118 (25.3).

The highway passes a gas station and beer hall and bears directly west with great long-distance views of the Santa Clara River plain. On the outskirts of Fillmore, cross Pole Creek (31.4) and pass a cluster of stores (market, restaurant, fast food). In one mile, turn north at State Hwy. 23 ("A" St.) and meander into Fillmore on Old Telegraph Rd. along a fenced Class I bikeway/walkway. A turn right (north) on Grand Ave. leads through more citrus to the Kenney Grove Park entrance on Oak Ave. (34.9).

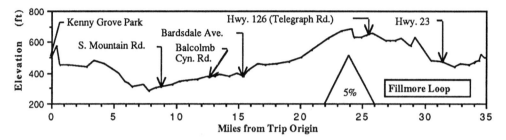

Somis Loop. Bike north to Los Angeles Ave., go right, and follow the busy Class X valley road eastward along Arroyo Las Posas. In 3.7 miles is Grimes Canyon Rd. and a turn north on an uphill past a variety of citrus crops and nurseries. Above, as with this generally isolated territory, are hawks "making lazy circles in the sky." At Broadway (7.3), begin a westwardly bent through more citrus-dotted foothills on roads which seem to change names every few miles. These are the Las Posas Hills. In 1-1/2 miles along Broadway/Stockton Rd. is the trip summit, with a distant view of the ocean and of an upcoming diet of more hills. A steady downhill through more citrus orchards on a lightly-used road leads past Waters Rd., where several mini-mansions stand out dramatically against the agricultural background.

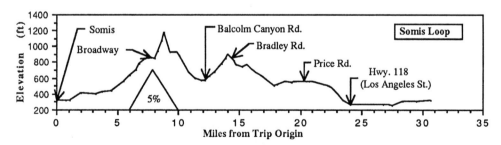

Turn right (north) on Balcolm Canyon Rd., follow a steady climb and then a downhill to Bradley Rd. (14.7), where Balcomb Canyon Rd. heads sharply right and dives down toward the Santa Clara River. Bear left on Bradley Rd. and stay on rolling hills, passing a European-style mansion in 1.3 miles (multi-faceted, steeple-topped, with trimmings and paintwork characteristic of Los Angeles' Alpine Village). A downgrade leads to a hard right at Berylwood Rd. (17.8), where you cycle past scattered eucalyptus stands on easy-going terrain through more citrus trees. On La Loma, visit a high plateau, pass Walnut Ave. and enjoy a nice downhill. The first view in a while of Los Angeles Ave. and the lower valley opens up in this area. At Los

Angeles Ave., head due east between South Mountain and the Camarillo Hills. In 6.6 miles on this busy, but wide-shouldered road, return to the start point in Somis (30.7).

Family Ride (Great American Tour de Heart)

Balcolm Canyon Connector. To do the "Crazy Eight," turn south at Balcolm Canyon Rd. at 12.5 miles into the Fillmore Loop. Pass some citrus groves and bike into the hills below South Mountain (RCA Satellite Tracking Station) and Oak Ridge. In 0.7 mile you enter the heart of Balcolm Canyon and, in another mile, start a steep winding uphill along the east flank of South Mountain. In the canyon below are numerous rusting automobile hulks and other assorted discards. The crest is reached in one mile and a 500-foot pumpathon (almost a 10% grade).

After a sharp curve right, reach a perch from which the citrus of the Las Posas Hills are spread below. A nice 0.7-mile downgrade takes the biker to Bradley Rd., which connects with the Somis Loop. Total commitment to do this uphill connector is 4.6 miles and 760-feet elevation gain. (Check your brakes before biking the steep return downgrade!)

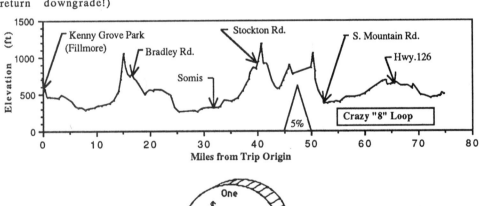

228

TRIP #60 - OJAI - SANTA PAULA LOOP

GENERAL LOCATION: Ventura, Ojai, Santa Paula

LEVEL OF DIFFICULTY: Loop - strenuous
Distance - 46.6 miles
Elevation gain - steep on Dennison Grade

HIGHLIGHTS: Definitely a great training ride, there are few stops and a lot of open terrain. This cycling tour passes along the City of Ventura periphery before heading north and mildly uphill to scenic Creek Rd. A six-mile moderate uphill through a rural setting puts the cyclist into the center of Ojai. Dennison Grade is the big challenge on the east side before reaching the massive, isolated Upper Ojai Valley. A grateful downhill returns you to Santa Paula. The final segment includes a lengthy Foothill Rd. tour into rolling citrus-covered hills. Take the Creek Rd. segment in autumn to enjoy the changing colors of the foliage. The Upper Ojai, Creek Rd. and Foothill Rd. segments make excellent workout tours in themselves.

TRAILHEAD: From U.S. Hwy. 101, exit north at Victoria Ave. and drive three miles to its terminus at Foothill Rd. Turn left, then right in 1/2-mile at the Arroyo Verde Park entrance. The north-south oriented day-use park is nestled on three sides into the foothills. This grassy bowl, that is the park, has picnic tables, barbecues, a playground and restrooms.

TRIP DESCRIPTION: Ojai-Bound. Going right (west) on Foothill Rd., the Class II path hugs the hillside to the north and passes through gentle rolling hills into the outskirts of Ventura proper, with ocean and valley vistas to the south and west. After a short downgrade, the road becomes Poli St., which you follow for the next two miles. (An option is to head south to Main St. at the California St. junction and visit the historical, and busier, part of town.) The reference tour continues past grassy, treed, city-block size Cemetery Park, in front of the classic Spanish-styled San Buenaventura City Hall and winds around the base of the hill below Grant Park. At Cedar St. and Prospect St., turn left (west) on the latter road, proceeding to Ventura Ave. (5.0).

A 1.7-mile Class III ride into the old, mixed commercial/residential north part of town leads to one of the few stop lights on this segment at Seneca St. Pass a small market at McKee St., enter flat land and go under State Hwy. 33, with distant views of the Santa Ynez Mountains framed by the valley hillsides. After passing Canada Larga Rd., cross back under Hwy. 33, and fuse with that highway (no longer a freeway at this point) (10.3). Foster Park and the Class I Ojai Valley Trail (see Trip #46) are to the west, but stay on the busy, wide-shouldered road. A gradual upgrade takes bikers past Casitas Springs through a stretch of tree-shrouded road and across San Antonio Creek.

At 2.4 miles from the Hwy. 33 entry is the turnoff to Creek Rd. (12.7). Bike a short downhill and begin a 5.8-mile gradual uphill into rural environs. Horse ranches, large residential lots, generous tree cover and the San Antonio Creek drainage to the east are the rule. This pleasing serpentine route passes Camp Comfort County Park. This sylvan retreat, which boasts picnic benches, barbecue facilities and restrooms is four miles from the Creek Rd. entry. Creek Rd. continues through this restful setting and, in 1.8 miles, reaches Ojai Ave.

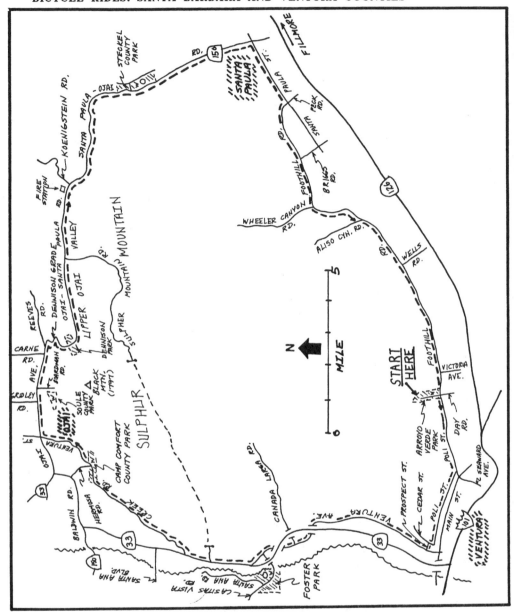

TRIP #60 - OJAI - SANTA PAULA LOOP

Ojai to Santa Paula. Head east, pass the Ojai Playhouse, old Spanish-styled U.S. Post Office and a modern shopping mall styled after the Franciscan-era architecture. The flat, busy Class X road crosses San Antonio Creek and reaches the entry to Soule County Park (see Trip #50) (19.8). The development thins as the land of citrus groves returns. (We spotted a coyote in this area.) At Reeves Rd. is a small cafe (last chance for goodies in the next 13.7 miles). A bend in the road (now called Ojai-Santa Paula Rd.) to the right announces the start of the tummy-tucking Dennison Grade.

The road narrows and there is a steep hairpin turn in 0.4 mile from Reeves Rd. In 1.2 miles and 340 feet of elevation gain is a scenic turnout point with a plaque identifying the major mountains to the north, including imposing Topa Topa Peak. Another 0.3 mile later is the tree-covered, picnicker's delight known as Dennison Park (closed when we passed through in mid-December) and, just beyond, a modest downgrade leading into the massive mountain-surrounded Upper Ojai Valley. Biking 2.2 miles on this majestic plain leads you to Sulphur Mountain Rd. near the trip's high point at Summit Trail (26.4). Continued pedaling takes bikers past more ranches and citrus orchards, then down a four-mile, 800-foot, drop to impressive Steckel Country Park (overnight camping, trees, barbecue facilities, restrooms, hiking trails, with Santa Paula Creek running through). In this segment is the little community of Sulphur Springs, numerous mountain vistas and several picture-postcard views of the Santa Paula Creek drainage. In 2-1/2 miles of downhill through scattered citrus groves are the Santa Paula outskirts and a small market at the city limits. Two miles of modest downgrade through a more developed area leads to the Santa Paula St. intersection (35.2).

Dennison Grade

Foothill Road Return. An initial Class II Santa Paula St. pedal is followed by the final segment which plies the dense citrus belt north of the Santa Paula River. The 9.6-mile Foothill Rd. portion is a serene, rolling-hills tour on the edge of civilization. The cyclist need only concentrate left (north) to a string of low mountains and right into the Santa Clara River drainage, staying observant of occasional traffic zipping by. The mostly straight-line road bends sharply south near Wheeler Canyon Rd. (40.0). The first far-off ocean views are seen beyond Kimball Rd., which is 1.8 miles short of the return entry to Arroyo Verde Park (46.6).

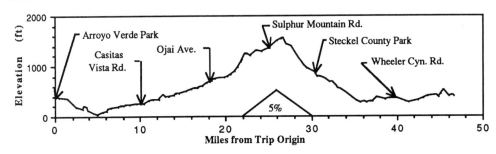

TRIP #61 ∘ SISAR CANYON (Mountain Bike)

GENERAL LOCATION: Summit (Upper Ojai Valley)

LEVEL OF DIFFICULTY: Up and back - very strenuous
Distance - 15.8 miles Sisar Canyon - Red Reef Trail Loop
Elevation gain - single continuous upgrade
(17% grade on Red Reef Trail)

HIGHLIGHTS: This trip, as related by Walt and Sally Bond, is one of Ventura County's best. The route is scenic and varied with a treed canyon, creek crossings, expansive vistas (particularly above the tree line) and a trek along Topa Topa Ridge with views of the Topa Topa Bluffs. No doubt this is an elevation workout, with nearly continuous steep-to-sheer upgrades. An especially tough segment on hot days is the 1-1/2 mile treeless stretch on the Red Reef Trail from the Sisar Canyon exit to Topa Topa Ridge. (Red Reef Trail is sheer--only for the most physically fit!) Return along Topa Topa Ridge with a turn south onto the upper reaches of Sisar Rd., followed by a tortuous downhill visit of Upper Sisar Canyon and a return to the Red Reef Trail junction. Then retrace the incoming route on Sisar Rd. to the trailhead.

TRAILHEAD: From the Ojai area, take State Hwy. 150 east to Upper Ojai Valley. Sisar Rd., in the community of Summit, is 2-1/2 miles west of Sulfur Mountain Rd. Follow this narrow road to the parking area near a set of water tanks. From the Santa Paula area, take Hwy. 150 north, pass Surphur Springs and drive 2-1/2 miles to Sisar Rd. Continue as described above.

Bring several quarts of water unless you want to chance the wet stuff from Sisar Creek. (We have become cautious of creek water sources near "people paths" and grazing lands.) White Ledge Camp has spring-fed water. On the Sisar Rd. return, there is a piped water trough from Wilsie Spring (1.5 miles downhill from the Topa Topa Trail departure point). Begin early in the morning on hot days, allowing for the shade of nearby slopes on the exposed upper reaches after the Red Reef Trail junction.

232

Mileage is approximate as the odometer quit working early on. Note that the trails are shared by cyclists, hikers and horse riders, so be careful and stay wary.

TRIP DESCRIPTION:
Sisar Canyon Road. The first uphill signals what is to come, as the narrow dirt road passes one gate (private) and reaches another, which blocks the road. The sign announces "White Ledge" (camp)-three miles and then "Horn Canyon" (junction)-four miles; these distances must be "as the crow flies," as they differ markedly from the U.S. Geological Survey topographic maps. Stay beside Sisar Creek under tree cover, making crossings near the 1/2- and 1-3/4-mile points. Numerous tributaries flow over the road in the canyon and can carry a lot of fast-moving water in heavy rainy periods; save the trip for better weather.

Sisar Road Creek Crossing

The fire road keeps switchbacking up Sisar Canyon and, near the 3.4-mile mark, reaches an out-of-place ivy-covered stone wall, a mini-jungle in the midst of forest country. Reach the Red Reef Trail (21W08) and the first of several decisions (3.5). The longest and least-steep approach is to stay on Sisar Rd. (see "Sisar Road Option").

Red Reef Trail. However, our outlined trip takes the right fork and follows Red Reef Trail on a steady, wind-sucking grade to White Ledge Trail Camp. (This is 1000-feet-per-mile territory, murderous even for hiking!) This tree-shaded mecca sits beside a creek, fed by a year-round spring: "The party's over" as the trail works further up into the first of mostly exposed and dry trail sections. A 1.5-mile sheer climb beyond the Sisar Canyon exit leads to a large barren plateau with spotty, low ground cover (5.6). This is the Topa Topa Ridge, where views span the horizon, and include Lake Casitas, Anacapa Island (on clear days), Ojai Valley below and the entire intervening coastal sections.

Topa Topa Ridge. At the junction with fire road 5N08 (Topa Topa Trail), an option presents itself. To the right (east) is a very steep-to-sheer, 0.3-mile climb leading to a saddle behind the Topa Topa Bluffs. For the adventurous, this diversion can be extended even further from the saddle by going south 0.6 mile on an unmarked trail to the top of the bluffs (peak 6367). Reportedly, this vantage point is a see-forever view of the south-tending bluffs and a 360-degree look at the surrounding peaks and canyons.

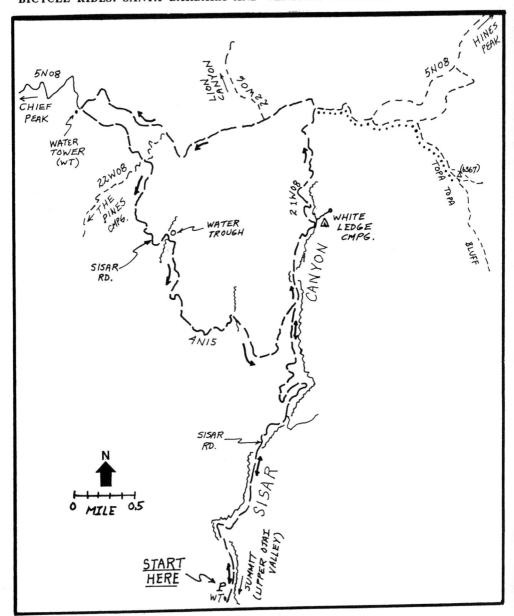

TRIP #61 - SISAR CANYON

Head left (west) instead and pedal a set of ups and downs on the ridgeline to the junction with Lion's Canyon Trail (22W06) (6.3). Continue downhill on 5N08 past the Horn Canyon Trail (22W08) junction (7.2), reaching Sisar Rd. (upper portion of 4N15) in another 0.6 mile at a water tower.

Creekside Rest Stop (Bob Alt Photo)

Sisar Road Return. The way back is to turn south (left) on 4N15 at this easternmost point. The winding road recrosses Horn Canyon and meets the like-named trail (8.6). (To the south about 1-1/4 miles and 1200-foot elevation loss from the junction is the Pines Trail Camp with a pine grove and piped-in water.) Sisar Rd. passes a potable water trough (thank Wilsie Spring for this!) (9.6) and negotiates a series of winding turns and switchbacks. Along the way is "Hot Rock," a name pinned on by outdoor adventurists for the rock's top, frequently used as a sun deck/rest spot. A wide "U"-bend particularly gets your attention in about one mile before dropping back into Sisar Canyon (12.3). Turn right on Sisar Rd, retracing the incoming route and coasting back to the trailhead in another 3.5 miles (15.8).

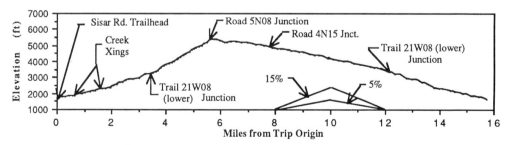

Sisar Road Option. On the incoming uphill leg, stay on Sisar Canyon Rd. past the 21W08 junction and either reverse the loop described (this means a sheer return on Red Reef Trail, balanced against a less stressing climb to Topa Topa Ridge), or ride

235

Sisar Canyon Rd. as an up-and-back trip. The up-and-back tour on Sisar Rd. to Topa Topa Ridge totals 16 miles. If the extension to Peak 6367 is included, add a total of six miles.

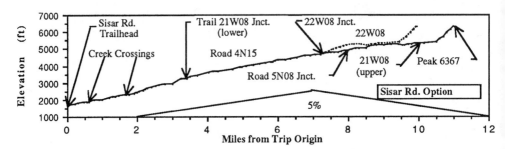

"Hot Rock" (Walt Bond Photo)

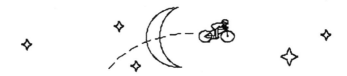

TRIP #62 - CASITAS PASS LOOP

GENERAL LOCATION: Ventura, Lake Casitas, La Conchita

LEVEL OF DIFFICULTY: Loop - strenuous
Distance - 46.2 miles (loop)
Elevation gain - periodic steep grades in Casitas Pass area

HIGHLIGHTS: A local classic, this 46-mile tour starts from Ventura's historic west side, works up to and around Lake Casitas, climbs into the East and West Casitas Pass areas, rockets down to U.S. Hwy. 101 and returns via the scenic oceanside Rincon Rdwy. The mixed-class route has all the elements of an exceptional bike ride: scenic views, mileage, backcountry, workout grades and quality roads. The pass areas have somewhat narrow and winding roads and the traffic is usually light. This is more than offset by the scenic vistas, particularly the snow-covered mountain views after winter storms. Another of the county's fine training rides, there are few stop signs or stop lights to break the pace. .

TRAILHEAD: Start from Plaza Park as described in Trip #46. Options are to start at Foster County Park (south of Ojai) or at Emma Wood State Beach County Park (west of the Ventura River in Ventura).

There is a 15-mile waterless stretch from the Lake Casitas Recreation Area to La Conchita, which encompasses the challenging and exposed Casitas Pass area. Bring several quarts of water.

TRIP DESCRIPTION: **Ventura to Lake Casitas.** Follow the Trip #46 directions to Santa Ana Rd. and Burnham Rd. (10.2). For this adventure, stay north on Santa Ana Rd. past Burnham Rd., cycling a progressively steepening uphill. A vista of the Santa Ynez Mountains' western edge opens up ahead with an over-the-shoulder view of the Ventura River Valley. The grade moderates as the Wadliegh Arm of Lake Casitas appears, then flattens and follows the lake contour past the Lake Casitas Recreation Area entry. This popular site has campgrounds, picnic areas, playgrounds, snack bar, bait and tackle shop, and boating facilities. (Word has it that bass, trout, and channel cats abound here!) Soon is a "T"-intersection at State Hwy. 150 (12.6), with Ojai about five miles east on Baldwin Rd. This tour heads west on Casitas Pass Rd.

Lake Casitas from Casitas Vista Road (see Trip #46)

237

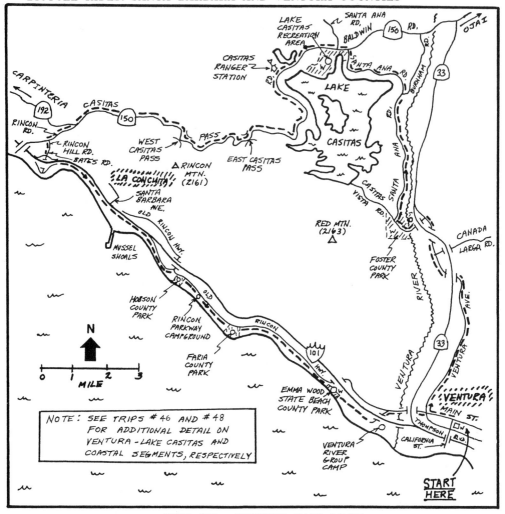

TRIP #62 - CASITAS PASS LOOP

Lake Casitas to State Highway 101. Casitas Pass Rd. transits a couple of modest hilly miles amid tree-spotted hills, crosses over a lake extension named Deep Cat Lake, passes the USFS Casitas Station, then cuts its way steeply upward on the north side of the Laguna Ridge. There are excellent lake vistas northward. The snaky, shore-hugging route returns to near-lake level twice, climbs back into the chaparral-covered hills and veers sharply west (17.2). A preview of the continuing, exposed steep climb to East Casitas Pass is provided by looking ahead to the roadside cutaway as it disappears well up the mountainside. In about 1-3/4 miles of steady pumping from near lake level, you reach the pass and take in the astounding view of distant Lake Casitas below.

A well-deserved downhill twists through the scrub-filled hillsides above a steep paralleling canyon, enters Casitas Valley with its scattered residences, then starts back uphill beneath the agricultural groves planted on the steep hillsides. This is the entry to what we have dubbed "Guacamole Valley." A rigorous one-mile climb past a berry farm and orchards leads to West Casitas Pass (21.1).   This is a joyous occasion to relish the 4-1/2 mile downhill spin to U.S. 101 which follows.

The next three miles prior to reaching the State Hwy. 192 junction is an exciting downhill through dense avocado orchards and above a canyon holding the Casitas Creek drainage.   Two miles below the pass is the first straightaway road in many a mile.   The east entry to Gobernador Canyon Rd. appears in 0.4 mile, followed by the Santa Barbara County Line and the Hwy. 192 junction in another 1/2 mile.   Go left and bike 1.0 mile on rural Rincon Rd.   A sharp left on easy-to-miss Rincon Hills Rd. takes the cyclist on a short, lightly-used, scenic road which becomes Bates Rd. just before reaching Hwy. 101 (25.7).

Lake Casitas Recreation Area

Highway 101 to Ventura.   Enter the southbound freeway and exit 4-1/2 miles later near Sea Cliff at Rincon Beach Park Dr.   Keep retracing the incoming route described in Trip #47 (Ventura to Santa Barbara: Southern Section map), going right onto a little Class I trail near where the old highway turns inland near Emma Wood State Beach County Park (42.5).   Return back to the bridge over the Ventura River in 2-1/2 miles and stay east on Class II Main St.   In one mile, turn right (south) on California St. and return to Plaza Park (46.2).

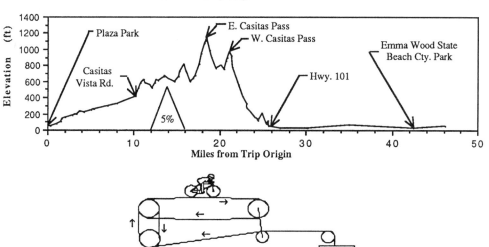

239

TRIP #63 - SULPHUR MOUNTAIN ROAD (Mtn. Bike)

GENERAL LOCATION: Ojai, Sulphur Mountain

LEVEL OF DIFFICULTY: Up and back - strenuous
Distance - 21.8 miles (up and back) 28.2 miles (loop)
Elevation gain - steady moderate-to-steep grades

HIGHLIGHTS: This is an alluring mountain-bike tour that plies the Sulphur Mountain ridgeline, gaining 2000 feet in 9.2 miles (average 4% grade). (Mileages are rough estimates as our odometer quit early in the tour.) Follow dirt/graded gravel-Sulphur Mountain Rd. for its full length, starting steeply near the trailhead in a forested area, then levels somewhat in exposed, oak-dotted hillsides for the trip's remainder. The route explores both north and south sides of the ridgeline, offering outstanding views of Ojai, Lake Casitas, the southside canyons, and distant Anacapa Island on very clear days. The return downhill is an absolute treat. An option to continue north past the Sulphur Mountain Rd. crest and complete the loop into Ojai on Creek Rd. is also provided.

TRAILHEAD: From Ventura, head north on the Ojai Fwy. (State Hwy. 33) past Casitas Springs. Beyond Nye Rd. is Sulphur Mountain Rd. on the right Drive to a large locked gate (with a moveable section for bikes) under shade trees--do not block the gate when parking. Bring 2-3 quarts of wet stuff since there are no sources on the up-and-back trip.

Sulphur Mountain Road with Ojai Backdrop

The county road is closed to motor traffic and is mostly dirt and graded gravel with some unstable, sandy and shale sections. Cyclists <u>must</u> stay on the main road; all side roads are smaller and gated (private property). Honor this consideration, since the

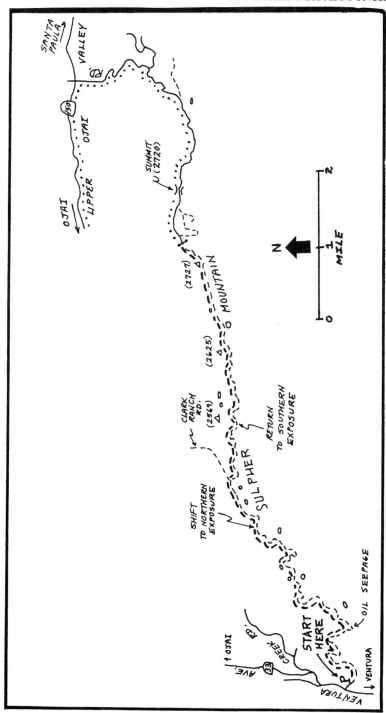

TRIP #63 - SULPHUR MOUNTAIN ROAD

owner is kind enough to allow bike traffic through some private sections. Our trip in June 1993 only took us through one closed gate, which is the biker's responsibility to close. There are several wide cattle guards to cross which demand your attention. The road is bikeable year-round, except during and immediately after rains. Best time of day to travel is early morning, when the temperature is modest and the west and north facing sections are shaded. There is only modest tree cover past the two-mile point. We saw few cattle, but were advised to travel low and slow in their presence, and to give them a patient right of way. We were greeted with cow pies and pesky flies on parts of the trail.

TRIP DESCRIPTION: Up. A few hundred feet beyond the trailhead is an aerobic "wake-up call" with a winding 1-1/2-mile upgrade, thankfully with tree cover. In the early part of the trip are views back to the trailhead and into Oak View, punctuated by a passage through a fragrant oil seepage near the first flat. Continue through an area that is a mix of exposed road and tree cover that hugs the slopes to the north and west. Scattered views of Ojai below open up which signal that a healthy chunk of elevation has been gained.

Continue along the Sulphur Mountain ridgeline and cross from southern to northern exposures (5.5). This translates into a change from far-away views of the canyons and mountains to the south to some spectacular views into Ojai, Lake Casitas and the powerful range of mountains to the north (Nordoff Peak to Topa Topa Bluff). This uphill traverse along the northside ridge involves some steeper road with rocks and shale that are a "pain in the pedal."

Mercifully, the road heads back to the southern ridgeline and a graded-dirt road that follows below the ridge top. Savor the views into Sulphur and Hammond Canyons and, on clear days, into Ventura, Oxnard and (with luck) Anacapa Island. At a crest is Rancho Vista Del Pacifica, a lone gated estate which overlooks Hammond and Aliso Canyons to the south. Continue east and upward on a 0.8-mile gravel-strewn asphalt traverse with wide-open southern vistas.

Rancho Vista Del Pacifica

Pass a water tower and barn-like structure and bike 0.7 mile on easy rolling terrain to a locked gate (10.9). This is a natural turnaround point for up-and back tourers. (There were roughly three miles of burned out slopes in this area when we revisited in Nov. 1993. As we understand, Mother Nature is making a comeback.)

Down. Return the way you came on an exciting let-it-out downhill with a couple of short and steep uphills for variety. There are some loose dirt patches on a few turns, a section of light shale/rock as noted, and a few deep ruts that demand full attention. Cycling may not get better than this downhill runout, a payback for the workout uphill.

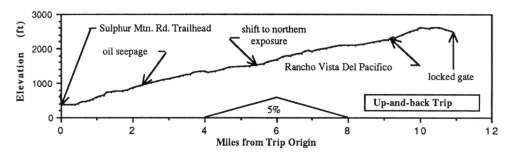

Ojai Loop Option-Downhill to Hwy. 33. (See Trip #60 map--mileages are from the trip origin.) At the locked gate, there is a frontal view of Topa Topa Mountain across the Upper Ojai Valley below as we begin four curvy miles on quality asphalt road beyond the locked gate. In another 0.8-treed mile is the road's crest and the start of a long downhill. Alternating views of Upper Ojai Valley and the southern canyons open up. In 3.6 miles from the gate, the tree cover gives way to more exposed terrain and farmland. Plunge into a canyon with a 180-degree switchback, then begin a 1/2-mile runout into a small valley to State Hwy. 150 (15.5).

Upper Ojai Valley. An easy-going westward 2-1/2-mile pedal in this serene valley of ranches and farms places the biker near Dennison Park. Beyond is a one-mile, 300-foot, drop through tortuous and wooded Dennison Grade and an outlet to Ojai Valley. Bocalli's Italian Restaurant (both a local and authors' favorite) at Reeves Rd. signals the entry into the Ojai outskirts (19.5).

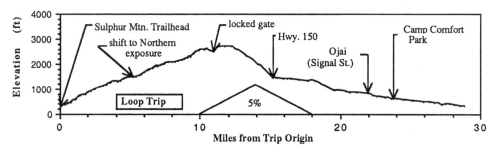

Ojai and Creek Roads. A continued flat ride transits citrus groves leading past Boardman Rd., the entry to Soule County Park. The first of several San Antonio Creek crossings lead past the Soule Park Golf Course and into Ojai proper. Pedal 0.8 mile past eateries and specialty shops into the heart of this popular tourist haven and reach Signal St. (22.0). Turn left and pass Libbey Park, then wander over to Ventura St. In 1/4 mile, the street becomes Creek Rd. and meanders downhill back and forth across San Antonio Creek in a shaded country setting. Past Hermosa Rd. is Camp Comfort Park (trees, picnic facilities, group camp, playground, restrooms, water). The winding road follows the canyon bottom through scattered horse ranches and developed pockets, reaches a low point, then starts a mild 1/2-mile climb back to Hwy. 33. A 0.8-mile flat spin take riders past Rancho Arnez (apples, cider) and Old Creek Rd. to the Sulphur Mountain Rd., the turnoff for the trailhead. (28.8).

Think about a return to Old Creek Rd. to celebrate the trip completion at the Old Creek Winery. Keep one hearty cyclist as a trusted driver on your return home.

243

TRIP #64 - PINE MOUNTAIN (Off-road)

GENERAL LOCATION: Pine Mountain

LEVEL OF DIFFICULTY: Up and back - strenuous
Distance - 5.9 miles to Reyes Peak Campground;
7.6 additional miles to Haddock Mountain
Elevation gain - continuous steep grades up to campground

HIGHLIGHTS: Though short in miles, this winding climb along the length of the Pine Mountain spine will test your stamina. The first 5.9 miles are shared with sparse auto traffic, many "blind" turns, but also provides a steady diet of spectacular vistas. This trip is best done on week days. Four miles of climb on exposed, alternating pocked-asphalt and packed dirt road gives way to a forested uphill past Pine Mountain Campground. Near the gated entry to the backcountry, about two miles farther, are the upper reaches of fantastic Reyes Peak Campground. The off-road tour after the gate is on good quality packed dirt for the 2.6 miles it takes to reach the flank of Reyes Peak. Another five more roller-coaster miles on a scenic trail with limited net elevation gain lead to a turnaround point below Haddock Mountain. (The trail beyond is for experts only.) On the latter segment, cyclists follow the Pine Mountain spine, weaving between and just below a steady line of peaks.

TRAILHEAD: From Ojai, head north on scenic State Hwy. 33 for 30 miles to the Pine Mountain turnoff at the Pine Mountain Summit (four miles north of the Pine Mountain Inn). For the reference trip, have a friend drop you off at this point. Another option is to start from the gate above Reyes Peak Campground, bike to Reyes Peak and "bomb" downhill back to Hwy. 33. An easy-to-moderate option is to bike from the gate to Haddock Mountain. This is the creme-de-la-creme segment of the trip. Bring several quarts of water for the "full-banana tour," as there are no available sources.

TRIP DESCRIPTION: To Reyes Peak Campground. From Hwy. 33, start an immediate upgrade on a narrow, rough asphalt road (6N06) winding into the mountains above the highway. There are scrub-filled hillsides, blind bends (watch for what little traffic there is), and patchwork road that varies from rough asphalt to packed dirt. The reward is ever-more-exciting views into the canyons which hold Adobe and Sespe Creeks (as well as Hwy. 33) and of the mountain ranges to the west. In 2.7 miles, views open to the north into the canyons that enfold Lockwood Valley Rd. below. Cross a saddle and pump a mile to reach the edge of the forested area of Pine Mountain ridge. Road conditions improve after entering a valley and passing the Pine Mountain Campground (tree cover, restroom, picnic tables, barbecues). Now in a high and inclined valley below the ridgeline, the asphalt ribbon runs through a 180-degree switchback and climbs to the first camp site of the Reyes Peak Campground. The next 0.6 mile has some of the best overnight campsites we have

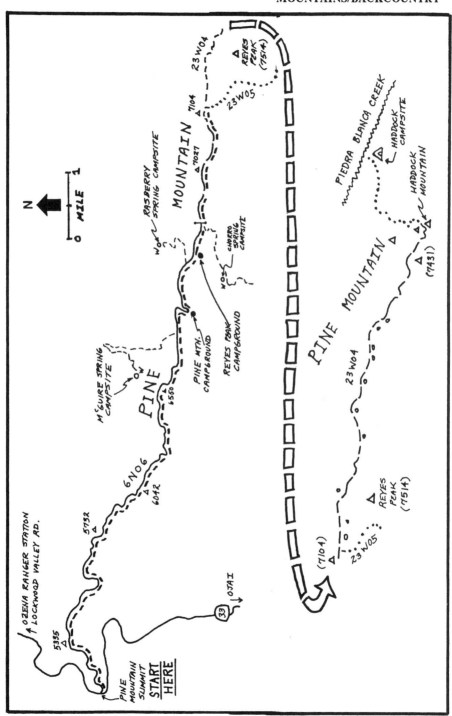

TRIP #64 - PINE MOUNTAIN

Reyes Peak Backdrop

occupied, all well separated and back-dropped by giant bolders (benches and fire grates, but no water). Sunset views of the western mountain ranges are nothing short of spectacular! At a gate, the Chorro Grande Trail heads south while the dirt road to Reyes Peak and Haddock Mountain continue east. Reyes Peak is clearly visible at this juncture.

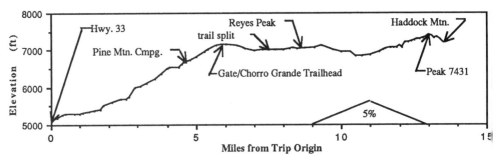

To Reyes Peak and Haddock Mountain. Pass the Chorro Grande trailhead (5.9) and bike east on a quality graded-dirt road, passing below nearby Munson Peak, then pedal on a flat grade to a trail junction beyond peak 7104 (7.6). The south fork goes 1.8 miles and dead ends on the south face of Reyes Peak. However, you follow the north fork trail (23W04) beyond a motorized vehicle barrier and head east below Reyes Peak (8.5). The trail to Haddock Mountain is a moderate teeter-totter ride with little net elevation change. There are transitions between somewhat-exposed and more heavily-treed sections, and periodic views east into the canyons which envelop

Piedra Blanca Creek. The turnaround point (13.5) is just below the Haddock Mountain summit. Beyond is some very treacherous downhill leading to Piedra Blanca, Lions and Reyes Creek Campgrounds. These are remote and reserved for the trail-wise and trail-hearty only. Consult other off-road books which deal with technical off-road cycling if this is your bag.

Chorro Grande Trail Option. Chorro Grande Trail (23W05) winds steeply down the Pine Mountain face, switchbacks past the Chorro Spring Camp (spring-fed water), and enters Chorro Grande Canyon. Further below is the Oak Campsite and a crossing near a waterfall, where the trail plummets to a junction with Hwy. 33 (mileage marker 36.60). Stay to the west (right) at the trail junction above Oak Campsite; the left junction wanders the lower ridges and dumps out further south on Hwy. 33. This trail is only for experienced off-roaders, since there are narrow and exposed sections with steep drops. This lively downhill drops over 3000 ft. in its 7.2-mile transit to scenic Hwy. 33 (an average 8% grade).

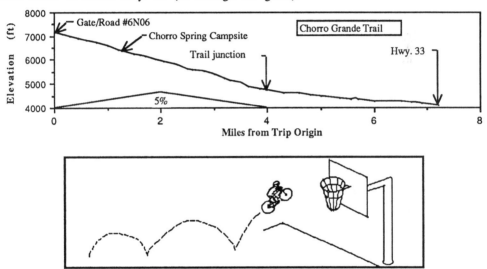

TRIP #65 - LAKE PIRU

GENERAL LOCATION: Piru, Lake Piru

LEVEL OF DIFFICULTY: Up and back - moderate to strenuous
Distance - 25.6 miles (up and back)
Elevation gain - moderate-to steep-grades

HIGHLIGHTS: Like Sisyphus and his labor, this is an opportunity to push an object (bicycle) up a hill, only to have it return to the base. After roughly 3-1/2 miles of level biking in scenic Piru Canyon, climb above the Santa Felicia Dam to enjoy an extended stretch of riding along, and mostly above, Lake Piru. The lake offers visitors great boating, trout and bass fishing, camping, water skiing, swimming and hiking. Pass two lake-level overnight camping areas with olive and oak trees. Beyond is a steep switchback signaling a climb back above the lake and an isolated several-mile mountainside trek before reaching the trip's end at isolated Blue Point Campground. On the way, cyclists enter a narrowing canyon where Piru Creek dumps into the lake. The trip is completed with a mostly downhill return to the start point.

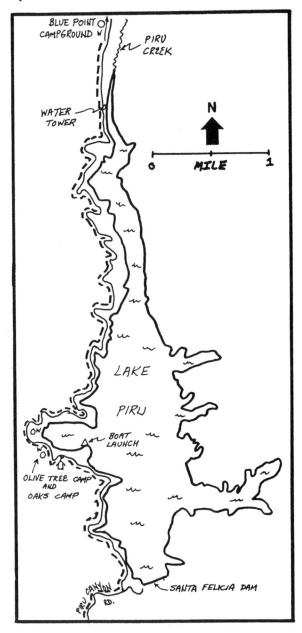

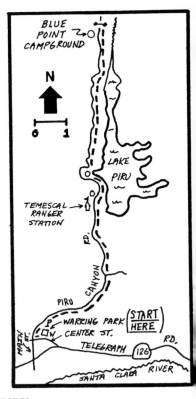

TRIP #65 - RIDE TO LAKE PIRU

TRAILHEAD: From State Hwy. 126 (Telegraph Rd.), go north at either Main St. (eastbound) or Center St. (westbound) and proceed one mile to Orchard St. and Warring Park. The day-use park has restrooms, a few shade trees, benches, baseball field, and a play area.

TRIP DESCRIPTION: To Santa Felicia Dam. Head right (east) from the park on Main St. and enjoy a 3.6-mile flat spin beside Piru Creek within Piru Canyon. Hug the contour of the mountains to the north and west for the entire ride. The early part is in a wide valley with trees and cattle. At 2.1 miles is the first view of the dam and, in another 1.5 miles, the initial ascent of that monolith. The grade then steepens dramatically and works its way 0.9 mile above the dam to a viewpoint of Lake Piru and Piru Canyon (4.5).

To **Blue Point Campground.** A short and steep pedal puts you at a crest. Then the road levels and proceeds steeply downhill on a sharp switchback above the lake. A series of rolling grades lead to the lake's entrance and a ranger station. Pass Olive Tree and Oaks Camps with the namesake trees scattered about. The overnight camps sport picnic facilities, fire pits, restrooms (with shower) and tree cover. The wide valley of groves and orchards nearby were planted by David C. Cook, founder of Piru, who wanted the area to be a second Garden of Eden. Across from the campground entry is the boat launch ramp and a market (5.8).

Lake Piru Boat Launch Area

Continuing north, pass the day-use picnic site (6.9) with covered eating areas, lawns, grills and tables. The road narrows, goes over a creek and follows a hairpin uphill by a dilapidated dwelling. The narrowing road follows along the western slopes, leaving Lake Piru further below. Leave the lake proper, continuing on a circuitous uphill above the Piru Creek Canyon. Cross a feeder creek at a canyon outlet, then climb roughly 200 feet in about a mile to the trip's high point (9.5). In this segment, you follow a "U"-bend within a canyon which is feed by both a runoff creek and Juan Fernandez Spring (tucked away in the hillside above). A refreshing downgrade, 3.3 miles of modest ups and downs (with several more feeder creek crossings) lead to Blue Point Campground (12.8) This is 1.1 miles beyond a water tower which is nestled between the road and Piru Creek. (There is a dynamite hike from the campground to the Pothole, a natural sink of lush grassland created by the Agua Blanca Fault.) All that remains now is to "cash in" all the uphill mileage with an easier return to the trailhead (25.6); beyond the trip's crest, the return segment is predominantly downhill.

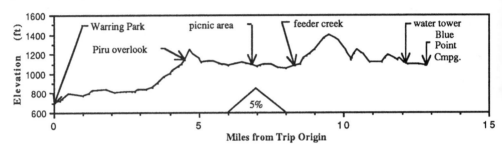

Start Point Options. Start from either Blue Point or Olive Tree Campgrounds, better options if overnight camping is a consideration. For the truly decadent, start from Blue Point Campground and cycle to Piru, then meet your waiting "chauffeur." (The road does continue beyond the Blue Point Campground; however, it is blocked to automobile traffic by a locked gate.)

TRIP #66 - LOCKWOOD VALLEY - POTRERO RD. - CUYAMA VALLEY LOOP

GENERAL LOCATION: Ozena Ranger Station, Lake of the Woods, Ventucopa

LEVEL OF DIFFICULTY: Loop - very strenuous
Distance - 85.2 miles
Elevation gain - periodic steep grades

HIGHLIGHTS: Not a tour for the weak-at-heart, this mountain-man special leaves the Ozena Ranger Station and climbs 2000 feet through the mountains of Los Padres National Forest to a summit. The winding road lets out at mile-high Lockwood Valley, where the cyclist is treated to a 6-7 mile "breather" in the mountain-surrounded environs prior to reaching Lake of the Woods. Following are a series of climbs and drops on Mil Potrero Rd. through tree country, which includes Cuddy Valley and leads to a summit at the Apache Saddle Ranger Station near Cerro Noroeste Rd. About 20 scenic downhill miles follow with a mix of trees and barren hills, fantastic deep canyon views and a pass by of Cowhead and Apache Potreros. In four miles is the entry into the Cuyama Valley region. The last 20 miles is on a steady, but mild, upgrade through the Cuyama Valley. Tracking the river plain to the west, distant mountain views are spread throughout the valley. The cyclist proceeds, sandwiched below the mountains, with only periodic crossroads and feeder creeks to interrupt the reverie. The tour ends after crossing Lockwood Valley Rd. and cranking a little further south to the ranger station.

TRAILHEAD: From the Ventura area, follow State Hwy. 33 north to the Ozena Ranger Station, which is about four miles past Pine Mountain Summit. Park at the station (which has water) and check road conditions, particularly if there has been a recent storm. Parts of this tour have road segments which can be flooded by creeks or blocked by winter snows. From the Santa Barbara area, follow State Hwy. 166 east and start from New Cuyama (see Trip #39). An option is to stay east on Hwy. 166 and travel south on State Hwy. 33 for seven miles to Ventucopa Station.

TRIP DESCRIPTION: Lockwood Valley Road. Pedal north and turn east on Lockwood Valley Rd. This starts a nine-mile plus, 1600-foot, upgrade to a summit. The surroundings transition from flat farmland to wooded, mountainous terrain as you pass the entry to several campgrounds. The last mile is very steep and the road hugs the tortuous contour of the imposing mountainside (10.2). Coast a modest two-mile downhill that includes several points where creeks run directly across the road. The twisting asphalt road hugs the mountain wall and provides sweaty-palm views deep into Park Canyon below San Guillermo Mountain. More creek crossings and a two-mile grade leads to a 5516-foot summit.

Mil Potrero Road Overlook

A steady downhill places you at the Pine Springs Campground turnoff at Mutau Rd. (15.8). The road straightens as you cruise into mountain-rimmed Lockwood Valley. An easy five-mile valley ride on rolling terrain leads past the dilapidated Owl's Barn bar (an old local favorite, now boarded up) and passes another uphill leading to a summit overlooking Cuddy Valley. A well-deserved downgrade takes you past the Chuchupate Ranger Station and the turnoff to the like-named campground. Cross the Kern County Line and reach the outskirts of Lake of the Woods, announced by the appearance of a cafe, realtor's office, bakery, and pizzeria; beyond is Frazier Park Rd./Cuddy Valley Rd. (26.8).

Mil Potrero Road. Turn left onto Cuddy Valley Rd., crank through Lake of the Woods and, in 1/4 mile, pass into the less-populated upper reaches of Cuddy Valley. This is in the heart of the San Andreas rift zone. Five miles of steady uphill through Cuddy Valley provides a pine-forest trek under the northern slopes of the Tecuya Ridge with Frazier Mountain and Mount Pinos dominating the southern landscape. The biker must make a conscious turn right onto Mil Potrero Rd. at the Mt. Pinos Hwy.

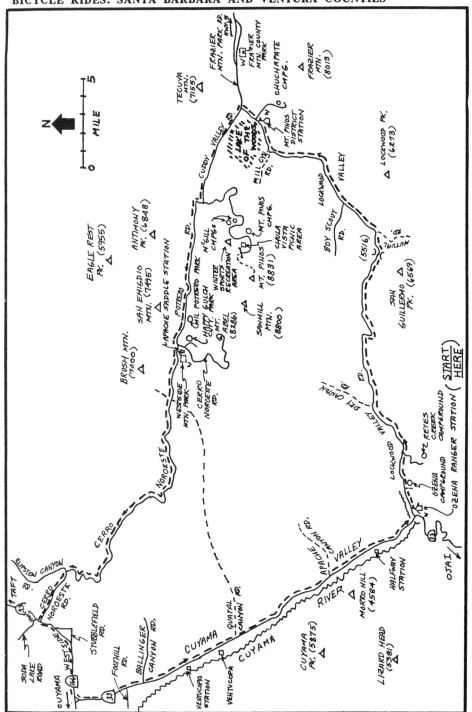

TRIP #66 - LOCKWOOD VALLEY - POTRERO ROAD - CUYAMA VALLEY LOOP

juncture (31.0) to follow the described tour (or else divert to a rugged uphill route to the Mt. Pinos recreation area). The road is totally immersed within a pine forest for the next nine miles. Three miles of downhill heads past Pine Mountain Club, with a 0.7-mile workout uphill to Ward Dr. A steep downhill canyon transit takes bikers to a valley floor and a four-mile uphill pull to Cerro Noroeste Rd. (39.8). Along the forested route is Village Center, with a general store, restaurant and Mil Potrero Park (water) off to the south. Cerro Noroeste Rd. is at Apache Saddle, the site of the Apache Ranger Station and Westside Mountain Park and is the trip summit.

Next is roughly 20 miles of almost total downhill. (Don's cycling companions have accused him of using the expression, "it's all downhill from here", too often") The route works to a massive down-sloping "plateau," providing views of the successive mountain ranges to the west. In a little over 2-1/2 miles from Apache Saddle are the first of many miles of views into the deep bowels of Santiago Canyon, with imposing Blue Ridge as a backdrop. Bike into a mix of scrub and trees skirting the north edge of massive Cowhead Potrero, ("Potrero" means pasture ground or a farm for rearing horses in Spanish.) with more striking views into the barren mountains to the north.

"Big Time" Watering Device in Cuyama Valley

In the next several miles (on what is now Cerro Noroeste Rd.) is an overwhelming collage of canyon and mountain vistas. The road roughly parallels the San Andreas rift zone, where one gets a first-hand look at the effects of millions of years of ground movement and mountain upthrusts. Coast along the north side of Apache Potrero, another gigantic meadow smack-dab in the middle of the array of mountains. On this stark plateau, the road leads further northwest and passes above the Valle Vista Campground (waterless) (48.8). The canyon vistas here are among the most impressive on this tour.

253

In a few pedal revs is the Los Padres National Forest boundary and more views into the massive rift zone. Proceed further downhill through the Bitter Creek National Wildlife Refuge and take in the first view of a transmitter station on a nearly dominant peak. Enter cattle country and circumnavigate the transmitter on a route which seems to follow all four compass points. This lonely passage through the treeless hills leads past the first near-road farmhouse in awhile, and drops down to Klipstein Canyon Rd. (58.0).

The downhill road straightens and meets Westside Hwy. (combined Hwys. 33 and 166) in 2.6 miles. To the north is a visible oasis at Reyes Station (snacks, liquid refreshments, antique shop). Turn left (southwest) onto the main highway, drop to a desert-like floor, cross the San Luis Obispo County Line and cruise to where Hwy. 33 junctions south into the Cuyama Valley (65.2). Hwy. 166 diverts west toward Cuyama.

Cuyama Valley. Turn onto Hwy. 33 and bike a 20-mile, 1000-foot, gain segment along the westernmost reaches of the Cuyama River. "The Place" is eight miles from the turnoff, a small restaurant in tiny Ventucopa. Cruise the valley and eyeball the surrounding distant peaks, including imposing Cuyama Peak and Morro Hill to the southwest. The steady valley pedal is broken by scattered connector roads from the eastern canyons and feeder creeks passing under the road to the Cuyama River plain. At Halfway Station is the Halfway Station Cafe and a rest area. Cross a major tributary in a few miles and greet Lockwood Valley Rd. A short hop south on Hwy. 33 takes you back to the ranger station (85.2).

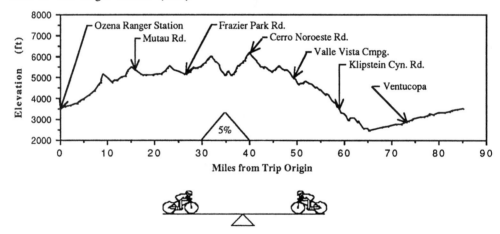

TRIP #67 - MOUNT PINOS LOOP

<u>GENERAL LOCATION</u>:   Los Padres National Forest

<u>LEVEL OF DIFFICULTY</u>: Loop - strenuous
  Distance - 14.4 miles
  Elevation gain - steep moderate-to-steep grade on
    Seymour Rd.

<u>HIGHLIGHTS</u>: This was one of the premier mountain-bike loops until we returned in June 1994 to verify that a two-mile section on Seymour Rd. had been shut off to the public by the new private owner. The Seymour Sage Flat area is fenced off to all

traffic. We have written this as a loop in the hopes that the easement sought by the U.S. Forest Service will soon reopen the route to cyclists. Meanwhile, other options are available that are described at the end of the loop trip description.

The full loop involves a moderate-to-strenuous eight-mile uphill, departing near the old Owl's Barn, transits the clear cut of Seymour Sage Flat (if the USFS easement is obtained), and winds aimlessly (or so it seems) up into pine forest under numerous peaks. A steeper one-mile upgrade leads to the Mill Canyon Rd. junction and follows a constricted canyon along Mill Creek on a steep downhill for several miles. The grade lessens as the canyon widens and the road drops down to a terminus at Lockwood Valley Rd. A paved-road return leads to Owl's Barn. Take into account that the entire route is above 5000 feet when planning your trip timeline.

TRAILHEAD: From Lake of the Woods, head southwest on Lockwood Valley Rd. The unmarked trailhead for Seymour Rd. (8N05) is near mile marker 22.6 across the highway from the old Owl's Barn bar. This dilapidated, boarded-up structure was a local hang-out. To start from Mill Canyon Rd. (9N04), follow Lockwood Valley Rd. to mile marker 24.0 (1-1/2 miles north of the boarded-up Owl's Barn bar) near the Plunderosa Ranch. To start from Mount Pinos Hwy., the trailhead is about 0.3 mile below McGill Campground (restrooms, water, barbecue facilities, overnight camping; closed in winter).

Lower Seymour Road

TRIP DESCRIPTION: Seymour Rd. The tree-sheltered, graded-dirt road (8N05) passes several off-shoots to homes and follows a "U"-bend starting at 0.3 mile. The road changes direction from southwest to north. Take the downhill junction right at 0.4 mile to keep on the road, follow along a feeder creek, swing west and come up

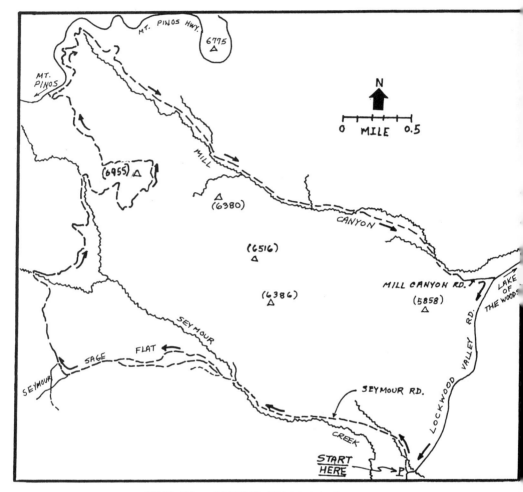

TRIP #67 - MOUNT PINOS LOOP

beside Seymour Creek (1.2). Navigate the first of several sand patches at the lower elevations and creek crossings throughout the trek. A posting notes private property on both sides of the road (1.7) and Seymour Creek disappears off the right. In 0.4 mile is a three-way road split, each blocked by gates and the lower two with signs noting electrified fences. If you gain permission, pass Seymour Sage Flat, a wide-open area punched out from the surrounding forest.

Seymour Rd. transits the flat westward, swings sharply north (3.4), passes a road junction left and begins a serious uphill through pines. No more major trail decisions are necessary from here to the Mill Canyon Rd. junction. For 3-1/2 miles, your direction changes many times and follows the contours of several 6000+-foot peaks. Take a wide swing to cross a large canyon (4.3), with additional crossings at the 5.0- and 5.5-mile points. These canyons carry the creeks that feed Seymour Creek. A tight switchback westward on a mostly flat terrain follows a one-mile, 360-degree, circumnavigation of peak 6955. The trail steepens for the last mile, then works northward to a three-way junction below Mt. Pinos Hwy. (8.0), where a left leads to the highway and McGill Campground.

Mill Canyon Rd. The right junction is the graded-dirt trail back to home base and has the appearance of the route up for the first 3/4 mile. Follow Mt. Pinos Hwy. from below, work back and forth across the compass, then pull away to the southeast and cross a ravine. This is Upper Mill Canyon, the route for the next 4.2 miles. Cross a ravine and pull beside Mill Creek, maintaining the rapid descent. The views down the canyon are distracting, so keep a wary eye on the path, or slow down and look. Keep to the north side of the creek, cross a major feeder creek (10.4) after passing to the west of a low hill, and follow a lesser grade for the remainder of the trip.

Within the enclosed canyon is another feeder crossing (11.3) and the first Mill Creek crossing near where the canyon widens appreciably. The slopes to the north fall away here (11.7). Accompany Mill Creek on its south bank after a set of trail/road junctions (12.3) and coast down to Lockwood Valley Rd. in 0.7 mile. Go right (south) and downhill for 1.4 miles and return to: a) the trailhead; or b) the Owl's Barn for an imaginary "cold one."

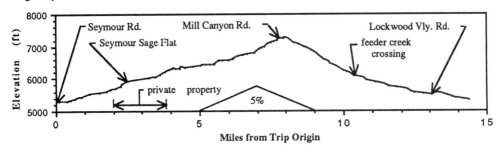

Trip Options. 1) Do an up-and-back trip in Mill Canyon; 2) arrange a car shuttle and cruise down Mill Canyon to Lockwood Valley Rd. from Mt. Pinos Hwy.; 3) do an up-and-back on Seymour Rd. from Mt. Pinos Hwy., doing a turnaround at the private property line; 4) attempt the full loop. Use the intercom at the gate below Seymour Sage Flat and ask for permission to pass (no one answered us); or 5) use Boy Scout Camp Rd. as the entry route to Mr. Pinos Hwy. and reconnect at Mill Canyon Rd. (many additional miles!).

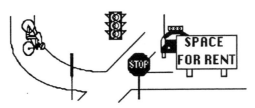

TRIP #68 - FISHBOWLS LOOP

GENERAL LOCATION: Los Padres National Forest

LEVEL OF DIFFICULTY: Loop - strenuous
Distance - 12.7 miles
Elevation gain - steep-to-sheer grade above Fishbowls
Campground

257

BICYCLE RIDES: SANTA BARBARA AND VENTURA COUNTIES

HIGHLIGHTS: We call this "the trip of many surprises." The mileage and elevation are nominal, but this is definitely a challenge of Mother Nature. Most of the trip is in sheltering forest and follows meandering Piru and Cedar Creeks. Along the route are numerous sandy sections, fallen trees across the trail and a myriad of river crossings. The summit climb is a challenge, very steep and on narrow trail. The downhill from the summit is also on a narrow trail with precipitous drops, and is difficult to ride on stretches. But leave no doubt this is a highly scenic ride and a worthwhile challenge!

TRAILHEAD: From Lake of the Woods, follow Lockwood Valley Rd. to the southern edge of Lockwood Valley. In two miles from Boy Scout Camp Rd., go south on a paved road to a marker announcing "Grade Valley" and other destinations (7N03). Drive on mixed road surfaces past Grade Valley to a tree-shaded flat, which normally is full of horsemen, horses and their trailers. If you reach the Piru Creek crossing, you've gone about 1/2 mile too far. The trailhead is visible about 100 yards south of the flat with a large metal gate set next to a prominent rock formation.

TRIP DESCRIPTION: Trailhead to Fishbowls. The first 1.8 miles is in a forest and on a rolling contour along Piru Creek. There are numerous sand patches. We called them "sand traps," then "sand devils," and eventually "#*$#* by the time we reached the outlet on Cedar Creek Trail. The first Piru Creek crossing introduces the first of many downed trees across the Fishbowls Trail, a result of a 1987 fire which burned from the Fishbowls area to Grade Valley Rd. The route stays with the main creek between low peaks on the south for 1.7 miles, crosses feeder creeks, sandy stretches and fallen timber. There are several closely-spaced crossings of Piru Creek and a big "U"-bend. After the bend is a bluff and an unobstructed 1/2-mile view up the Piru Creek drainage.

Above Piru Creek, Early in the Trip

At about the five-mile point, a major creek dumps into Piru Creek on the opposite bank. Piru Creek turns south and starts to snake in a narrowing canyon under a tree canopy. This begins a segment of many creek fords. In another 0.6 mile, a second major creek drops into Piru Creek. Keep a careful eye on the trail and remember to head upstream past the junction. (As we discovered, there are a multitude of small spur paths in this area.) Another crossing to the west bank leads to Fishbowls

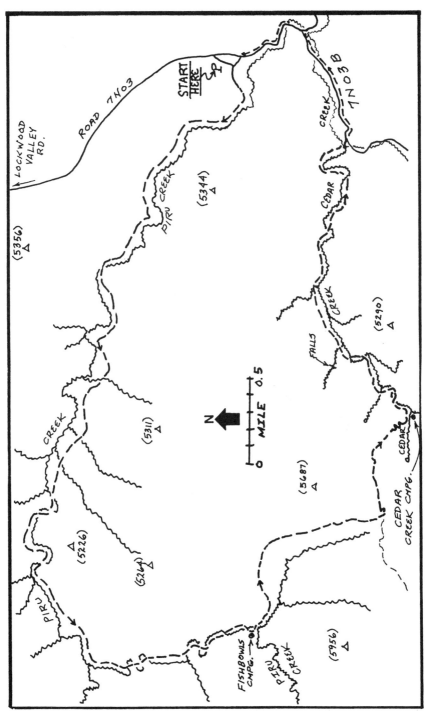

TRIP #68 - FISHBOWLS LOOP

Campground with abundant tree cover and scenic surroundings. The Fishbowls themselves are reportedly found by hiking 100 yards or so upstream from camp. They are 20-25-foot deep pools carved out of the sandstone by the creek (6.3).

Fishbowls to Grade Valley Road. After recrossing Piru Creek, a quick and steep passage over a small ridge leads to a narrowing trail, turns east and leaves Piru Creek. Several feeder creek crossings lead to switchbacks. The trail from here to the ridge's top is so steep, and the trail so narrow and rough, that pushing your bike uphill may be required. Through thinning tree cover, reach an exposed saddle with the first of many long-range vistas.

Climb 1/2 mile up a ridgeline that will bring tears to your eyes and fire to your quadraceps. A surprise awaits past the summit (7.7)! Now under a tree canopy, the narrow trail hugs the mountain, with steep drop-offs into the canyon, and crosses several ravines on a varying steepness downhill. We walked our bikes in some areas and rode with a leg extended on the mountain side, used to either speed up or slow down progress. (Our maps indicated a trail (22W10) fork to the right just beyond the summit--we did not see it.)

Mountain Biking or Tree Climbing??

The now-unshaded trail rockets down a steep ridgeline, switchbacking down the south side and then north side, staying well above the steep drop-away canyon. Cross a saddle and switchbacks to spring-fed Cedar Creek. (If you are a gambler, this may be an option to resupply your water, if necessary. The smarter option is to pack in your own water supply. A crossing leads to Cedar Creek Camp under a mantel of conifers. The Cedar Creek Trail outlet is almost a replay of the early incoming segment of the Fishbowls Trail, with sand traps, creek crossings, but no downed trees. This 2-1/2-mile, level and forested section crosses and recrosses Cedar Creek numerous times before reaching Grade Valley Rd. (11.5).

The Blessed Return. We felt ready for anything when we reached the road. To our surprise, there were no more surprises, just an easy 1.3-mile return on wide, graded road. With photo-taking and rest-and-exploration stops, this little off-road "beauty" took us over seven hours!

Saddle Below the Trip Summit

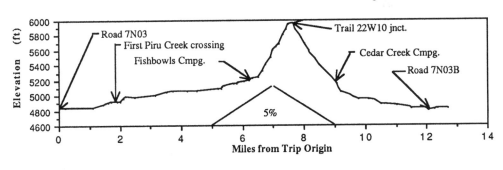

261

INDEX: SANTA BARBARA COUNTY

ATTRACTION, POINT OF INTEREST	TRIP NUMBER(S)
Mission Santa Ines	15,20,21
Mono Campground	13
Mono Creek	13
Montecito	1,3,8
Mountain Drive (Santa Barbara, Montecito)	1,3,8
Museum of Art (Santa Barbara)	3
Museum of Natural History (Santa Barbara)	3
Nipomo Regional Park	38
Nojoqui Falls	19,22
Nojoqui Falls County Park	15,19,22
Ocean Beach County Park	29
Old San Marcos Road	10,19
Orpet Park	3,8
Oso Flaco Lake	38
Paradise Road	16,17,18
Paradise Store and Grill	16
Pendola Ranger Station	13
Pershing Park (Santa Barbara)	1
Pine Mountain	64
Pismo Dunes State Vehicular Recreation Area	38
Plaza Del Mar Park (Santa Barbara)	1
Point Conception	27
Point Sal Ridge	36
Point Sal State Beach	35,36
Purisima Hills	32
Rancho Del Cielo (Reagan Ranch)	14,15
Rancho Oso Resort	16
Refugio Beach State Park	14,15,19
Refugio Pass	14,15
Reyes Peak/Reyes Peak Campground	64
River Park (Lompoc)	26
Romero Canyon Rd.	11,12,13
Romero Saddle	11,12,13
Rocky Nook County Park (Santa Barbara)	1,2,8
Ryon Park (Lompoc)	28,29,30
San Antonio Creek	7
San Antonio Valley	31
Sandpiper Golf Course (Goleta)	2
San Marcos Pass	12,19
Santa Barbara Botanic Gardens	1,2,10
Santa Barbara City College	3,5
Santa Barbara Harbor/Marina	1
Santa Barbara Polo And Racquet Club	9
Santa Barbara Yacht Club	3
Santa Barbara Zoological Gardens	3
Santa Cruz Trail	18
Santa Maria River	39
Santa Maria Valley	34,35,36,37,38
Santa Rosa Rd.	23,26,38
Santa Ynez Earthquake Fault	17
Santa Ynez Park	22
Santa Ynez Peak	14
Santa Ynez River	10,12,15,16,19,26,29,30
Santa Ynez Valley	19,20

INDEX: VENTURA COUNTY

ATTRACTION, POINT OF INTEREST	TRIP NUMBER(S)
Santa Rosa Valley	56
Santa Susana Park (Simi Valley)	54,55
Santa Susana Pass	54,55
Seabee Museum (Port Hueneme)	42
Seymour Rd. (Lockwood Valley)	67
Silver Strand County Beach (Port Hueneme)	43
Sisar Canyon	61
Soule County Park (Ojai)	46,60,63
Steckel County Park (Santa Paula/Sulphur Springs)	60
Strathern Historical Park (Simi Valley)	56
Summit	61
Sunset Hills Park (Thousand Oaks)	52
Sulphur Mountain Rd.	63
Surfers Point Park (Ventura)	47
Sycamore Canyon	58
Sycamore Cove/Canyon Campgrounds	48,58
Teague Park (Santa Paula)	56
Tierra Rejada Valley	56
Topanga State Beach (L.A. County)	48
Topa Topa Bluffs	61
Topa Topa Mountain	61,63
Upper Ojai Valley	60,63
U.S. Naval Construction Battalion Center (Port Hueneme)	42
Ventura College	44
Ventura County Fairgrounds (Ventura)	46,47
Ventura County Government Center (Ventura)	43,44
Ventura County Historical Museum (Ventura)	46
Ventura Harbor	44,45
Ventura Pier	45
Ventura River	46,47
Ventura Yacht Club	45
West Casitas Pass	62
Westlake Lake	30,51
Westlake Village	51
White Ledge Trail Camp	61
Will Rogers State Beach (L.A. County)	48
Zuma County Beach (L.A. County)	48

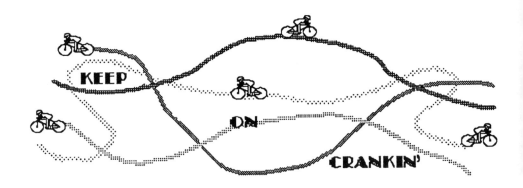

Swimming Hole on the Santa Ynez River

Foxen Canyon Road Vineyard (Susan Cohen Photo)

Mystical Point Sal Beach

End of a Beautiful Day on West Camino Cielo

Romero Canyon Road Below East Camino Cielo

East Camino Cielo Near Arroyo Burro Road

271

Little Pine Mountain from Camuesa-Buckhorn Road

Camuesa-Buckhorn Road-Bikers Returning to Upper Oso Camp

Heading for the Upper Santa Ynez River Playground

Nothin' to It!

NOTES: